POLITICAL GAIN AND CIVILIAN PAIN

POLITICAL GAIN AND CIVILIAN PAIN

Humanitarian Impacts of Economic Sanctions

Edited by
Thomas G. Weiss, David Cortright,
George A. Lopez, and Larry Minear

Foreword by
Lakhdar Brahimi

ROWMAN & LITTLEFIELD PUBLISHERS, INC.
Lanham • New York • Boulder • Oxford

ROWMAN & LITTLEFIELD PUBLISHERS, INC.

Published in the United States of America
by Rowman & Littlefield Publishers, Inc.
4720 Boston Way, Lanham, Maryland 20706

12 Hid's Copse Road
Cummor Hill, Oxford OX29JJ, England

British Library Cataloguing in Publication Information Available

Library of Congress Cataloging-in-Publication Data

Political gain and civilian pain : humanitarian impacts of economic
    sanctions / edited by Thomas G. Weiss . . . [et al.] ; foreword by
    Lakhdar Brahimi.
        p.   cm.
    Includes bibliographical references (p.   ) and index.
    ISBN 0–8476–8702–3 (alk. paper). — ISBN 0-8476-8703–1 (alk.
paper)
        1. Economic sanctions.   2. War victims—Legal status, laws, etc.
    3. Economic sanctions—Moral and ethical aspects.   I. Weiss, Thomas
    George.
    KZ6373.P65   1997
    337—dc21   97–25040
                                                                          CIP

ISBN 0–8476–8702–3 (cloth : alk. paper)
ISBN 0–8476–8703–1 (pbk. : alk. paper)
Printed in the United States of America

∞ ™ The paper used in this publication meets the minimum requirements of
American National Standard for Information Sciences—Permanence of Paper
for Printed Library Materials, ANSI Z39.48–1984.

Contents

Part III: Conclusions

Illustrations

Tables

Foreword

Thomas G. Weiss, David Cortright, George A. Lopez, and Larry Minear have assembled in *Political Gain and Civilian Pain* a well-documented and most welcome contribution to the debate about the use of economic sanctions as a means of achieving foreign policy objectives.

The first of this book's many merits is that it takes stock of much of what has been written or said by policymakers—inside and outside of the United Nations (UN) and other diplomatic arenas—as well as by scholars, journalists, and officials from both intergovernmental and nongovernmental organizations (NGOs).

As the editors write at the outset, "Comprehensive reviews of many social groups and situations and of current or projected situations for an entire people across a diverse set of economic, social, and health indicators have been rare." This work therefore offers a useful starting point for anyone wishing to take a closer look at the complex issues raised by economic sanctions, which tend to be used in quasi-routine fashion by the international community as a whole or by some of its members as a policy instrument that supposedly prevents conflict, restores peace, and otherwise secures compliance with desired norms of behavior from recalcitrant targeted states or factions within them. As usual, the real world is distinct from the theoretical version.

Such use—some say abuse—of economic sanctions has created uneasiness among UN member states and within the ranks of international civil servants and NGO staff. The preoccupations and views of all those concerned by economic sanctions are accurately and fairly reflected in the pages of this volume. Field-workers from various UN agencies and NGOs will be particularly grateful, I believe, for the genuine sympathy and understanding shown by the editors and the authors of case studies when they describe the frustrations and numerous problems with sanctions as their "bite" increases along with the humanitarian needs of civilians in targeted countries. Also well highlighted is the peculiar situation of the United Nations that, far too often, finds itself entrusted with contradictory mandates: enforcing sanctions with one hand, and providing humanitarian relief to the victims of those very same sanctions with the other.

Three basic questions arise with reference to the imposition of economic sanctions. Is it legal? Does it work? At what price and who foots the bill? The editors and other contributors to this book shed much light on each of these questions, concentrating, quite rightly, on the last one, which is the central theme of their analyses as well as the most important issue in this context.

The legality of sanctions is challenged, in the first place, by the party that is targeted. This is predictable enough—whether the culprits are from Iran, Yugoslavia, Haiti, Sudan, Burundi, or, for that matter, the European Union, Japan, or Canada (in the case of U.S. legislation threatening to extend to third countries several American sanctions against Cuba or Iran). They all have a wealth of arguments aiming to demonstrate that Article 41 of the UN Charter is not applicable, or that the measures contemplated are abusive and incompatible with principles of international law.

In the Lockerbie case, for example, Libya has gone to the International Court of Justice (ICJ) and argued that the Security Council has overstepped its boundaries and ignored international law (in particular the 1971 Montreal Convention for the Suppression of Unlawful Acts against the Safety of Civil Aviation), which contains adequate provisions to deal with the accusation directed against two Libyan nationals. Tripoli argues that there was no justification for the imposition of sanctions because it was willing to cooperate fully with the pursuit of international law.

Sudan's vehement and indignant denial of any involvement in the assassination attempt in June 1995 against President Hosni Mubarek of Egypt in Addis Ababa, Ethiopia, was not found convincing simply because of Khartoum's known association with several groups allegedly guilty of terrorist activities in several neighboring countries, including Egypt. The evidence produced by Ethiopian authorities supporting their claims against Sudan's assassination attempt was insubstantial, to say the least. Hence the hesitations of the Security Council and the resistance of some of its members to support even limited sanctions that would affect only Sudan Air's international flights.

Another unprecedented case regards Burundi, where yet another military coup was staged in July 1996. Burundi's neighbors convened a summit conference in August and decreed comprehensive sanctions against Major Pierre Buyoya's regime. This decision was not formally endorsed but only "supported" by the Security Council. The government of Burundi, to quote from a memorandum distributed by its prime minister, considers that "this embargo amounts to a comprehensive blockade and violates the rules governing interstate relations" [cet embargo se revéle être un blocus total et viole la reglementation sur les rapports entre états]. The group of countries that initiated this action (Ethiopia, Kenya, Rwanda, Tanzania, Uganda, Zaire, and later Zambia) does not constitute a regional organization. It is, at best, an informal subregional group and, according to Burundi, has no valid legal grounds to take such a decision. According to Burundi, this decision amounts, in fact, to an act of war.

These and other legal arguments put forward by targeted countries fall on deaf ears most of the time, not necessarily because they lack substance but because other governments as well as the public at large do not relish the prospects of being associated with the likes of Saddam Hussein, Colonel Muammar Qadhafi, the repressive military forces of Burundi, or Islamic fundamentalists in the Sudan. Nor would anyone wish to be considered as showing sympathy with suspected terrorists who might have been involved in such outrageous acts as the Lockerbie incident and the 1988 UTA (Union des Transports Aériens) disaster in Chad. In the case of the two Libyan nationals, guilt has not been definitively established by a court of law; and in theory, a basic right under any legal system in the world is that they should be presumed innocent until a due process proves otherwise. But in this particular case, the two are, one might say, "guilty by association," as result of the negative public image of their country's leader.

Legal principles, moral values, and human rights generally encounter predictable resistance by those governments whose national interests are at stake. Third World countries, including China as one of the Security Council's permanent members, have often refused, or at least hesitated, to support sanctions that are viewed as infringing on the national sovereignty of the targeted country. The legal and moral arguments invoked are real enough, but their attitude also has another motive—namely, the fear that today's punitive measures against one state may be a dangerous precedent for tomorrow's intervention in their own internal affairs. Naturally, more powerful and more affluent states have fewer such fears, although they may have other interests. Russia, for example, is making no mystery of its view that sanctions should be lifted from Iraq—for reasons of principle and also so that Baghdad can resume repaying its substantial debts to Moscow. The European Union, Canada, and Japan, for their parts, immediately challenged U.S. legislation that threatened to extend to their business firms American sanctions against Cuba and Iran.

The debate is far from finished, but concerns about the expanding resort to sanctions are genuine and growing both in government circles around the world and among the public at large. Discussions continue within committees in the General Assembly, and it seems that recommendations are contemplated with a view to set stricter guidelines for the imposition of economic sanctions by the Security Council. The essential issue of the debate is, of course, the impact of sanctions on vulnerable civilians in targeted countries who are men, women, and children—real people, not merely agenda items. The four countries singled out for detailed examination in this book—South Africa, Iraq, the former Yugoslavia, and Haiti—are spread over four continents, have contrasting backgrounds, and therefore represent a wide spectrum of situations that allows the editors and case-study authors to pose appropriate and extremely vital questions and suggest pertinent responses to many of them.

Cases not analyzed in the volume add other dimensions. Burundi, the latest country to be subjected to economic sanctions, is, as indicated earlier, a case without precedent in that the decision to apply sanctions was taken neither by the Security Council, as had been the case with Iraq and Yugoslavia, nor by the established Organization of African Unity (OAU) as the salient regional organization, as had been the case with sanctions against Haiti by the Organization of American States (OAS) that were later endorsed by the United Nations.

The Sudan also presents other interesting features. Although Security Council Resolution 770 was adopted almost a year ago, sanctions have not become effective, because Sudan has complied with some of the council's demands. Moreover—and this is more significant—some members of the Security Council have insisted that a report be submitted to them on the humanitarian consequences of sanctions; and other members of the council have argued that sanctions should be applied for a limited period of time and be automatically lifted at the end of a fixed period without a new decision. This is concrete evidence that the Security Council, in particular, and the international community, more generally, are aware of the terrible consequences of economic sanctions on people who were not meant to be hurt by them. Indeed, it is a cruel irony that dictators and their henchmen grow obscenely rich as a direct result of sanctions that are meant to punish them. Meanwhile, helpless civilians—especially the most vulnerable groups among them—are made to suffer hunger, disease, or even death as a result of those very same sanctions that are said to help them. And, to add insult to injury, the targeted regime will claim that all the things that went wrong—from inflation to a plane crash, a disappointing harvest, or even an earthquake—are caused by sanctions. The leaders of the targeted regime will assume the mantle of the gallant defenders of national sovereignty and the champions of human dignity.

Opposition groups often support the imposition of sanctions on their own country. The African National Congress (ANC) of Nelson Mandela wanted sanctions to remain in force until elections were actually held and the hated apartheid system officially and effectively dismantled. The supporters of Jean-Bertrand Aristide clamored for sanctions when they understood that there was insufficient political will for more vigorous international action, especially military intervention. In Sudan, opposition groups are claiming that the imposition of sanctions will help precipitate the fall of the regime and will therefore not hurt the civilian population for very long. Many observers are skeptical and point out that the Sudanese opposition leaders have been predicting for several years the imminent collapse of the fundamentalist military regime.

Iraq is a painful case without substantial political gain. Those opposition groups that enjoy active support from the most powerful foreign enemies of Saddam Hussein have been predicting the imminent collapse of the Baghdad regime for six very long and painful years. However, many highly respected Iraqi members of other opposition groups have, from the beginning, warned the international community that sanctions will not work and that their country's present harsh regime will not change its ways because the international community has joined in punishing the Iraqi people. They, along with numerous non-Iraqi observers, have also warned that, one day, with the regime of Saddam Hussein still in place, the international community may find it difficult to lift sanctions because it would be seen as a victory for Baghdad and a defeat for its enemies. In times of severe budget cuts and grave financial difficulties for the United Nations and its organizations, the international community puts itself in a situation in which donors devote a large portion of meager resources to help Iraq, a rich country that should be giving, rather than receiving, humanitarian assistance.

It is no wonder, then, that the editors find that "concerns are mounting that the short-term humanitarian consequences and the long-term structural effects of economic sanctions are often themselves as harmful as war itself, if not more so. In addition, the negative humanitarian consequences of sanctions plausibly outweigh whatever political objectives may have been accomplished." They also quote former UN Secretary-General Boutros Boutros-Ghali, who "captured many of those concerns in his 1995 *Supplement to An Agenda for Peace*. He noted that sanctions are a 'blunt instrument' that inflict suffering on vulnerable groups, complicate the work of humanitarian agencies, cause long-term damage to the productive capacity of target nations, and generate severe effects on neighboring countries."

There is every reason to feel confident that these acute preoccupations also will be shared more and more universally. When economic sanctions are agreed, they should be accompanied by the careful calculations and humanitarian safeguards that the editors recommend. *Political Gain and Civilian Pain* breaks new ground for applied scholarship. I commend it to diplomats, UN and NGO officials, and academics alike. It is a "must" for anyone active in this field.

—LAKHDAR BRAHIMI
Under-Secretary-General
for the Secretary-General's
Preventive Peacemaking Efforts

Preface

Each of us serves in numerous ways as an author or editor of this volume. Each of us has conducted original research about many of the crucial areas of activity that provide the central framework for this book. We have also spent considerable time working within, or consulting with, international organizations. Each took primary responsibility for a section of this book and in serving as first-draft author of particular chapters. Tom Weiss took responsibility for overall editing of the volume and for negotiations with contributors and the publisher; George Lopez drafted the introduction and most of chapters 1 and 2 with rewriting by David Cortright. Larry Minear drafted the conclusions in chapter 7. Yet, each of us has commented so extensively and rewritten all chapters so thoroughly that pride of authorship has yielded to collective judgment, making this book a team effort. Our collaboration has, we hope, not only discouraged ill-informed and parochial points of view, but also produced a synergy and a better text than any one of us could have written on his own.

We are pleased that this project has brought to bear the collective analytical strengths of three institutions: the Fourth Freedom Forum of Goshen, Indiana; the University of Notre Dame's Joan B. Kroc Institute for International Peace Studies; and the Humanitarianism and War Project of Brown University's Thomas J. Watson Jr. Institute for International Studies. This type of collaboration is unusual in policy and academic circles, and we are proud of our efforts.

As is customary at the outset of such volumes, we would like to acknowledge the efforts of numerous colleagues who have contributed to the quality of what follows. The enthusiasm and logistical support provided by our editor, Jennifer Knerr of Rowman & Littlefield Publishers, was indispensable in bringing the volume to fruition. Outside referees, unknown to us, provided insightful comments on the manuscript.

We would particularly wish to thank Lakhdar Brahimi, who has graced this volume with his insightful foreword. As a former foreign minister and ambassador of Algeria, he has followed international politics from a distinct vantage point. As under-secretary-general for the Secretary-

General's Preventive and Peacemaking Efforts, he has conducted numerous missions for the United Nations. As special representative of the UN secretary-general, he led two UN missions that are among the cases under analysis in this volume. In spring 1994, he headed the UN Observer Mission in South Africa (UNOMSA) for the elections that ended apartheid and saw the birth of a nonracial South Africa. And from September 1994 until March 1996, he headed the UN Mission in Haiti (UNMIH) that followed the U.S. Multinational Force and contributed to the return of the democratically elected government of Jean-Bertrand Aristide, the organization of peaceful legislative and presidential elections, and the peaceful handover of power from one democratically elected president to another for the first time in Haiti's tormented history. It would be hard to imagine a person who is better qualified to introduce this book, and we are very grateful that Lakhdar Brahimi took time from his busy schedule to write his foreword.

Discussion groups helped us to frame issues in 1995 and 1996. Although only the authors are responsible for the final versions of chapters, we would like to acknowledge with gratitude the time and effort that more than two dozen present and former UN officials, humanitarian practitioners, and scholarly experts put into improving our work during two meetings that we organized in New York: David Bassiouni, Lori Fisler Damrosch, Jennifer Daskal, Juergen Dedring, Graciana del Castillo, Claude de Ville de Goyet, Marie-Andrée Diouf, Margaret Doxey, Jon Ebersole, Kimberly Ann Elliott, Winifred Fitzgerald, Peter Küng, Manfred Kulessa, Ed Luck, Stephen Marks, Melissa Martinez, Anita Mathur, Roger Normand, Jack Patterson, Joel Rosenthal, Joseph J. Stephanides, Claudia von Braunmühl, and Andrew Yarrow.

We would like to express our special gratitude to those staff members of the Watson Institute who—with good humor and professionalism—retyped, edited, and helped shape various versions of this manuscript and the accompanying tables and illustrations. Thanks are in order for Fred Fullerton, Greg Kazarian, Amy Langlais, and George Potter. Laura Sadovnikoff should be singled out, for the final texts would have been considerably slower in appearing and certainly less well presented without her patient and careful attention to editorial details.

Cindy Collins, a graduate student in the Department of Political Science at Brown University, was a very useful helping hand at the outset of this process. We especially thank Julia Wagler, senior researcher at the Fourth Freedom Forum, whose dedicated investigative and editorial services contributed greatly to this enterprise. We also acknowledge the important contributions of Fourth Freedom Forum staffers Jennifer Glick,

Ann Miller Pedler, and Miriam Redsecker. Appreciation also goes to Jaleh Dashti-Gibson, a graduate student at the University of Notre Dame, who coauthored the chapter on the former Yugoslavia and also helped at various stages in interviewing, checking facts and endnotes, and compiling the bibliography.

A complicated joint undertaking of this sort could only materialize through significant outside financial support provided by the Program on Peace and International Cooperation of the John D. and Catherine T. MacArthur Foundation and the United States Institute of Peace. In addition, four institutions of the United Nations system through the Inter-Agency Standing Committee (the UN Department of Humanitarian Affairs, the UN Children's Fund, the UN Development Programme, and the World Food Programme) have financed related work, which has been helpful in our own writing of this book. We are also indebted to the generosity of Howard Brembeck, founder and chairman of the Fourth Freedom Forum. This substantial support permitted us to collaborate intensively, to commission the case studies in the volume, to organize evaluation sessions, and to gather data while maintaining our analytical independence. To each of these sponsors and benefactors we are truly grateful.

It is probably worth mentioning at the outset that the four of us are sympathetic to multilateral organizations in general, and to the United Nations in particular. We believe that the UN fits into a complicated world situation that does not often yield to unilateral undertakings. We believe that the first Clinton administration recognized this reality when initially describing its foreign policy as one that pursued "assertive multilateralism." Although it retreated from this rhetoric, it has been reluctant to act without collective approval and support. Madeleine Albright, now secretary of state for the second Clinton administration but then U.S. permanent representative to the United Nations, stated clearly in 1993 what remains valid today: "There will be many occasions when we need to bring pressure to bear on the belligerents of the post–Cold War period and use our influence to prevent ethnic and other regional conflicts from erupting. But usually we will not want to act alone—our stake will be limited and direct US intervention unwise."[1]

However, our orientation is not accurately described as "Wilsonian idealism," and it certainly does not reflect a knee-jerk and uncritical support for transnational efforts. Our preference for multilateral diplomacy, through sanctions among other means, is not idealistic. To the contrary, unilateralists promoting an image of unbridled state control over events are the real utopians of the twenty-first century. Multilateral diplomacy

can be complicated and messy, but much unilateral action can be dangerous and destructive. In spite of well-publicized threats to the United
Nations emanating from Washington,[2] we feel compelled to state our own
position at the outset of this volume.

The theoretical analyses and case studies of economic sanctions in this
volume point out the weaknesses of the UN system and, indeed, the
ambiguities of international coercion. We do not hesitate to discuss how,
when, and where the so-called international community has not measured up to reasonable expectations. After all, multilateralism is not a
religion. It is something not to be worshipped but to be critically analyzed. Although circumscribed by international law and the UN Charter,
decisions to impose multilateral economic sanctions are primarily affected by the foreign policies of member states. We hope this volume makes
a contribution to how leaders in those member states, as well as officials
at the United Nations, approach economic sanctions in the future.

Notes

1. Quoted in the *Washington Post, National Weekly Edition*, 21–27 June 1993, 16.
2. See, e.g., Jesse Helms, "Saving the U.N.: A Challenge to the Next Secretary-
General," *Foreign Affairs* 75, no. 5 (September/October 1996): 2–7. For a bipartisan
overview on the eve of the 1996 presidential elections, see George Soros, chairman
of an independent task force, *American National Interest and the United Nations*
(New York: Council on Foreign Relations, 1996). For more academic overviews,
see John Gerard Ruggie, *Winning the Peace: America and World Order in the New Era*
(New York: Columbia University Press, 1996); and Charles William Maynes and
Richard S. Williamson, eds., *U.S. Foreign Policy and the United Nations System* (New
York: Norton, 1996).

Abbreviations

ADRA	Adventist Development and Relief Agency
AFSC	American Friends Service Committee
ANC	African National Congress
CIA	Central Intelligence Agency
CRS	Catholic Relief Services
CSCE	Conference on Security and Cooperation in Europe (later Organization for Security and Cooperation in Europe)
DHA	Department of Humanitarian Affairs
EC	European Community
EPI	Expanded Program on Immunization
EU	European Union
FADH	Forces Armées d'Haiti
FAO	Food and Agricultural Organization
FRAPH	Front for the Advancement and Progress of Haiti
FRY	Federal Republic of Yugoslavia
GDP	gross domestic product
GNP	gross national product
HIV	human immunodeficiency virus
IASC	Inter-Agency Standing Committee
ICJ	International Court of Justice
ICRC	International Committee of the Red Cross
IDP	internally displaced person
IFOR	Implementation Force
IFRC	International Federation of Red Cross and Red Crescent Societies

IIE	Institute for International Economics
IMR	infant mortality rate
INGO	international nongovernmental organization
IRCU	Iraq Relief Coordination Unit
JNA	Yugoslav People's Army
MIF	Multinational Inspections Force
MOU	memorandum of understanding
MPP	Mouveman Peyizan Papaye
NAM	nonaligned movement
NGO	nongovernmental organization
OAPEC	Organization of Arab Petroleum Exporting Countries
OAS	Organization of American States
OAU	Organization of African Unity
OPIC	Overseas Private Insurance Corporation
OSCE	Organization for Security and Cooperation in Europe
PAHO	Pan American Health Organization
SADF	South African Defence Force
SAM	sanctions assistance mission
UNHCR	United Nations High Commission for Refugees
UNICEF	United Nations Children's Fund
UNPREDEP	United Nations Preventive Deployment Force
UNPROFOR	United Nations Protection Force
USAID	United States Agency for International Development
WFP	World Food Programme
WHO	World Health Organization

Part I

Theoretical and Historical

Perspectives

Introduction

Thomas G. Weiss, David Cortright, George A. Lopez, and Larry Minear

This volume reflects upon the convergence of two major policy trends in the immediate aftermath of the Cold War's end. The first is the dramatic increase in the resort to international economic sanctions as a means of multilateral coercive action against states or political authorities that violate basic norms of international relations.[1] The second is the increased international willingness to mount international responses to humanitarian emergencies in civil wars, one of the defining characteristics of which is the inability or unwillingness of national or local political authorities to cope.[2] The four editors have worked separately on these issues, but this volume presents the opportunity to bring them together.

Context

At first glance, there is no logical reason why these two policy concerns would collide. In its best light, the "sanctions era" that dawned in 1990 signaled the end of a stalemated United Nations (UN) Security Council.[3] The breakthrough in the impasse between the superpowers opened up the potential that nonforcible, but coercive, approaches such as sanctions could be employed as an alternative to coercion through military force in dealing with aggressors and others who violated fundamental principles of international law. Whereas the period from 1945 to 1990 had witnessed some sixty sanctions cases, only two of these were multilateral and imposed by the Security Council: against Rhodesia in 1966 and South Africa in 1977. During this period more than two-thirds of the sanctions cases were initiated and maintained by the United States. Of these, nearly three-quarters involved U.S. unilateral action.[4]

The change in this unilateral pattern has been pronounced. In the

1990s, the Security Council passed partial or comprehensive sanctions against Iraq, the states of the former Yugoslavia, Libya, Liberia, Somalia, Haiti, Rwanda, and the Sudan. These cases were particularly striking because of the range of purposes and circumstances for which they were imposed. The Security Council has placed sanctions on states for a variety of reasons: to overturn direct aggression against another state; to prompt the restoration of democracy; to condemn human rights abuses; and to punish the harboring of terrorists and others charged with international crimes.[5] In unprecedented action, the council also imposed sanctions on two nonstate actors: the Khmer Rouge in Cambodia (formerly Kampuchea) and the National Union for the Total Independence of Angola (UNITA).

Despite the diversity of sanctions episodes and their greater multilateral character, one dimension of sanctions policy remains unchanged. Conventional wisdom assumes that the imposition of economic coercion will exercise sufficient "bite" that citizens in the targeted country will exert political pressure to force either a change in the behavior of the authorities or their removal altogether. Although analysts have long characterized this underlying assumption as naive, inflicting civilian pain in order to achieve political gain remains the modus operandi of sanctions policy.[6] Implicit in this approach, and often presumed to be substantiated by historical evidence for the majority of sanctions cases before 1990, has been the claim that such sanctions, while inflicting pain, will be much less damaging to the economy generally, to civilian livelihood, and indeed to life itself than the alternative of war. This assumption, reviewed in the light of recent experience, is reflected in the title, *Political Gain and Civilian Pain.*

Developing parallel to the increased attractiveness of economic sanctions has been burgeoning attention to human suffering. This focus, too, has been liberated from the strictures of the Cold War. For decades, these concerns—such as hunger, population displacement within national borders, and human rights abuses—were considered within the domestic jurisdiction of sovereign states and were regarded as off limits to the international community. In stark contrast, the years since 1990 have witnessed numerous and largely unprecedented humanitarian initiatives undertaken by the United Nations that have expanded the legitimate area of international action. Prominent among these have been the creation of safe havens for Iraqi Kurds in 1991, military intervention to guarantee the unimpeded delivery of food supplies to starving Somalis in 1992, and the restoration of the elected authorities in Haiti in 1994. Efforts in Bosnia and Rwanda, although less successful, also marked a radical departure from time-tested reluctance to challenge opprobrious domestic practices.[7] The former UN secretary-general made humanitarian action during these emergencies a pivotal element in his two major policy analyses of peace and security in 1992 and 1995.[8] This new concern for human suffering, even when nested within societies in conflict, is reflected in the subtitle of this volume, *Humanitarian Impacts of Economic Sanctions*.

The harbinger of these two newly prominent policy realities of international life—the wider use of multilateral economic sanctions and a more assertive humanitarianism—took shape in the international response to Iraq's invasion of Kuwait in 1990. Moving swiftly to counteract the Iraqi military advance, the UN Security Council first imposed economic sanctions in August then approved military action by a coalition of states in January. Further, in the aftermath of the war, the world organization launched a major humanitarian effort to assist Kurdish populations in northern Iraq that came under pressure from the Saddam Hussein regime. At the same time, the UN continued stringent sanctions as leverage for enforcing one of the most prominent features of the Gulf War peace agreement—that Iraq dismantle its production and storage facilities for weapons of mass destruction and that it turn over to the UN's International Atomic Energy Agency (IAEA) documents related to this program.

Observations by officials from UN organizations and other humanitarian groups, reinforced by high-visibility media coverage, including a May 1996 segment of the CBS News program *60 Minutes*, spotlighted the devastation of war and especially of the economic sanctions continuing after the war to Iraq's economic and social infrastructure. In UN inner circles, and often even among those concerned with Iraq's lack of compliance with the work of the IAEA, diplomats expressed grave reservations about the impact of the sanctions on civilians and on the carrying capacity of Iraqi society. During negotiations spanning more than two years, they pressed for arrangements under which Iraq could sell oil to generate revenue to purchase foodstuffs.[9] Thus the humanitarian impacts of sanctions on Iraq, as well as their political effectiveness, became the subject of widespread challenge.[10]

Some of these concerns, like the analysis of Bashir Al-Samarrai, a member of the Iraqi Democratic Opposition, framed the pain-and-gain nexus quite clearly:

> Economic sanctions have targeted the wrong party in Iraq, i.e., the poor, the helpless, and the children. Most Iraqis question the logic of this policy by wondering how it is possible for a helpless nation to overthrow one of the world's most ruthless dictators, when the U.S. and its allies could not, or

would not, remove Saddam from power during the war. How much suffering must innocent Iraqis endure before the UN ends its strangulation policy or before Saddam is removed? Is the world willing to stand by and watch a whole nation be starved and strangled? To continue the present policy is analogous to blowing up an aircraft with all passengers aboard to kill the hijacker. In this standoff eighteen million Iraqis are the passengers.[11]

The question of how much pain the community of states is willing to inflict on civilians in the quest for political gains was raised also in the imposition of sanctions against the former Yugoslavia and Haiti. In earlier years, opponents of sanctions and divestment in South Africa also had sought to dramatize the potential negative impact of sanctions on the economy and on the black majority. In all of these instances, it was clear that the international community[12] had discovered a blunt though stinging weapon but had yet to achieve clarity about the ground rules for its utilization. There was confusion about both the pain and the gain sides of the equation. In fact, some challenged the assumption that the use of the term "equation" was accurate or appropriate at all.

In any event, questioning the civilian costs of sanctions and achieving clarity about those costs are two fundamentally different matters. As sanctions have become more multilateral, the UN secretariat and several UN agencies, including the Food and Agricultural Organization (FAO) and the United Nations Children's Fund (UNICEF), have conducted impact studies in particular targeted countries. These studies have focused on specific segments of the population, such as children, and have examined impact in particular sectors, such as health. Comprehensive reviews of many social groups and situations and of the current or projected situation for an entire people across a diverse set of economic, social, and health indicators have been rare.[13]

Moreover, some recent studies have been controversial. As will be noted in several cases, reports by UN emissaries such as Prince Sadruddin Aga Khan and Marti Ahtisaari on Iraq and by the Harvard Center for Population and Development Studies on Haiti were quickly caught up in a swirl of debate between those who would like to see sanctions continued and those who believe that their costs are disproportionate and even immoral. Others have argued, in contrast, that some of the claims about child deaths in Iraq are erroneously based on extrapolated estimates rather than hard data.[14] An accepted methodology has yet to be devised that provides comparable information that could be the basis for reasoned, as opposed to ideological, debate; this methodology is a topic in chapter 2 of this volume. Moreover, given the political pressures on those carrying out sanctions research, safeguards have yet to be devised to protect the integrity of such research, whether it is accomplished by intergovernmental and governmental organizations or by private research groups.

Available reports provide relatively little information about the winners and losers who emerge in the competition and reallocation of scarce resources in a target state.[15] They offer even less about the mix of short-term and long-term effects of sanctions on a nation's economic and social infrastructure, impacts with a bearing on the quality of civilian life in the near and medium-term future. Better data and analytical frameworks are critically important to member states of the United Nations and to humanitarian agencies as future sanctions are contemplated.

Content

The rationale for this volume is twofold. First, we seek to obtain some very specific information on selected episodes of multilateral sanctions—South Africa, Iraq, the former Yugoslavia, and Haiti—to understand their humanitarian and political impacts better. Second, we seek to develop a methodology for assessing the humanitarian impact of sanctions wherever they are contemplated and/or imposed. These two tasks reinforce each other. Many of the tensions in the humanitarian and political nexus of sanctions were apparent to us at the outset. We were aware of the host of conceptual, methodological, and measurement problems associated with such an investigation. However, consultations with public officials, experts, policy analysts, and aid personnel have dramatized anew for us the practical dilemmas in assessing and mitigating the most harsh and unintended effects of sanctions.

Our own prior research work and policy dispositions on this problématique meant that each of us as editors brought to this collaboration views that were more or less already formed. Cortright and Lopez, the two of us most deeply involved in sanctions work from an academic base, believed that once we had reviewed the human costs of sanctions, our study would move quickly to examine more humane and efficient means of imposing sanctions. They were particularly interested in whether financial, communication, and transportation controls might be imposed in a coordinated and systematic manner as key elements in "smarter" sanctions. Because of in-depth fieldwork in war zones as part of the Humanitarianism and War Project team, Minear and Weiss were already familiar with the devastation wrought by sanctions and predisposed to delimit as narrowly as possible the conditions under which sanctions could be imposed.

This book demonstrates how a careful analysis of available information and even limited empirical data, combined with continuous frank exchange of views, can lead investigators to conclusions that differ from their original inclinations. Enriched by a year and a half of collaboration, the four editors are not unanimous on the advisability of economic sanctions as a policy instrument. However, we now have a clearer idea about the issues that should be taken into account when sanctions are under consideration, are in place, or should be lifted. Moreover, the research presented here—including our first two chapters, the four case studies, and our conclusions and recommendations in the final chapter—provides steps toward a template for monitoring humanitarian impacts of sanctions in future cases.

This book reflects a research design that has attempted to be inductive, oriented toward cases, and sensitive to policy. We have scrutinized the literature of economic sanctions with an eye toward learning as much as possible about impacts. We have sought to connect our review of humanitarian impacts and political results with each other. From the outset, we have maintained a steady dialogue with officials of United Nations agencies, nongovernmental organizations (NGOs), and other groups. For the case studies in particular, we have enlisted the participation of individuals who were willing to place their country expertise within the context of our broader search for a serviceable methodology to facilitate the evolution of individual and improvisational sanctions responses into a more consistent and accountable sanctions regime. Our purview is confined to the humanitarian impacts of sanctions within target states, not among third parties. We acknowledge the difficulties that are encountered by neighboring states and the trading partners of targeted countries when sanctions are imposed, and we recognize that serious political and humanitarian problems are created by these secondary effects.[16] Certainly the range of issues associated with Article 50 of the UN Charter (compensation to third parties that are affected by sanctions) warrants sustained policy research in its own right. To keep the current volume to manageable length, however, we have focused our investigation on direct effects within sanctioned countries.

Part I of the book provides the conceptual and analytical framework. Chapter 1 presents a conceptual discussion of sanctions as instruments that, in the process of achieving the political objective of changed behavior in the target nation, have humanitarian consequences in five specific regards. Chapter 2 is more methodological, specifying the contours of the case studies, identifying indicators to be examined in measuring the impact of sanctions on civilians, and analyzing the political context of economic coercion. It also analyzes the difficulties of disaggregating the effects of sanctions from other factors and of taking into account adjustments made by a targeted government.

Part II comprises case studies that review the individual experience of sanctions in South Africa (chapter 3), Iraq (chapter 4), the former Yugoslavia (chapter 5), and Haiti (chapter 6). Each analysis draws as much as possible on the framework outlined in Part I within the constraints imposed by research conditions and the uniqueness of each case. Each of the chapters includes persons who have conducted firsthand research in the areas reviewed. New fieldwork was carried out specifically for this volume only in South Africa.

Chapter 3, by Neta Crawford, examines the economic, social, and political impacts of the longest-running case of sanctions, those against the apartheid government of South Africa from 1977 until 1994. An assistant professor of political science at the University of Massachusetts, a frequent visitor to South Africa over the last decade, and a longtime observer of developments there, Crawford examines the only case in the volume that predates the end of the Cold War. Set against substantial civilian pain from economic coercive measures are demonstrable political gains in the form of a democratically elected black majority government. Crawford details steps taken by the white minority government to deflect the impacts of sanctions, some of which yielded unexpected benefits for the majority population.

Chapter 4, by Eric Hoskins, chronicles the devastating impacts of sanctions on human conditions in Iraq, unmitigated by significant changes on the political front. A physician and independent consultant who was a member of the original Harvard study team that engaged in the first household-based study of the effects on the people of Iraq of the Gulf War and sanctions, Hoskins chronicles the deepening distress of civilians since August 1990. Since the chapter was completed, negotiations have been concluded to allow for some of the proceeds from the limited sale of Iraqi oil to underwrite relief activities in Iraq.

Chapter 5, by Julia Devin (an international lawyer and consultant) and Jaleh Dashti-Gibson (a Ph.D. candidate in government and international studies at the University of Notre Dame), examines the multiple contexts in which sanctions came to play a role in attempts to dissuade Slobodan Milosevic and the Serbian regime in Belgrade from supporting the war of Bosnian Serbs against Muslims in Bosnia-Herzegovina. On the political side, the case occupies something of a middle position between the success of sanctions against South Africa and their failure in Iraq. Factors other than sanctions—in particular, battle fatigue and a new military balance—played significant roles in facilitating the 1995 Dayton agreement. The civilian pain associated with sanctions in Serbia and Montenegro was substantial and, combined with the devastation wrought by the war, poses daunting difficulties for future reconstruction.

Chapter 6 is by Sarah Zaidi, a trained political scientist who is the science director at the Center for Economic and Human Rights in New York. She examines perhaps the most oscillating of sanctions policy episodes, that of Haiti. The on-again, off-again pattern makes it difficult to assess the precise impact of sanctions, as do the general poverty and underemployment of a large proportion of the Haitian population. The political objective of sanctions—the restoration of the elected government of Jean-Bertrand Aristide and the elimination of the de facto military junta led by Raoul Cédras—was accomplished, but the determining role was played by overwhelming U.S. military force rather than economic coercion. Sanctions were discredited over time; and Haitian civilians, who had initially accepted the privation that sanctions entailed in exchange for the international solidarity that they conveyed, emerged disillusioned and poorer for the experience.

Chapter 7 makes up Part III and provides a set of policy recommendations that reflect our own engagement with the issues and our reading of the recurrent themes in the case studies. These recommendations are also part of an ongoing dialogue with the many experts and practitioners consulted for this study.[17] The recommendations themselves, however, emanate from our independent effort alone and seek to present a range of options and strategies to policymakers who impose sanctions, as well as to humanitarian agency officials who will operate in sanctioned environments.

Notes

1. See David Cortright and George A. Lopez, eds., *Economic Sanctions: Panacea or Peacebuilding in a Post–Cold War World?* (Boulder, Colo.: Westview, 1995), 3–17; and John Stremlau, *Sharpening Economic Sanctions: Toward a Stronger Role for the United Nations,* report to the Carnegie Commission on Preventing Deadly Conflict (New York: Carnegie Corp., November 1996), 12–18.

2. See esp. Larry Minear and Thomas G. Weiss, *Mercy under Fire: War and the Global Humanitarian Community* (Boulder, Colo.: Westview, 1995); and *Humanitarian Politics* (New York: Foreign Policy Association, 1995).

3. For a discussion of this trend, see George A. Lopez and David Cortright,

"The Sanctions Era: An Alternative to Military Intervention," *Fletcher Forum for World Affairs* 19, no. 2 (Summer/Fall, 1995): 65–86.

4. Previous research has concentrated largely upon the utility of sanctions as a foreign policy tool of the United States, exercised for the most part unilaterally. See Gary Clyde Hufbauer, Jeffrey J. Schott, and Kimberly Ann Elliott, *Economic Sanctions Reconsidered: History and Current Policy* and *Economic Sanctions Reconsidered: Supplemental Case Histories* (Washington, D.C.: Institute for International Economics, 1990), which updated *Economic Sanctions in Pursuit of Foreign Policy Goals* (Washington, D.C.: Institute for International Economics, 1983). See also David A. Baldwin, *Economic Statecraft* (Princeton: Princeton University Press, 1985); and Theodore Galdi and Robert Shuey, *U.S. Economic Sanctions Imposed against Specific Countries: 1979 to the Present* (Washington, D.C.: Congressional Research Service, 1992). The use of multilateral economic sanctions has recently become the subject of analysis. See, e.g., Lisa Martin, *Coercive Cooperation: Explaining Multilateral Economic Sanctions* (Princeton: Princeton University Press, 1992); and Lisa Martin, *Political Symbol or Policy Tool? Making Sanctions Work* (Muscatine, Iowa: Stanley Foundation, 1993).

5. The analysis of the meaning of such trends, both for the UN and for the United States as a key supporter of sanctions, is just beginning to be the subject of serious scrutiny. Two assessments of such trends are available in Stremlau, *Sharpening International Sanctions;* and Bruce W. Jentleson, "Economic Sanctions: Post–Cold War Policy Challenges," working paper prepared for the National Research Council's Committee on International Conflict Resolution, Washington, D.C., June 1996.

6. The terminology and original critique were developed by Johan Galtung, "On the Effects of International Economic Sanctions, with Examples from the Case of Rhodesia," *World Politics* 19 (April 1967): 378–416. For a far-reaching analysis of the limitations in Galtung's thinking about the domestic political and economic impact of sanctions, see David Matthew Rowe, "Surviving Economic Coercion: Rhodesia's Responses to International Economic Sanctions" (Ph.D. diss., Duke University, 1993), esp. 59–110.

7. See Thomas G. Weiss and Cindy Collins, *Humanitarian Challenges and Intervention: World Politics and the Dilemmas of Help* (Boulder, Colo.: Westview, 1996).

8. Both the 1992 document *An Agenda for Peace* and the 1995 *Supplement to An Agenda for Peace* by Boutros Boutros-Ghali are republished in *An Agenda for Peace 1995* (New York: United Nations, 1995).

9. This culminated in Security Council Resolution 986, whose implementation has attracted the attention of sanctioners and humanitarians alike.

10. For one compilation of comment and criticism by major international institutions and prominent individuals, see *The Children Are Dying: The Impact of Sanctions on Iraq* (New York: World View Forum, 1996). This volume reprints a 1995 report, "Evaluation of the Food and Nutrition Situation in Iraq by the FAO," by Ramsey Clark to members of the UN Security Council on the civilian impact of UN sanctions, and "An International Appeal to the U.S. Government and the U.N. Security Council."

11. Bashir Al-Samarrai, "Economic Sanctions against Iraq: Do They Contribute to a Just Settlement?" in *Economic Sanctions*, ed. Cortright and Lopez, 138.

12. This nebulous moniker is somewhat abused shorthand. However, in the chapters written by the editors, it refers to the collectivity of political authorities who maintain formal ongoing relationships with one another during a particular historical period for a particular set of activities. Such authorities always include national leaders and diplomats from states as well as officials from the intergovernmental organizations that are financed by member states. In the humanitarian arena, staff members from NGOs are often included because their activities are increasingly financed with public resources and they also cooperate under a UN umbrella in field activities; so too are the international media, whose reporting frequently helps lead to policy changes and resource mobilization.

13. The FAO reports (there were several) are mentioned in the British publication *The Lancet*, 346, no. 8988 (2 December 1995): 1439–85. On Haiti, see the UNICEF-commissioned study by the Harvard Center for Population and Development Studies, *Sanctions in Haiti: Crisis in Humanitarian Action* (Cambridge: Program on Human Security, November 1993). On Iraq, see Ahmed Al-Hadi and Omer Obeid, "Report on the Nutritional Status of Iraqi Children: One Year Following the Gulf War and Sustained Sanctions" (New York: United Nations Children's Fund, June 1991); United Nations, *Report to the Secretary-General on Humanitarian Needs in Iraq by a Mission Led by Sadruddin Aga Khan, Executive Delegate of the Secretary-General*, 15 July 1991 (Geneva: Office of the Executive Delegate of the Secretary-General for a United Nations Inter-agency Humanitarian Programme for Iraq, Kuwait and the Iraq/Turkey and Iraq/Iran Border Areas, 1991); and United Nations, *Report to the Secretary-General on Humanitarian Needs in Kuwait and Iraq in the Immediate Post-Crisis Environment by a Mission to the Area Led by Mr. Martti Ahtisaari, Under-Secretary-General for Administration and Management*, 20 March 1991 (New York: United Nations, 1991).

14. See Kim Richard Nossal, Lori Buck, and Nicole Gallant, "Sanctions as Gendered Instrument of Statecraft" (paper presented at the British International Studies Association, Durham, England, 17 December 1996), 18 n. 53. See also the comments by researchers from the London School of Hygiene and Tropical Medicine in response to claims of Iraqi child deaths, letter to *The Lancet* 347 (20 January 1996), 198.

15. One of the few exceptions is Rowe's *Surviving Economic Coercion*, because of its examination of the economic and political impacts of sanctions on Rhodesia. Rowe examines governmental decisions on how to deal with sanctions and surveys the changing policies and actions of government as it worked with key industries and trade sectors in the country. Some of his findings are discussed in chapter 1.

16. Among the many UN reports and documents on the subject are United Nations, *Report of the Special Committee on the Charter of the United Nations and on the Strengthening of the Role of the Organization: Draft Resolution Proposed by the Chairman of the Working Group, Implementation of the Provisions of the Charter of the United Nations Related to Assistance to Third States Affected by the Application of Sanctions*, A/C.6/51/L.18, 25 November 1996; United Nations, *Report of the Special Commit-*

tee on the Charter . . ., Implementation of the Provisions of the Charter of the United Nations Related to Assistance to Third States Affected by the Application of Sanctions under Chapter VII of the Charter, Report of the Secretary-General, A/50/361, 22 August 1995; United Nations, *Strengthening of the Coordination of Humanitarian and Disaster Relief Assistance of the United Nations, including Special Economic Assistance: Special Economic Assistance to Individual Countries or Regions: Economic Assistance to States Affected by the Implementation of the Security Council Resolutions Imposing Sanctions against the Federal Republic of Yugoslavia (Serbia and Montenegro), Report of the Secretary-General,* A/49/356, 9 September 1994.

17. In fact, this volume is one stage in a multiyear process of consultation and collaboration. The editors are working with the UN Inter-Agency Standing Committee to develop a checklist for monitoring the humanitarian impact of economic sanctions by the UN system and other interested parties.

1

Economic Sanctions and Their Humanitarian Impacts: An Overview

Thomas G. Weiss, David Cortright,
George A. Lopez, and Larry Minear

Circumstances and conscious political decisions have made the 1990s a time when nonforcible sanctions have become a major means for dealing with a myriad of what Chapter VII of the UN Charter refers to as "threats to international peace and security." The end of the Cold War created a climate within the United Nations Security Council in which comprehensive and partial sanctions have become a viable policy option and no longer the virtual dead letter that they had been for forty-five years.[1] More than a dozen state and nonstate actors have been targeted with sanctions since the beginning of the decade. Ironically, the growing globalization of trade and finance renders any nation—but especially poor and weak states or ones with high dependence on exports and imports— vulnerable to economic coercion. Sanctions can realize their full potential for political gains in a targeted country, but only when powerful sender economies cooperate to reinforce these coercive measures.[2]

In this changing geopolitical environment, sanctions have grown more attractive because they permit countries with quite different foreign policies a kind of "mini-max" opportunity to forge shared responses in crises in which they might otherwise disagree. Nonforcible sanctions also give national leaders the ability to "do something" while simultaneously allowing them to refrain from high-risk military engagements. Although many people favor economic sanctions as more humane than military force, the preference for nonforcible (economic) over forcible (military) sanctions often has little to do with humanitarian values. Rather, it is due to the low domestic political cost combined with the low risk of lost credibility in case of failure. The attractiveness of military action to redress grievances has declined in the minds of many policy elites. Constraining factors include the unwillingness of Western publics to sustain casualties in overseas military operations when critical national interests are not seen as being involved. The destructive power of sanctions may also represent a deterrent of sorts to potential targets. Their lower cost and lower risk have made sanctions an increasingly attractive alternative to the use of force. At the same time, a certain irony is involved in the reality that economic sanctions in Iraq, the former Yugoslavia, and Haiti gave way to substantial military action.[3]

These political and economic realities of sanctions have become further complicated by humanitarian considerations, especially concern about the harmful effects of sanctions on the effective functioning of health and other social support services. Damages to the social safety net have been most thoroughly documented in Iraq but are present in all cases, illustrating the disturbing irony that appears to operate in the use of economic sanctions. On the one hand, such measures are imposed with greater regularity, often with an expressed rationale of avoiding the ostensibly more inhumane application of military force. On the other hand, the short-term humanitarian consequences and longer-term structural effects of economic sanctions in some cases would often appear to be as harmful as war itself, if not more so. This apparent irony frames our central research questions: How pervasive are the negative humanitarian consequences of sanctions? Does this damage outweigh whatever political objectives may have been accomplished in imposing sanctions? These research questions for multilateral sanctions stand in stark contrast to the already existing findings of the devastating humanitarian impacts of some unilateral cases, where sanctions are essentially punitive. The most thoroughly documented case in the literature is U.S. sanctions against Cuba.[4]

Recent research and policy discussions regarding multilateral economic sanctions have also recognized that such measures carry a host of primary and secondary goals, some more attainable than others.[5] Keeping pressure via sanctions on an apartheid regime is one thing; ousting Saddam Hussein is quite another. Although there is widely held skepticism about the utility of economic sanctions in achieving certain political objectives, they appear superficially attractive relative to alternative instruments of policy.[6] At the same time, there is growing reticence about sanctions, given a lack of consistency and an absence of formalized and effective mechanisms for their monitoring, enforcement, and evaluation.[7]

Among those who apply economic sanctions (hereafter referred to as policymakers and sanctioners) and those who seek to minister to the casualties of their application (humanitarian practitioners), certain concerns converge. To date, this convergence has not resulted in consensus about recognizing when the adverse impact of sanctions on civilians becomes a humanitarian emergency. Nor has it yielded agreement whether sanctioners and practitioners should develop a common strategy for anticipating and dealing with this eventuality.

Concern about humanitarian consequences has been sparse in the academic literature but has always been part of the ongoing policy debate within international organizations.[8] However, the discussion has become more heated as sanctions have gained currency. In 1992 UN High Commissioner for Refugees Sadako Ogata urged that sanctions operate "without making the disadvantaged even more disadvantaged."[9] Similar issues were raised in an October 1993 message to then UN Secretary-General Boutros Boutros-Ghali from his under-secretary-general for humanitarian affairs, Jan Eliasson. The tensions between political gain and civilian pain are framed in a statement by the UN Inter-Agency Standing Committee, a roundtable of humanitarian organizations that consulted in the process with the UN's political and peacekeeping units. "Humanitarian and political objectives do not always coincide and even may be contradictory. Economic sanctions, for example, often have negative consequences for vulnerable groups and often directly affect the poorest strata of the population."[10]

Boutros-Ghali captured the increasingly untenable tensions between civilian gain and political pain in his 1995 *Supplement to An Agenda for Peace.* He noted that sanctions are a "blunt instrument" that inflict suffering on vulnerable groups, complicate the work of humanitarian agencies, cause long-term damage to the productive capacity of target nations, and generate severe effects on neighboring countries. Although he did not reject the use of sanctions, the secretary-general pleaded for reforms in their implementation to minimize humanitarian suffering and for special assistance for vulnerable populations. He called for a new UN "mechanism" to monitor and assess sanctions impact, ensure the delivery of humanitarian assistance to vulnerable groups, and help maximize the political impact of sanctions while minimizing collateral damage.[11]

The International Federation of Red Cross and Red Crescent Societies (IFRC) has voiced concern as well. In a 1995 report, it concluded that sanctions against Iraq, Haiti, and Serbia-Montenegro "have paid only minimal political dividends at a very high price in human terms." The IFRC did not reject sanctions outright but urged that they "should operate within prescribed limits" and that efforts be made to focus "the political and economic impact of sanctions on those in power."[12]

These concerns over the humanitarian impact of sanctions exhibit differences in their placement of responsibility for various negative impacts on sanctions and sanctioners. One perspective maintains that the disjunctures of society as a result of sanctions are an integral part of this policy instrument. As such, the leaders of targeted states control the negative humanitarian impacts, both by how they allocate resources made more scarce and by whether they alter the behavior that generated sanctions in the first place. Under these conditions, the role of the international humanitarian system is compensatory. To protect civilians, aid organizations are obliged to mount additional assistance efforts, sometimes on a triage basis, until the sanctions impasse ends.

One central query posed by this line of argument involves when and how humanitarian actors decide that sanctions are having an unacceptable impact on civilians, in particular the most vulnerable. Recently some analysts have attempted to establish criteria for making such determinations. Lori Fisler Damrosch argues that the inevitable imposition of hardship on the people of a target nation is ethically justifiable if and when it is carried out for a higher political and moral purpose, such as halting aggression or preventing repression. She argues that a sanctions regime, to retain legitimacy, must not drive living standards below subsistence levels.[13] Working from a just-war perspective, Drew Christiansen and Gerard Powers assert that although a certain amount of civilian hardship is unavoidable, sanctions may not deprive people of the basic human right to life and survival. They also note that nations imposing sanctions have a responsibility to provide humanitarian assistance to vulnerable populations.[14]

In a second line of argument, the unintended consequences of sanctions should be tolerated in light of the desirable goal. Implicit in this argument is the notion that whatever the negative impacts of sanctions, the targeted economy and society will recover after their lifting and in some cases will be strengthened because the scarcity of resources under sanctions may have induced greater efficiency in the economic system. There is a parallel to claims made by economists and officials with international banks and lending agencies as they discuss the harsh effects resulting from externally imposed economic austerity programs. And like structural adjustment, there are human costs that make it difficult to have a "human face," or even to keep policymakers aware of those suffering from such international measures.[15] This logic has the ring of the philosophical principle of double effect, whereby the good that can be achieved through sanctions is in tension with the harm that occurs, however unintended. The plausibility of such logic can be tested by the experience of the four cases examined in this volume.

A third set of concerns views humanitarian impacts as so directly related to political gain that sanctioners have an obligation to remove the sanctions when the likelihood for political gain wanes. In the words of one UN humanitarian official who monitored the impacts of sanctions in the Federal Republic of Yugoslavia, it is necessary to establish "the humanitarian limits of sanctions." By this she meant "the point at which the suffering you've imposed is enough to achieve certain stated political results but not so much as to create a humanitarian emergency that can't be tolerated by the international community." Jack Patterson of the American Friends Service Committee (AFSC) argues that sanctioners have not only a responsibility, but also an obligation, to provide humanitarian aid and protect the lives of vulnerable populations. He also raises the important issue of sanctions as an alternative to war. Too often, he notes, sanctions are a prelude to war rather than an alternative. To be morally acceptable, he asserts, sanctions must stand in sharp distinction to the use of military violence.[16]

Without question, nonforcible measures exist for both analysts and practitioners in tension with humanitarian action. However, the view that sanctions and humanitarianism involve a more fundamental contradiction is strongly debated. Situations look quite different to member states of the Security Council seeking to convey a political message, aid organizations concerned about the welfare of affected populations, and targeted populations themselves. The farmer who operates the harrow and the toad beneath the blade have different perspectives. Because sanctions have political repercussions, the debate about their impact is readily distorted by political and humanitarian agendas, both open and hidden. Careful review of historical experience too rarely informs debate or influences discussions of future strategies, in part because of difficulties in establishing consistency or comparability among multiple episodes of economic sanctions.

Policymakers often focus narrowly on the question of effectiveness—that is, whether sanctions are achieving the announced political objectives—while ignoring or disregarding humanitarian effects. National political leaders and intelligence officials emphasize the consequences of sanctions on a target nation's economic activities and policy judgments or on the cohesion of an international political coalition, but not necessarily on the health and well-being of civilians. This overemphasis on policy outcomes is misplaced: the issues of effectiveness and humanitarian impact are more intimately connected than is often acknowledged.

Rather than either a tension or a contradiction, the interconnection between political gain and civilian pain may be more accurately represented on a continuum. On one end, sanctions imposed by the Security Council should be expected to have minimal or negligible impact on human rights or humanitarian conditions. After all, the council is mandated to protect human rights as well as international peace and security. To be effective, sanctions may need to generate moderate levels of inconvenience, discomfort, or disruption. How else will leaders be persuaded to reassess the policies that have occasioned sanctions? This middle position on the continuum already points toward the other end. To make their bite felt by insensitive regimes, sanctions necessarily will have a profoundly negative impact on the socioeconomic sectors of the targeted nation to the point of creating, regrettably but necessarily, a humanitarian emergency.

The four cases examined in this volume are attempts to determine whether the recent experience with sanctions has shifted the debate along the continuum. Do advocates of the view that political gain can be achieved at little humanitarian cost have more difficulty in making their case in light of this experience? Do advocates of the view that heightened civilian pain is justified by increased political gain lack persuasiveness in the absence of clear political results associated with massive human suffering?

Several other factors have emerged to stay the Security Council's hand at precisely the point where it might otherwise be prepared to proceed with a pain-and-gain approach to sanctions. Among these, one of the most prominent is that the council lacks the institutional capability to monitor and enforce sanctions. Its various sanctions committees are charged with managing the implementation of its decisions, but their efforts to carry out programs and assess impacts lag far behind the realities on the ground.[17] Because of this, the council lacks the information necessary to fine-tune (that is, make more humane) sanctions arrangements while they are in force. Combined with the unprecedented duration and harsh consequences of recent sanctions, a backlash against sanctions has taken shape in some quarters. Challenges to the council's functioning in this area are sometimes linked to other criticisms, including its overresponsiveness to the political agendas of its permanent members and a perceived lack of accountability.

These current policy concerns appear very much at odds with the recent theoretical literature on sanctions and multilateral coercive action. In particular, recent studies have maintained, either directly or implicitly, that multilateral sanctions are facilitated by strong international institutional arrangements. Operating in the four cases initiated by the Security Council that are considered here, these arrangements are likely to be more effective in achieving their objective *and* will inflict less damage on the target's economy than will unilateral or bilateral sanctions. As Lisa L. Martin has demonstrated, effectiveness is increased because the international institution fosters a cooperation among sanctioners that, among other impacts, maintains such high coalition commitment that these countries are willing to absorb some of the economic pain of the policy to obtain the professed goal.[18] This claim is an inversion of sorts of the pain-and-gain linkage explored in this volume.

In this situation, sanctioners can achieve their objective, with only limited economic damage to a target country, because economic interdependence permits a focused effort with a clear message. But the prospects for such outcomes are greatly reduced if the sanctions episode and leadership of the multilateral effort are "captured" by a major state sanctioner within the international institution authorizing the action. When a powerful state or states use sanctions more for national than international goals, the pain-and-gain advantage weighs more heavily on the former, possibly in contradiction to the original multilateral policy goals.[19] This is precisely what happened when the UN sanctions against Iraq were captured by the United States and Great Britain after 1991.

Against the backdrop of these recent developments and discussions, three issues require careful analysis: (1) the ways in which sanctions create civilian pain; (2) their impact on humanitarian programs; and (3) the identification of indicators to monitor the civilian impact.

The first two issues are addressed in this chapter, and the third in chapter 2.

Assessing the Full Impact of Sanctions

The parameters for understanding the negative consequences of sanctions for civilian populations emerge from two themes. The first concerns the meaning of "success." In addition to the obvious difficulties in establishing widely agreed criteria for such an ostensibly subjective notion, this theme reveals a great deal about the goals of sanctions, the context in which they are adopted, and the manner in which they are implemented and evolve. Success may be understood in ways that either obscure humanitarian impacts or frame their discussion antiseptically so that civilian pain disappears.

The second theme involves empirical generalizations that have emerged from a variety of recent analyses. These generalizations provide the major categories for policymakers to debate expectations about the potential political gain from particular policies. This literature also serves as a guidepost for knowing which outcomes sanctioners await—and why they wait as long as they do—before acknowledging the acute civilian pain resulting from economic sanctions in a target country.

The literature about sanctions is driven by the notion of success. Paradoxically, however, policy analysts appear not very confident about judging the success rate of sanctions. Margaret Doxey, whose work on sanctions has been published in multiple editions, states emphatically that "sanctions will not succeed in drastically altering the foreign and military policy of the target."[20] Even scholars such as Richard Falk who eschew military intervention and advocate more nonviolent and multilateral means concede that "the difficulty with sanctions is that they cannot be effective, or that it is hard to make them effective."[21] The major empirical study in the field, undertaken by Gary Hufbauer and his colleagues at the Institute for International Economics (IIE), showed an overall success rate for all cases of only 34 percent.[22] The caution about economic sanctions among policy elites reflects the apparent assumption that this rate is simply too low, especially when compared with the assumed higher success rate for forcible military sanctions.

The prominence of the concern with success in the literature has not been matched by self-critical assessment of this emphasis, except in rare cases. For example, Alan Dowty has argued convincingly that "the 'success' of sanctions depends on what goals they are measured against."[23] To their credit, the IIE analysts distinguished success rates of sanctions across diverse primary goals.[24] But even with this qualification, their analyses fail to recognize that a primary goal of sanctions may be more than that embodied in the instrumental outcome. Sanctions often serve multiple purposes, each of which needs to be assessed. The official or publicly declared purposes of sanctions, which usually define the specific policy change that the targeted state must make, are considered primary goals.[25] Yet other objectives also can be identified: establishing deterrence, demonstrating resolve to allies or domestic constituents, sending symbolic messages, and the like. Moreover, these objectives often change over time.[26]

One factor directly relevant to attaining the objectives of sanctions, which is also linked to consequences but underestimated in the literature, is the type of sanction. For certain targeted nations, an arms embargo may have a major, positive impact in curtailing a bloody internal conflict but little if any effect on the national economy. Full-scale trade embargoes, the most often enacted form of sanctions, are designed to take an immediate toll on a target and will have multiplier effects in a variety of social and humanitarian sectors of the country over the medium to long term. Sanctions that suspend direct economic aid and access to development bank loans may have less immediate economic impact but can be devastating over time to infrastructure growth and economic strength. Obviously, partial trade embargoes, especially of high-technology items, will have proportionally less impact on the economy generally or average citizens in particular, but they may deprive the ruling elite of goods critical to their perceived economic or military success. Freezing financial assets and isolating a country by cutting off its commercial transportation and communication links historically have come after other types of sanctions have been imposed. They are also likely to have far more consequences for societal elites than for the general population. The four case studies in this volume attempt to trace particular consequences to specific types of sanctions, but such causal connections are often elusive.

The dominant focus of the literature with the most influence on policy has concentrated on primary goals, narrowly construed, and on the success of the instrumental objectives. Thus in the case of the initial sanctions against Iraq, the primary goal was to force Saddam Hussein to withdraw from Kuwait. In the case of U.S.-led sanctions against Libya, the goal has been to coerce the government of Muammar Qadhafi to extradite the individuals who allegedly engaged in airline terrorism. In neither instance have sanctions alone achieved their objective. If the analysis remains focused literally on primary goals, sanctions indeed have only limited effectiveness. The record demonstrates clearly that sanctions by themselves are seldom able to roll back military aggression, have limited ability to impair a targeted regime's aberrant behavior, and have never toppled a dictator. The U.S. General Accounting Office has accordingly concluded that "the primary goal of sanctions is usually the most difficult to achieve."[27]

But primary goals are not the only ones relevant in assessing consequences. Although symbolic goals may be the simplest to understand owing to their transparency, they also elude easy evaluation. When a leader joins in imposing sanctions to satisfy domestic concerns that his or her government "do something," public opinion polls can be used to determine whether such a policy is successful. When sanctions are meant as a signal of international disapproval of a particular regime, or of the violation of norms, leaders can often cite the solidarity of many states in imposing sanctions as a manifestation of success.[28] Yet because these criteria are so subjective and imprecise, they may lose any connection to the desired changes in the targeted regime. And in some cases, as has been frequently discussed with regard to UN sanctions against Iraq, multiple signals and domestic pressures to maintain sanctions can combine to create a sanctions episode where the goalposts continue to move. Under these conditions, a common definition of success would appear to be very elusive, with the concomitant impact on a society likely to be devastating.

Several studies suggest that sanctions achieve their stated political goals (that is, they have an impact that damages the target economy) when:

- the cost of the sanctions to the target economy exceeds 2 percent of its GNP;

- a large economic size differential exists between the primary sender and the target (a GNP ratio of 10:1);

- the target has a high trade concentration with the sender (greater than 25 percent of target's total trade);

- sanctions are imposed quickly, with maximum harshness and with the full cooperation of trading partners who otherwise might circumvent such mechanisms; and

- the ongoing cost of sanctions for the senders is low.[29]

As firm as this empirical ground may appear, most sanctions cases until very recently have been unilateral, as noted in the introduction. Thus, extrapolation from these findings to the success rates of multilateral sanctions should be made with some caution. As additional data are collected and analyzed on the latest multilateral cases, some of the commonly accepted empirical generalizations about sanctions may change, although the propositions presented here are likely to remain valid.[30]

One of the more intriguing findings from this previous research concerns the utility of financial sanctions. Sanctions involving primarily financial measures, such as freezing loans and assets held in foreign banks, have a higher political success rate (41 percent) than do the more widely imposed trade sanctions (25 percent).[31] In theory, financial sanctions may be most likely to produce the desired political changes within a government because they can be effectively targeted against the economic groups benefiting most from that regime's policies. When elites feel the pinch, they are more likely to lobby for political change and may even help orchestrate it.[32]

When combined with tight controls on transportation and communications, these measures are called "smart sanctions," as they are supposed to isolate key financial assets of leaders, avoiding disproportionate impacts on the most vulnerable members of society. Exactly how these measures will be framed and implemented and assessed for effectiveness, however, remains unclear.[33] During the 1995–96 debate about whether to impose sanctions on the Abacha regime in Nigeria after a new wave of repression, which included the execution of several environmental activists, the United States and other governments succeeded in avoiding the traditional reflex of initiating sanctions with a general trade embargo. However, they failed to find or choose ways to sharpen the effective bite of sanctions, and the Nigerian regime experienced little economic pain other than the rhetoric of condemnation for their abuses.[34] Such examples may indicate that smart sanctions are more workable in theory than politically acceptable in practice.

Finally, sanctions take time to work, often longer than those who impose them anticipate or allow. The cases of the last forty years show that sanctions require an average of nearly three years to achieve their political goals.[35] Analysts are quick to point out, however, that the greatest impact of sanctions typically occurs in the first year.[36] Although the impact may level off in the second and third years, social and humanitarian reverberations continue and often are exacerbated. In the four cases examined in this volume, UN sanctions persisted for seventeen years in South Africa, more than six years in Iraq, three and a half years in Serbia and Montenegro, and about three years in Haiti. In these cases, there is no obvious relationship between the longevity of sanctions and their effectiveness, or lack thereof. Clearly other factors play an equal or greater role in the prospects for "success." The severity of civilian pain is also a function of multiple variables, including actions by sanctioned leaders and by the international community.

Despite empirical generalizations such as these, policymakers are frustrated when economic sanctions devastate a target economy without producing the desired change in political behavior. The patience of sanctioners is often outlasted by the obduracy of sanctionees. Changed behavior is difficult to achieve exclusively through the use of sanctions, particularly because such behavior usually assumes that leaders of targeted states will behave "rationally" as defined by the sanctioners. Different actors place different values on political and economic outcomes. This uncertainty in attempting to measure the political gain from sanctions makes the task of weighing the accompanying civilian pain extremely difficult. It is hard to justify civilian pain, especially severe human suffering, when the political gain that supposedly justifies this hardship is itself so elusive.

This uncertainty poses a practical as well as a theoretical dilemma for those who advocate sanctions as a robust, yet nonviolent policy. It is especially problematic that the unevenness in application and thus in effectiveness of sanctions defies the use of a calculus for assessing the pain-and-gain balance. Further, if sanctions are to be effective in halting objectionable policies, they must be harsh, comprehensive, and immediate. The logic of the instrument recommends a hard-and-fast policy. Paradoxically, then, economic coercion may appear less bloody than military force, but over time the civilian pain, especially among the most vulnerable, may make sanctions a less humane course of action.

The conventional political psychology of both coercion and persuasion accordingly calls for a much more graduated application of pressure to end objectionable behavior. Thomas Schelling provided the classic argument for this approach in calling for the incremental application of force combined with the clear and imminent threat to inflict more pain in the future. The escalatory nature of such policies, linked to the threat of further action, would leave the target with a sense of impending "pain beyond endurance."[37] Faced with this prospect, according to Schelling, the target would alter behavior to avoid the threatened escalation of pain.[38]

The notion of advantageous, incremental action is shared by those who emphasize peaceful conflict resolution and preventive diplomacy. Recasting the terms of a dispute and implementing "trial-and-error" policies often helps defuse violent confrontation and resolve disputes.[39] Yet while the incremental ratcheting up of pressure may be key, experience suggests that economic sanctions by themselves are unlikely to change behavior because their strength has been sapped from the outset by such gradualism. Furthermore, policymakers who seek to impose sanctions gradually to maximize future coercive or conflict-resolution options also tend to oversell domestic constituents, and probably one another, on what sanctions can deliver.

Assessing the impact of sanctions on civilians is also difficult because of tunnel vision among policymakers, who often assess sanctions only in terms of whether they are achieving expected political gains and without attention to negative humanitarian consequences. National leaders publicize the devastating impact of sanctions on a target country's industrial output and exports, but not on its health care system or daily caloric intake. Even when the latter documentation is provided by humanitarian personnel on the ground, there is little evidence that such information is considered relevant or persuasive by governments whose representatives are hardly keen to announce with great fanfare how their policies are hurting vulnerable civilians.

Achieving visible political gains in a target becomes even more important to sanctioners over time because of their own domestic political constituencies. Thus when the domestic political ante about the perceived success of a policy of economic coercion is raised, sanctioning states may downplay somber data regarding civilian pain, which is presented as regrettable but necessary. As a result, policymakers are understandably reticent to confirm that sanctions have created an emergency of substantial proportions; that the humanitarian consequences are so negative that they decrease the chance of achieving the primary policy goals of a policy; and that the wider political gains being sought via sanctions are being dramatically discounted as the human toll necessary to achieve them increases.

It would appear that given the momentum of policies in place and the institutional stakes of those promoting them, midterm corrections are unlikely. The burden in public debate is on those who recommend change, not on those associated with existing policies, however dysfunctional from a humanitarian perspective. That burden is increased by the reality that once in place, sanctions narrow available options and alter the political dynamics for both the sanctioner and the target. That sanctions in the 1990s have lasted longer than any of the cases since 1945 may indicate that they have not proved more effective, but that policymakers have lacked the flexibility to reformulate or discard strategies that are not working. The duration of a given sanctions policy and the gradual increase in civilian pain in an effort to achieve elusive political gain lends credence to the view that inflicting pain often becomes an end in itself rather than a means to an end. What began as a commitment to sanctions policy to achieve certain goals often evolves into a commitment to maintain a sanctions policy, even if it veers away from its goals.[40]

Challenges to Humanitarian Programs

In addition to creating or exacerbating civilian pain, sanctions pose major challenges for humanitarian organizations. First, such measures complicate the effective discharge of the groups' mandates to assist civilians in distress. Functioning within states whose links with the outside world are limited, aid agencies experience difficulties in importing relief material, carrying out routine financial transactions, and posting and supporting international personnel. Most multilateral sanctions authorized by the Security Council provide "passthrough" arrangements for humanitarian items. However, the allowable items vary from situation to situation, and the administrative procedures through which approval is granted can be cumbersome, time-consuming, and arbitrary, and the review process uneven and secretive.[41]

Second, humanitarian organizations working within a country facing sanctions are presented with an identity crisis of the first order. They are seeking, and are expected to convey, a sense of solidarity between themselves as members of the international humanitarian system and those in distress by helping to meet emergency needs for food, health care, and shelter. They do so, however, at precisely the time when the Security Council is seeking to isolate and stigmatize political authorities of the country where those in distress reside. As a result, mixed messages are conveyed. That some humanitarian organizations belong to the same United Nations that has imposed sanctions heightens the difficulty. However, even private organizations not associated with the world body are affected. Day-to-day interactions between international agencies and political authorities become more highly charged in sanctions environments. Artifices such as painting aid vehicles white and disassociating UN aid organizations from the UN Security Council do not reestablish the integrity of humanitarian actors.

Third, humanitarian activities are supported largely by contributions from governments, whether they are channeled through UN organizations, bilateral aid programs, NGOs, or the International Committee of the Red Cross (ICRC). As a result, aid programs are subject to influence from the same governments that seek to isolate a target regime. UN agencies are most vulnerable to such vagaries. But NGOs face a kind of double jeopardy. Private funding from the concerned international public is affected by the efforts of governments to ostracize a regime, as is direct government aid to NGOs. In some instances, aid levels may rise for activities in areas not controlled by reprobate authorities—for example, in northern Iraq during the years 1991–96—while activities to assist vulnerable groups in government-controlled areas suffer. Distinct pluses or minuses aside, a cardinal tenet of humanitarian action in international law and in the ethics of professional practice is that its fundamental purpose is to assist people in need, not to carry out a political agenda or advance political objectives. Although this principle has come under increasing attack as outmoded in the politicized arena of the 1990s, it nonetheless remains a stated ideal and objective for many humanitarian agencies.[42]

Fourth, as noted in the previous discussion, sanctions create additional human need. Indeed, that is their purpose, based on the assumption that civilian pain will produce political gain. Under sanctions, the quality of life of average citizens may deteriorate from difficult to unmanageable. The most vulnerable members of society risk being catapulted from a precarious marginal status to a full-scale emergency. Because humanitarian organizations are on the front lines witnessing and assessing these hardships (as well as charged with helping to eliminate them), understanding the depth of negative humanitarian impacts and how to measure them over time has become a crucial organizational task. This measurement lies at the heart of the case studies and is the primary motivation for this volume.

Finally, sanctions intersect with humanitarian concerns at another juncture—their long-term, structural impact on a target economy. This intersection is distinct from the immediate impacts of sanctions on the quality of life of citizens, especially their health and livelihood. At issue is whether sanctions destroy or damage basic features of target economies to such an extent that they will not be able to recover their productive capacity in a postsanctions situation. Economic development may be reversed or so retarded by economic coercion that the effects are irreversible. Sanctions can place a society in a state of permanent crisis due to displacement of labor (through migration) or changes in the mix of the factors of production. They can stimulate development of a parallel (or illegal) market for goods and concomitant corruption and criminality, producing vested interests in keeping various economic sectors of the country monopolies or oligopolies even in a postsanctions environment.

In short, sanctions represent a challenge, not only to the logistical capacity of aid organizations, but also and more fundamentally to their identity, their mission, and their would-be impartiality.[43] Aid agencies confront a proliferation of needs, ranging well beyond the scale and severity of what existed before sanctions. At the same time, their efforts to cushion the worst consequences of sanctions are viewed with suspicion by some members of the international community as undercutting the chances that economic coercion may result in political gain.

The case studies that follow illuminate the difficulties experienced by humanitarian organizations in four country settings. They demonstrate that all humanitarian organizations are affected by sanctions, although the effects differ because of specific country circumstances, the framing of sanctions and their humanitarian exemptions, as well as the scope, duration, and enforcement of the economic coercion. In each of the sanctions episodes, the coercion authorized and the administrative procedures established by the Security Council tend to argue for individualized conclusions, although some improvements have been made in recent years that are applicable across cases. The need for additional changes is examined in chapter 7, which also analyzes the four individual experiences in a broader context.

Conclusion

Sanctions and humanitarianism often collide. Although in theory sanctions are motivated by an implicitly humane rationale, their implementation often wreaks great havoc and civilian suffering. Inherent in sanctions policy are uncomfortable and, for the moment, still imprecise calculations about inflicting civilian pain to achieve political gain. Where tolerable civilian discomfort ends and full-fledged humanitarian crisis begins is an elusive boundary, particularly because presanctions conditions in many countries are often so marginal. The next chapter offers some indicators that attempt to capture these different conditions in sanctioned environments.

The link between sanctions and humanitarianism is further clouded by the usual bureaucratic and political judgments that tend to downplay the impact on vulnerable groups as a critical variable in policy assessments. Civilian pain is often presented antiseptically, to be rationalized as necessary to achieve the requisite political gain.

The intersection of sanctions and humanitarianism also raises a host of issues about structural change in the economies of targets, about the likelihood of military action should sanctions fail, and about the identity and work of the international agencies that provide a buffer against a target country's total collapse. Each of these themes is explored in the ensuing case studies. They also raise numerous methodological questions, which are the subject of the following chapter.

Notes

1. For a discussion of the historical development of the charter within the United Nations, see Thomas G. Weiss, David P. Forsythe, and Roger A. Coate, *The United Nations and Changing World Politics* (Boulder, Colo.: Westview, 1994); Chad Alger, *The Future of the United Nations System* (Tokyo: United Nations University Press, 1997); Karen A. Mingst and Margaret P. Karns, *The United Nations in the Post–Cold War Era* (Boulder, Colo.: Westview, 1994), esp. 15–36, 65–106; Thomas Erlich and Mary Ellen O'Connell, eds., *International Law and the Use of Force* (Boston.: Little, Brown, 1993), 289–398; W. Michael Reisman, "Allocating Competencies to Use Coercion in the Post–Cold War World: Practices, Conditions, and Prospects," and Oscar Schachter, "Authorized Use of Force by the United Nations and Regional Organizations," in *Law and Force in the New International Order*, ed. Lori Fisler Damrosch and David J. Scheffer (Boulder, Colo.: Westview, 1994), 26–48, and 65–93, respectively.

2. For a detailed discussion of these and other circumstances associated with the increase in the use of sanctions, see George A. Lopez and David Cortright,

"Economic Sanctions in Contemporary Global Relations," in *Economic Sanctions: Panacea or Peacebuilding in a Post–Cold War World?* ed. David Cortright and George A. Lopez (Boulder, Colo.: Westview, 1995), 3–17. A special focus on cooperation of sanctioners as a criterion for sanctions success is provided in Lisa L. Martin, *Coercive Cooperation: Explaining Multilateral Economic Sanctions* (Princeton: Princeton University Press, 1992).

3. For discussions of combined military and economic sanctions in these cases, see Larry Minear et al., *United Nations Coordination of the International Humanitarian Response to the Gulf Crisis, 1990–1992,* Occasional Paper No. 13 (Providence, R.I.: Watson Institute, 1993); Richard H. Ullman, ed., *The World and Yugoslavia's Wars* (New York: Council on Foreign Relations, 1996); and Robert Maguire et al., *Haiti Held Hostage: International Responses to the Quest for Nationhood, 1986–1996,* Occasional Paper No. 23 (Providence, R.I.: Watson Institute, 1996).

4. See Michael Krinsky and David Golove, eds., *United States Economic Measures against Cuba* (Northampton, Mass.: Aletheia Press, 1993); Kamran Nayeri, "The Cuban Health Care System and the Factors Undermining It," *Journal of Community Health* 20, no. 4 (August 1995): 321–34; and Richard Garfield et al., "The Impact of Economic Crisis and Embargo on Health in Cuba," *American Journal of Public Health* 89, no. 1 (January 1997): 15–20. With reference to the U.S. embargo against Nicaragua, see William M. LeoGrande, "Making the Economy Scream: Economic Sanctions against Sandinista Nicaragua," *Third World Quarterly* 17, no. 2 (1996): 329–48.

5. Although research on multilateral sanctions in the 1990s is still at the early stage, two assessments of such trends are available in John Stremlau, *Sharpening International Sanctions: Toward a Stronger Role for the United Nations* (New York: Carnegie Commission on Preventing Deadly Conflict, 1996); and Bruce W. Jentleson, *Economic Sanctions: Post–Cold War Policy Challenges,* working paper prepared for the National Research Council Committee on International Conflict Resolution, Washington, D.C., June 1996.

6. Some of the attraction may be explained by the reality that sanctions, despite appearing to be an alternative to direct use of force, are always meant to convey punishment for the target's behavior. See Kim Richard Nossal, "International Sanctions as International Punishment," *International Organization* 43, no. 2 (Spring 1989): 301–23.

7. See Paul Conlon, "The UN's Questionable Sanctions Practices," *Aussen Politik* [*German Foreign Affairs Review*] 46, no. 4 (1995): 327–38.

8. Among the few exceptions is the discussion of the linkage about strengthening UN sanctions capacity undertaken by the Carnegie Commission on Preventing Deadly Conflict and reported in Stremlau, *Sharpening Economic Sanctions,* 40–45. Also see Margaret P. Doxey, *International Sanctions in Contemporary Perspective* (New York: St. Martin's, 1996).

9. Quoted in Claudia von Braunmühl and Manfred Kulessa, *The Impact of UN Sanctions on Humanitarian Assistance Activities: Report on a Study Commissioned by the United Nations Department of Humanitarian Affairs* (Berlin: Gesellschaft für Communication Management Interkultur Training mbH–COMIT, 1995), 2.

10. United Nations, Inter-Agency Standing Committee, *Respect for Humanitarian Mandates in Conflict Situations* (New York: United Nations, 1996), sec. 12.

11. Boutros Boutros-Ghali, *Supplement to An Agenda for Peace*, paras. 66–76, reprinted in *An Agenda for Peace, 1995* (New York: United Nations, 1995).

12. Peter Walker, "Sanctions: A Blunt Weapon," *Red Cross, Red Crescent*, no. 3 (1995): 19.

13. Lori Fisler Damrosch, "The Civilian Impact of Economic Sanctions," in *Enforcing Restraint: Collective Intervention in Internal Conflicts*, ed. Lori Fisler Damrosch (New York: Council on Foreign Relations, 1993), 281–82.

14. Drew Christiansen and Gerard Powers, "Economic Sanctions and the Just War Doctrine," in *Economic Sanctions*, ed. Cortright and Lopez, 97–117.

15. See Richard Jolly and Ralph van der Hoeven, eds., *Adjustment with a Human Face—Record and Relevance*, special issue, *World Development* 19, no. 12 (December 1991).

16. Jack T. Patterson, "The Political and Moral Appropriateness of Sanctions," in *Economic Sanctions*, ed. Cortright and Lopez, 89–96.

17. Two different approaches to this harsh reality include Conlon, "UN's Questionable Sanctions Practices"; and Jaleh Dashti-Gibson, "Sharpening the Bite: Monitoring Multilateral Sanctions in the Post–Cold War World" (Ph. D. diss., University of Notre Dame, forthcoming).

18. See Martin, *Coercive Cooperation;* and Lisa L. Martin, "Credibility, Costs, and Institutions," *World Politics* 45 (April 1993): 406–32.

19. Such an argument is made in the comparative book review essay of Edward D. Mansfield, "International Institutions and Economic Sanctions," *World Politics* 47 (July 1995): 575–605.

20. Doxey, *International Sanctions in Contemporary Perspective*, 92.

21. Richard Falk, "The Use of Economic Sanctions in the Context of a Changing World Order" (paper presented at the Conference on International Economic Sanctions in the Post–Cold War Era, Philadelphia, 17 October 1992), 1.

22. See Gary C. Hufbauer, Jeffrey J. Schott, and Kimberly Ann Elliott, *Economic Sanctions Reconsidered: History and Current Policy*, 2d ed. (Washington, D.C.: Institute for International Economics, 1990), 2.

23. Alan Dowty, "Sanctioning Iraq: The Limits of the New World Order," *Washington Quarterly* 17, no. 3 (Summer 1994): 192.

24. See Hufbauer, Schott, and Elliott, *Economic Sanctions Reconsidered*, 93 ff.

25. General Accounting Office (GAO), *Economic Sanctions: Effectiveness as Tools of Foreign Policy* (Washington, D.C.: GAO, 1993), 11.

26. See Hufbauer, Schott, and Elliott, *Economic Sanctions Reconsidered*, 93 ff for the issue of fluid objectives; Nossal, "International Sanctions as Punishment," would argue that despite such shifting objectives, the punitive reality of sanctions is their central characteristic, if not goal.

27. GAO, *Economic Sanctions: Effectiveness*, 11.

28. This reality has led Nincic and Wallensteen to observe that "of all the ends that sanctions can plausibly be intended to promote, it is here that such policies may be most effective." In Miroslov Nincic and Peter Wallensteen, eds., *Dilemmas of Economic Coercion: Sanctions in World Politics* (New York: Praeger, 1983), 8.

29. The sources for these generalizations include Hufbauer, Schott, and Elliott, *Economic Sanctions Reconsidered*, 49–73; GAO, *Economic Sanctions: Effectiveness;* Margaret P. Doxey, *Economic Sanctions and International Enforcement* (New York: Oxford University Press, 1980), 77–83; and James M. Lindsay, "Trade Sanctions as Policy Instruments: A Re-examination," *International Studies Quarterly* 30 (June 1986): 153–73.

30. The opportunity to investigate whether or how such empirical patterns change will emerge in 1998 when the IIE research team publishes an updated version of the previously cited 1990 edition of *Economic Sanctions Reconsidered*.

31. Hufbauer, Schott, and Elliott, *Economic Sanctions Reconsidered*, 63 ff.

32. See William H. Kaempfer and Anton D. Lowenberg, "Theory of International Economic Sanctions: A Public Choice Approach," *American Economic Review* 78 (September 1988): 792–93.

33. For example, the researchers at the IIE who observed the relatively high success rate of financial sanctions in achieving their objectives noted that financial strictures are almost always imposed *after* a trade embargo has been in place. The "smart sanctions" strategy front-loads these measures, whose outcome is unpredictable because of insufficient historical data.

34. For an early argument for such an approach, see George A. Lopez and David Cortright, *"Smart" Sanctions on Nigeria*, working paper of the Joan B. Kroc Institute for International Peace Studies, Notre Dame, Ind., April 1996. See also Desmond Tutu, "Tough Sanctions Could Topple Nigerian Regime," *Baltimore Sun*, 10 December 1995.

35. Doxey, *Economic Sanctions and International Enforcement*, 101.

36. Nincic and Wallensteen, *Dilemmas of Economic Coercion*, 109.

37. See esp. the chapter "The Diplomacy of Violence," in Thomas Schelling, *Arms and Influence* (New Haven: Yale University Press, 1966), 63 ff.

38. Although her analysis of sanctions analyzes the conditions associated with, and institutional arrangements necessary for, successful multilateral sanctions, much of the context of Martin's *Coercive Cooperation* fits within this theory of compulsion.

39. A good example of recent research in this mode is Louis Kriesberg, Terrell A. Northrup, and Stuart J. Thorson, *Intractable Conflicts and Their Transformation* (Syracuse: Syracuse University Press, 1989).

40. This "commitment to the commitment" is not a new phenomenon in foreign policymaking. It was first outlined in detail in describing the momentum of policy in Vietnam decisionmaking by Leslie Gelb and Richard Betts, *The Irony of Vietnam: The System Worked* (Washington, D.C.: Brookings Institution, 1979).

41. We are aware that analysts and UN officials have some disagreement regarding the scope of these and the level of crisis they create in humanitarian action. Compare, for example, Conlon, "Questionable Sanctions Practices," with James C. Ngobi, "The United Nations Experience with Sanctions," in *Economic Sanctions*, ed. Cortright and Lopez, 17–28.

42. The most controversial analysis is Rakiya Omaar and Alex de Waal, *Humanitarianism Unbound? Current Dilemmas Facing Multi-Mandate Relief Operations in Political Emergencies* (London: African Rights, 1994), Discussion Paper no. 5. There

is also a rapidly growing literature on the political dimensions of humanitarian action and peacekeeping, e.g., Jarat Chopra, "The Space of Peace-Maintenance," *Political Geography* 15, nos. 3/4 (1996): 335–57; and Antonio Donini, *The Policies of Mercy: UN Coordination in Afghanistan, Mozambique, and Rwanda,* Occasional Paper No. 22 (Providence, R.I.: Watson Institute, 1996). There also is a growing interest in this subject among political philosophers, e.g., a special issue "Rescue—The Paradoxes of Virtue," *Social Research* 62, no. 1 (Spring 1995), esp. Michael Walzer, "The Politics of Rescue," 53–66. See also David Rieff, "The Humanitarian Trap," *World Policy Journal* 12, no. 4 (Winter 1994–95): 1–11; and Amir Pasic and Thomas G. Weiss, "The Politics of Rescue: Yugoslavia's Wars and the Humanitarian Impulse," *Ethics and International Affairs* 11 (1997), forthcoming.

43. See Larry Minear and Thomas G. Weiss, *Humanitarian Politics* (New York: Foreign Policy Association, 1995).

2

Toward a Framework for Analysis

**Thomas G. Weiss, David Cortright,
George A. Lopez, and Larry Minear**

In recent years, the growing trend to impose economic sanctions has
been met with a growing concern about the results of doing so. Policymakers, humanitarian practitioners, analysts, and the public have
expressed uneasiness about the pain meted out to civilians who are not
responsible for the foreign and domestic policies of targeted governments
and who have very limited leverage to change repressive authorities. The
disquiet has been fueled by analyses of the effects of sanctions on children, the most vulnerable members of societies. Concerns also have been
expressed about the unevenness in political gains achieved by sanctions
and about the lack of consistency in their application. A dispassionate
review of recent experience is clearly required.

However, such an examination is no small task. This chapter sketches
a modest framework that permits an initial comparative assessment of the
humanitarian impact of economic sanctions. The methodological challenge is formidable, raising issues of causation, specification, and comparison. Especially in comparing, we are well aware that simply the com-
monality of the four selected multilateral cases of the 1990s may be
irrelevant in light of the particular experience from each country, and generalizations may be arduous. At this stage of the investigation, the objective is to develop an analytical structure and to identify useful indicators
that approximate the complex economic, social, and political spheres in
which sanctions operate. The challenge to this volume is whether the
framework can yield a template that is useful in comparing cases and is
relevant in terms of policy to sanctioners and humanitarians.

The approach rejects the conventional counsel from many policymakers
who automatically endorse sanctions and from many practitioners who
equally automatically condemn them. An open-ended research design
was constructed to allow case investigators to pose a wide range of

appropriate questions and to let the data from recent experience begin to speak for itself. A leap of faith in this research design is that such data, when properly marshalled, carefully analyzed, and accurately assessed, should indicate whether there are manageable tensions or fundamental contradictions between sanctions and humanitarian concerns. Further, such comparative case-study data, while uneven and fragmentary, are a requisite first step that should help guide subsequent scholarly analyses and inform policymaking.

The research strategy within the overall design was simple. Each researcher was asked to review relevant literature and experience to catalogue available data and identify plausible conclusions about the extent and sources of civilian pain. The indicators identified in this chapter were to serve as guides. The four major episodes of multilateral sanctions in the 1990s—South Africa, Iraq, the former Yugoslavia, and Haiti—were expected to provide useful cross-case comparisons. As this scrutiny commenced, there was a bonus in three of the cases (the former Yugoslavia being the exception) as investigators traveled to each of the countries.

Researchers also were asked to consider a second, more elusive factor: the political gains sought and achieved by sanctions. A review of the international and domestic political context of sanctions provides opportunities and constraints for both sanctioners and targeted regimes. Contextual variables, such as the type of regime and the nature of the conflict and economy, along with a description of the international political situation and the scope of sanctions for each country, were examined in order to be sensitive to the wider environment in which sanctions functioned. Some of these broader contours detail not only how the imposition of sanctions was interpreted by senders and targets but also how the humanitarian impacts of sanctions were felt and interpreted by political groups in and out of power within the targeted nation. Thus, herein may lie the unique contribution of each of the case studies in this book; such context has seldom been explored in the study of sanctions.[1]

Central to this research design is that the investigation of recent sanctions experience ought to embody the pain-and-gain linkage as closely as possible. There is no intention to eschew macroeconomic analysis that would focus on long-term impact, but it is only a small part of the pain-and-gain dynamic. Thus, a wide range of indicators of the status of civilian life is examined; some of these indicators are quite sensitive in short-term time frames. Whatever the difficulties associated with measuring how much economic sanctions have caused civilian suffering and how much they have achieved stated political objectives, the framework offered affirms the importance of viewing neither pain nor gain in a vacuum. Under these conditions, research findings may advance discussions in the international relations literature on coercion and sanctions and will serve the policy process as an important step in the debate about how to make necessary improvements in the concept and implementation of economic sanctions.[2]

Previous Attempts to Assess Humanitarian Impacts of Sanctions

The chorus of concern regarding humanitarian impacts of sanctions heard in policy circles is so recent that it has generated relatively few attempts to document and analyze this pain-and-gain link. Since these few attempts have been undertaken since 1993, and most as commissioned reports for international agencies, virtually none of them has appeared in any form in scholarly or policy journals. Thus, the parlance of pain-and-gain has been limited indeed.

Primary among the sparse literature are those reports that document the effect of sanctions on the most vulnerable sectors of the population. The studies vary in size and scope and in their ability to establish a direct pain-and-gain link.[3] Moreover, while such studies are sometimes credible attempts to piece together diverse, if not divergent, information, they are undertaken in societies where independent and unbiased information gathering is neither a priority nor standard professional practice. Asserting the pain-and-gain link becomes problematic owing to data quality and the lack of clarity about how much inference or extrapolation the researcher might be permitted in using such data.[4] But a number of recent studies have influenced the approach in this volume, more often because of their claims about the pain-and-gain link than because they have found and interpreted actual data substantiating this phenomenon.

In a seminal paper, "The Impact of Economic Embargoes on Health," Richard Garfield of Columbia University summarizes a variety of different, smaller case studies that examine what happens to national health under sanctions. He claims that an economic embargo can affect health mainly through three mechanisms:

1. It can reduce the quality and quantity of goods available to satisfy a person's need to eat, drink, and dispose of wastes.

2. It can reduce the capacity of the public health system to maintain food, water, air, and medicines of adequate quality.

3. It can reduce the capacity of the system of curative medical care to respond to limitations and failures in (1) and (2) above.[5]

Garfield further notes that societal adjustments to these resource changes, health education, and a wide variety of other factors ultimately will influence the precise medical impact of sanctions on a population. Generally, he concludes soberly, sanctioned countries that are not ruled by leaders with a commitment to quality of life (virtually all conceivable cases of sanctions) are going to experience increased levels of morbidity and mortality, especially among the vulnerable sectors of the population.[6]

The most recent analysis of this type approximates most closely the goals and methods in this book. Eric Hoskins, author of the Iraq case study in this volume and former member of the Harvard Study team, has produced a draft report for the United Nations Children's Fund (UNICEF) that attempts to develop a framework and set of measurable indicators for a "child impact assessment" of sanctions. On the basis of the UNICEF mandate for implementing the Convention on the Rights of the Child and other international human rights codes, such as the Universal Declaration of Human Rights, Hoskins catalogues a number of the "sanctions sensitive indicators" that emerge from a careful reading of these sources of human rights law.[7]

In addition to a differentiated list of indicators, Hoskins also introduces two notions that will be important to use in subsequent studies. First, he envisions sequencing sanctions' impact through a series of phases. At imposition, sanctions have an immediate, direct impact on the economy because of dramatic changes in export earnings, and often because of the curtailment of communications and travel (depending, of course, on how comprehensive the measures are). Intermediate or short-term effects are experienced by the population generally, but by children in particular, in the health and food security sectors of the economy, especially if these sectors have a heavy concentration of imports. Long-term effects of sanctions encompass an array of chronic conditions in the health and social support systems, as well as more indirect effects caused by an overall economic decline.

Second, Hoskins argues that in analyzing these phases, the unit of analysis for sanctions impact should be the household. Two factors determine this: the household is the societal unit most likely to include the vulnerable, that is, women, children, and the elderly; and the household is the unit least able to resist deprivation and deterioration across the different phases of sanctions. Thus household data must be seen in contrast to regional- or national-level indicators, which simply are too highly aggregated and insufficiently sensitive to real quality-of-life variations in short time periods.[8]

Another critical approach to the humanitarian impact of sanctions is the major study undertaken in 1995 for the Department of Human Affairs (DHA) of the United Nations. The authors of this report, Claudia von Braunmühl and Manfred Kulessa, took a particular angle of vision on the pain-and-gain link: they explicitly shied away from establishing either a methodology or a set of indicators for assessing the humanitarian impact of sanctions. They asserted that because sanctions always have some serious negative impact on a population and because various actors within and outside the target state manipulate these consequences for their own purposes, it would be unprofitable to examine humanitarian effects in any strict sense. It would be more sensible, they suggested, to follow closely the work of NGOs and other humanitarian actors to assess how their work changed because of sanctions. Thus, these analysts consider the operational indicator of the level of humanitarian impact (that is, civilian pain) that results from sanctions to be the increased action of humanitarian actors in the targeted country and in frontline states experiencing adverse effects of sanctions.[9]

An alternative approach, which broadens Hoskins's covenant- and rights-based approach, seeks to measure the condition of a targeted population against stated baseline criteria. As elaborated by Lori Fisler Damrosch, these would begin with established data measurements of the society at the time that sanctions are imposed. The international community also would consider a threshold level of humanitarian concern, such as the poverty line, below which sanctions should not plummet the population. Then, sanctions monitoring would assess the effect of sanctions over time. When their effect is to drive various segments of the civilian population below the poverty-line threshold, sanctions become unsupportable. Presumably, the sanctioners are left with only two alternatives: lift the sanctions or inject massive amounts of humanitarian relief to push the indicators back over the line of acceptable civilian pain.[10]

Following closely along this strategy and line of reasoning are the claims of Roger Normand, who contends that a baseline advocated by analysts should not sit within economic and social indicators. Instead it should reside in a set of legal standards that provide a guarantee to civilians that their basic rights and minimal standards of quality of life will not be violated by sanctions. Normand concludes:

> Most importantly, the imposition of sanctions by the Security Council, as well as by individual states, needs to be governed by an explicit legal regime, drafted by a panel of international experts and informed by both human rights and humanitarian law principles. Under this regime, future

cases of sanctions could be assessed according to universal criteria, in contrast to the current situation in which sanctions increasingly are imposed
without reference to any legal or ethical standard.[11]

Probably the most far-reaching study of sanctions' economic impact—
but one without explicit humanitarian categories or criteria—is David
Rowe's dissertation study of the adaptation of the Rhodesian government
and its industries to international sanctions.[12] Rowe's central concern is
how these externally imposed sanctions change the nature of the political
and economic relationships between the national government and economic elites, some of whom may not support the government in exactly
those policies that generated the sanctions. He finds that the Ian Smith
government helped critical economic sectors adapt to sanctions in quite
different ways—thus ultimately strengthening, over the short to medium
term, the white-minority regime's political hand. Owing to its centralized
control of the economy, the government had the ability to withstand the
worst shocks from trade sanctions and to manipulate the effects of sanctions in ways that demobilized political opposition. In addition, the
Rhodesian government was capable of creating new institutions to
respond to the harsh effects of sanctions, buffering negative impacts and
providing new political leverage, even in the face of declining popularity
at home. Rowe's work underscores the importance of examining the political context of sanctions, especially this creative manner in which a sanctioned government can create a new base of support and additional "rally
round the flag" effect.[13]

Causation and Indicators

Because the central research question "How pervasive are the negative
humanitarian consequences of economic sanctions?" attempts to assess
impact, it raises questions about how causality is understood within this
project. As causality has attracted renewed attention among international
relations researchers and social science methodologists of late,[14] the
dynamic embedded in the research puzzle here warrants consideration
under these headings.

- Conditions of multicausality operate in each case. Any number of
  other ongoing, discrete factors could have led (and probably did lead)
  to negative humanitarian impacts either in a more powerful way or in
  a dynamically interactive manner with the contribution of sanctions.

- Sui generis considerations are present in each case. The distinctive features of each of the four situations and the large-scale differences among the individual sanctioned nations are acknowledged. Yet a comparative method that is sensitive to such discrepancies yet is likely to yield generalizations is used to examine more or less the same set of indicators in each of the four case studies.

- The outcome variable, negative humanitarian impacts, requires multifaceted measurement, often nuanced, across a large list of discrete indicators.

Each of these parts of the problem deserves comment. First, the four cases concern countries in which multiple causes exist: war (Iraq and Yugoslavia), political and economic repression (Haiti, South Africa), and changing world economic circumstances affecting their economies (Yugoslavia and South Africa), to name just the most prominent of the more critical forces that would compete with sanctions as a "cause" of negative humanitarian impacts. An ideal research world would contain variables (like those just mentioned) for which precise and meaningful data existed and a sufficiently large number of cases would permit a statistical analysis across cases. Recognizing that the inability to create such an ideal research world limits the ability to apportion precise levels of causation of any of the "critical forces," it is important to explain why it is credible to hypothesize that sanctions in fact had negative humanitarian impacts.

One useful way to address this crucial issue is to examine sanctions from the perspective of counterfactual claims or conditions. As an insightful approach to causal assessment using limited numbers of cases, counterfactual analysis permits a particular perspective on the question of the impact of sanctions. In particular it permits the rejection of claims that sanctions fail to result in political gains and that they should not be among the factors considered in studying deteriorating economic and social conditions in economically unstable nations.[15]

On the gain side of the calculation, the counterfactual approach prompts such questions as: If sanctions, however comprehensive or partial, had not existed, would apartheid in South Africa not have ended in 1993? Or, if sanctions had not existed, would Milosevic not have brought Bosnian Serbs and himself as Serbian president to the bargaining table at Dayton in 1995? Regarding the pain dimension, if there had been no sanctions, would there have been no ongoing humanitarian crisis in Iraq after the Gulf War? Even though the U.S. bombing during the war wrecked the social and humanitarian infrastructure of Iraq, closer scrutiny produces a useful counterfactual nuance even in this difficult case: The war immobilized Iraqi society, possibly creating a humanitarian emergency. But without sanctions, rehabilitation and a return to minimal normalcy, especially in health and sanitation, would have been possible. Counterfactual reasoning permits an assessment of the manner in which sanctions are linked in a pain-and-gain mode, even when total precision is lacking, because to dismiss their influence would lead to a void in causal explanation.

The second dilemma concerns sui generis problems. To refine the notion of causal links, it is necessary to narrow the wide variation among possible impacts that sanctions may have on humanitarian conditions in the targeted state. To help make meaningful distinctions, three different sanctions impact conditions are specified at the outset. In the first hypothesized relationship, sanctions serve as a catalyst for worsening socioeconomic and related conditions. They do so by setting in motion a series of serious shortfalls and economic dislocations so that the support structure or cornerstone of the socioeconomic dimensions of a society is damaged, with the most vulnerable portions of the population sent into disarray or crisis. At various times, this appears to be precisely the situation of sanctions in Haiti and Iraq.

In contrast to the catalyst and its rather direct impact, sanctions also may serve to exacerbate one or more deteriorating conditions that already exist in the economic sphere, resulting in further negative trends in the humanitarian sector. In this sense, sanctions may serve as the straw that breaks the camel's back, pushing a society that may already be in humanitarian need to a condition of humanitarian emergency. As a third distinct effect, sanctions may generate structural change in the economy by shifting resources and the means by which they are distributed. This often results from the targeted government's decisions about economic policy, but it may also happen "privately," as in the rise of criminal elements and black marketeering brought on by the changing resource mix. In structural change, the negative humanitarian impact of sanctions is less immediately felt in the society, but it is likely to be deeper and broader when it is felt over the medium to long term.

Given the aim here to assess impact and causality, the decision to examine four cases of multilateral economic sanctions in the 1990s pushes contributors to employ a structured and focused comparison mode of inquiry. Consistent with this approach, the cases, and a comparative investigative strategy, meet three criteria:

- In each of the cases, it is possible (through direct statement or counterfactual claims as made above) to posit some clear causal patterns that may or may not hold under close scrutiny but that initially illustrate variation across the cases.

- The comparison of cases is structured so that the same general guiding queries and the same variable indicators are used to guide data collection.

- The cases are compared in a focused manner, according to the pain-and-gain dimensions, rather than attempting to examine every economic, social, and political impact of sanctions.[16]

Finally, a word is in order about the third methodological difficulty, which concerns devising a serviceable way to measure the humanitarian impact of sanctions. The task is difficult for a variety of reasons, some of which have been suggested in these first two chapters. Establishing a series of indicators that reflect changes in the status of civilian populations is a social science challenge of the first order. Moreover, data in sanctioned countries are frequently sparse, unavailable to international organizations, and/or manipulated for political purposes. In addition, multiple factors are involved in the worsening of the population's status, including government policies as well as the sanctions themselves. These make it difficult to pinpoint how much sanctions are implicated.

Attempts to move toward an agreed framework about humanitarian effects are complicated by the absence of a generally accepted definition in international law of humanitarian assistance for which exemptions are normally allowed when sanctions are imposed. The International Court of Justice (ICJ) has identified the activities of the International Committee of the Red Cross (ICRC) as humanitarian, but the relevant opinion provides more a tautological description than a definition.[17] Dictionary definitions evoke multiple associations from very positive ("heroic and unselfish service to mankind") to very negative ("naive" and "interventionist"). As a result, a range of doubtful policies can be justified as "humanitarian." For example, the Reagan administration in 1985 requested, and the U.S. Congress approved, "humanitarian assistance" to the Nicaraguan insurgents. Or, closer to the focus of this book, the work of the UN Security Council's Sanctions Committee has been complicated by a lack of consensus as to whether such individual items as health kits, fertilizer, children's playthings, or spare parts for water purification plants qualify as "humanitarian."

In spite of this controversy, a reading of the literature and interviews with policymakers point toward a commonsensical working definition of "humanitarian" that includes the minimal conditions for life, health, and dignity. To the extent that economic well-being determines the ability of individuals to enjoy life, health, and dignity, basic economic opportunity also deserves a place within the array of such concerns. Thus, humanitarian assistance consists of those emergency efforts by outsiders or local populations to improve the life, health, and dignity of noncombatants suffering from natural disasters, wars, or such international political decisions as economic or military sanctions.

Can the impacts of sanctions be disaggregated from negative humanitarian consequences resulting from war, political repression, military spending, domestic social policies, and economic impoverishment? A large portion of this problem was addressed above, but it is useful to recognize that "pure" disaggregation in any meaningful sense of establishing a precise accounting of impacts simply cannot be ascertained. What can be undertaken with some care and accuracy, as the cases demonstrate, is a modified form of process tracing, whereby economic factors, including types of sanctions in effect that beset an economy and society, are assessed in a Geertzian-like "thick description" of the depth of impact.[18] Such an approach, in combination with the comparative method selected, acknowledges that each sanctions imposition, like each target country, has a number of unique dimensions. It is essential to note for each sanctions case how these singular features affect the assessment of humanitarian impacts.

Central to the analytical task, then, is establishing a cluster of indicators that guide data collection for case studies, both those in this volume and those undertaken in the future by other researchers. Although a wealth of indicators can be collected about a given population, data gathering for this volume has been structured in terms of two general categorizations. The first is collecting information across four category clusters: economic, sociodemographic, health/medical, and sociohumanitarian. For the most part, the first three indicator sets aim to assess the direct and secondary economic, social, and health impacts of sanctions on individuals; the fourth, while containing some individual data, aims to measure societal coping with the stress that sanctions (and/or other factors) have placed on populations.

The second categorization attempts to assess these four clusters of indicators in terms of two basic measures: the physical integrity of life of individuals and the often more subjective quality-of-life indicators. Physical integrity means those variables that relate to whether people can actually live and survive; quality of life is a "more or less" sensitive indicator, in which baseline data are important in determining deterioration generally and the portion that can be attributed to sanctions in particular. The combination of trends in both indicators (such as declining rates of both) provides researchers with a sense of when a society moves from discomfort to humanitarian need to humanitarian crisis.

A suggested full list of indicator variables appears in table 2.1 and was the comprehensive guide provided to the case-study researchers. In gathering information, they were asked to have particular interest in measurements that are sensitive to incidence in the population, to rates of change over the short run, and, where sensible, to standardized data. Ideally, research would permit measurement of these indicators on distinct sectors of the population, with the most notable discriminations based on age, gender, urban/rural, and ethnic variations. It is essential in diverse contexts to define which sectors suffered the most and the least in order to understand better which populations were able to minimize or avoid the negative humanitarian consequences of international economic coercion.

Since the purely economic impacts of sanctions frequently have indirect but clear humanitarian consequences, it is important to gather societywide data about important macroeconomic indicators. These include the rate of inflation, the situation of the currency internally and worldwide, employment/unemployment data, industrial and agricultural outputs, and consumer purchasing power. Changes in the economic infrastructure of a society also need monitoring to determine the economic winners and losers and how relationships with neighbors changed. Three areas of inquiry link economic and humanitarian concerns and are particularly important for gathering nonquantitative information about the fourth and key category, the sociohumanitarian infrastructure. Of special interest are:

- the differential effects of various types of sanctions (for example, trade embargoes, arms embargoes, oil embargoes, financial sanctions, communication and transportation blockage) on the most vulnerable and relatively less vulnerable populations;

- the kinds of sanctions that hurt elites the most while having the least impact on vulnerable, nontarget populations;

- the types of sanctions that produce the most serious long-term impacts on an economy.

Finally, in order to fill in more fully the pain-and-gain picture, it is essential to ask two sets of questions:

Table 2.1
Indicators of Humanitarian Impact of Economic Sanctions

Economic	
Physical Integrity	Quality of Life
• household purchasing power (cost of "basic food" basket) • changes in wage rate • changes in the number of people living at or below the poverty line	• existence of black market • per capita GDP • consumer price index • percentage of industry operating at capacity • unemployment rate • inflation rate • trends in savings and investment • government expenditures (e.g., education)

Sociodemographic	
Physical Integrity	Quality of Life
• crime/personal security • displacement • psychological well-being • housing/shelter availability	• human rights situation • degree of civil society • changes in environment (nonhealth) • rationing programs • dropout rate in schools • changes in land use

Health and Medical	
Physical Integrity	Quality of Life
• access to health care and basic drugs • availability of clean water and sanitation • morbidity and mortality rates • birth statistics for children	• environmental damage • adequacy of intermediate and advanced care • isolation • fuel sources

Sociohumanitarian	
Physical Integrity	Quality of Life
• adequacy of support system for the vulnerable (women, children, the elderly) • family/household violence	• social services demand • INGOs present • migration rates of skilled personnel • access to transportation and communications • changes in government capacity to meet basic needs

- What has been the recent experience regarding lifting sanctions? Has the achievement of stated objectives been followed by the prompt removal of sanctions, or have the goalposts been moved to reflect evolving political agendas? This is one of the research questions that has an important policy-related flip side, namely, should the likelihood of political difficulties associated with lifting sanctions be taken into account in deciding whether or not to impose them in the first place? Certainly the mood among a number of UN member states points in the direction of such an approach before serious consideration will again be given to comprehensive sanctions against a particular country.

- What has been the recovery after the removal of sanctions? Has the economic infrastructure been altered in ways that retard the possibility of recovery to presanctions levels? Have illegal or parallel markets developed that negatively affect the general economic picture?

The task of assessing the impacts of sanctions on the work of humanitarian agencies is based less on such aggregate indicators than on a subjective appreciation of expanded human needs and reduced agency effectiveness. In particular, it is important to ascertain whether current humanitarian exemption procedures are adequate or whether they should be replaced. What procedures were used to exempt items from embargoes or to make them otherwise available for humanitarian assistance? How well have those procedures worked? What types of leakage occurred?

A central concern is discovering whether the negative consequences of economic coercion can be offset by the compensatory benefits of additional international assistance. Mapping the demography of the humanitarian challenge before sanctions, the relationship of the targeted state to the region prior to the imposition of sanctions, and the quality of the working relationship between the targeted government and aid agencies is essential. A related issue involves the extent and value of continued dialogue between sanctioned authorities and outside aid groups. Did this dialogue—or ongoing political negotiations—have any effect on the treatment of the target by the international humanitarian system, or vice versa?

A final question regards international relief organizations charged with counteracting the burden of sanctions on neighboring countries. Would the consequences be different if sanctions had been imposed with explicit and effective cushioning measures for third parties? Did humanitarian assistance help in mitigating the effects of sanctions on third parties? Such queries open up a series of larger policy concerns that are addressed in the final chapter. Among them is determining how realistic are calls to strengthen the implementation of Article 50 of the UN Charter. Specifically, can the preassessments proposed by the United Nations secretary-general consider such effects as well?

Toward Understanding the Political Effects of Economic Sanctions

An assessment of sanctions must include an understanding of the political context in which they operate. Recent sanctions episodes suggest that individual countries often have quite different motives and national interests at stake in supporting the imposition of sanctions and in ensuring their actual implementation. Yet the stability of a coalition may depend on the extent to which the partners share views rather than paper over differences with diplomatic language in resolutions. Recent cases are too divergent to establish whether sanctions are more effective against a target (or, alternatively, attract greater international support and cooperation) when invoked to punish violators of international human rights standards, to persuade states to denuclearize, or to convince the leaders of a country to change their decision to harbor suspected international terrorists.

Data suggest that sanctions are more likely to be successful in deterring aggressive action and in creating conditions for arms negotiations than in removing leaders from political office. Therefore, when sanctions are geared to achieving the last objective, their impacts on civilians are likely to be more serious and risky, especially unless provision for humanitarian exemptions has been made. Such an approach to economic coercion would seem to condemn a civilian population to a deteriorating quality of life, except in the unlikely event that it is willing to undertake revolution—for which there is no historical precedent.

In cases where sanctions serve realizable political objectives and provision has been made for humanitarian relief, researchers should assess the degree of accountability and transparency in enforcement and administration. This can be done in part by institutional mechanisms that ensure that sanctions are administered by international civil servants with maximum equity and minimum politicization. A related task is to explore whether sanctions are more likely to be successful when they are a component of a larger, coherent strategy that includes other means of persuasion, such as the possible use of incentives to end sanctions. It is useful to ask whether sanctions stand alone as *the* policy against a targeted state or are part of a larger mix of policies—some of which may be more carrot-like (involving persuasion and incentives), some of which may be even more sticklike (involving coercion through military force). These and related issues are addressed in the concluding chapter.

At the domestic level in a targeted country, three variables are relevant when judging how raw data about humanitarian consequences suggest how civilians might react to their own plight. The first involves one of the better known outcomes of sanctions in a targeted state: "rally round the flag." Leaders of a sanctioned regime are able to use the shared sense of human misery brought on by sanctions to broaden their political support. The sense of endurance and camaraderie of the citizenry is enhanced by standing fast—and together—against the evil external sanctioners.[19]

The second domestic variable deals with the reaction of leadership to the humanitarian consequences of sanctions beyond the "rally round the flag" effect. Is a particular government stronger because it can condemn opponents and reward supporters through the allocation of scarce resources and government stockpiles of goods? What differential impacts or manipulation of sanctions by the targeted government take place? Did sanctioners anticipate, and move to preempt, these?

The third domestic variable links international sanctions with internal change. Sanctions may contribute positively or negatively to conditions for viable political opposition or reform by a sanctioned leadership. Relevant questions include the following: Do sanctions stimulate or hinder the prospects for internal political actors to organize and engage in political opposition? Under which conditions do existing opposition groups support sanctions? Does the impact of sanctions stifle other desirable developments in civil society? Does the severity of civilian pain change the assessment and influence the resolve of the international community to continue or to rescind sanctions?

Examining the alternative contextual factors by which a sanctioned state sees its choices should permit better informed judgments about when sanctions are likely to be effective or counterproductive. The four case studies in the next part of this volume illustrate how such contexts shape the impact of sanctions, especially as regards human suffering, as well as how humanitarian action affects the stated objectives of any policy of economic coercion.

Caveats and Conditions

In light of the embryonic and uneven state of data and knowledge, cross-national comparisons clearly present a formidable challenge. Three factors disturb the ideal set of circumstances and research strategies that scholars would have wanted. First, mechanisms for data collection on the impact of sanctions vary considerably. Data on households is pivotal in assessing coping mechanisms of suffering populations. Such data, however, may simply be unavailable, or when it is available, it may not lend itself to comparisons.

Specifically, in the four case studies that follow, information is derived from earlier fieldwork by the researchers and others and does not involve newly generated data. Moreover, in all cases, authors analyze the impact of sanctions on children or other vulnerable segments of the population, but again statistics are incomparable across cases. To the extent possible, contributors seek to mitigate the worst effects of such differential data by presenting and analyzing a range of available data for each case.

A second factor involves the aforementioned difficulty in apportioning the effects of sanctions on a population relative to other conditions, policies, and events. For South Africa, the pressures of an extractive economy suffering under a global recession were overlaid by a comprehensive international embargo. For Iraq, the challenge involves disentangling the impacts of sanctions from those of the Iran-Iraq war, of government policies during the 1990s, and then of the Gulf War itself. For Haiti, the situation was complicated by on-again, off-again sanctions targeting the poorest and most stratified economy in the Western Hemisphere. In the case of the former Yugoslavia, the issue involves how much sanctions contributed to the deterioration of civilian life in Serbia and Montenegro as compared with the ill effects of their sponsorship of the war in Bosnia. Such analytical complexities and ambiguities notwithstanding, the chapters convey the considered judgment of researchers who are able to identify to a surprising extent the role played specifically by sanctions in civilian pain.

However much the four cases warrant and require comparison, there are many constraints to providing a systematic scheme for understanding the humanitarian impacts or the political context of economic coercion. This volume therefore represents at most a limited step toward greater analytical clarity. As the case studies demonstrate, the framework is useful in assessing humanitarian consequences and offers a template of sorts for international agencies that have become increasingly concerned with assessments. It can serve as a guide to preassessments of the likely consequences of sanctions as policy is debated.

There does not yet exist a uniform research protocol, much less a comprehensive methodology, for judging the impact of economic sanctions on political, social, and economic life in target countries. This chapter has attempted to deal with the many methodological issues that are involved in such a research task. In addition, it has provided a rationale for this research that builds from ongoing work on humanitarian impacts that, while relevant, has remained mostly in the purview of a few agencies and experts. Finally, the text provides a general set of guiding indicators for monitoring the humanitarian condition of vulnerable populations within targeted states.

There is no substitute for new fieldwork, undertaken by a diverse team of country, functional, and disciplinary experts, using a template such as that proposed in table 2.1. The present research may heighten interest in, and expectations for, what such in-country studies could provide. It may also whet the appetite of private and public sources of funding to support such necessary research and increase the interest of policymakers in reviewing its findings and recommendations.

With these caveats and conditions in mind, it now is appropriate to proceed to the individual case studies. The next four chapters analyze the most serious and long-standing cases in which multilateral sanctions have been imposed, applying the indicators and framework to the extent possible. These cases constitute a sort of test of the adequacy of the questions and categories provided. They also provide examples of the methodological difficulties that this chapter raised and that will face future research. As the reader no doubt will have surmised, the conclusions and recommendations in the final chapter necessarily will be tentative.

Notes

1. Earlier work by two of the editors suggested, but did not develop, this important theme. See David Cortright and George A. Lopez, "Research Concerns and Policy Needs in an Era of Sanctions," in *Economic Sanctions: Panacea or Peacebuilding in a Post–Cold War World?* ed. David Cortright and George A. Lopez (Boulder, Colo.: Westview, 1995), 201–4.

2. In particular, the editors have in mind the work of Lisa Martin, *Coercive Cooperation: Explaining Multilateral Economic Sanctions* (Princeton: Princeton University Press, 1992); the classic treatise of David A. Baldwin, *Economic Statecraft* (Princeton: Princeton University Press, 1985); and the standard texts portraying the coercive use of force of which sanctions are a part: Gordon A. Craig and Alexander George, *Force and Statecraft: Diplomatic Problems of Our Time* (New York: Oxford University Press, 1990); and Alexander George, *Forceful Persuasion: Coercive Diplomacy as an Alternative to War* (Washington, D.C.: United States Institute of Peace Press, 1991).

3. These reports have been conducted in the societies that comprise the four cases and constitute much of the information that appears in chapters 3 through

6; they thus are not reviewed here.

4. The most contentious example is that regarding the reporting by the Food and Agricultural Organization (FAO) of the death of more than 560,000 Iraqi children between 1991 and 1995 as a result of sanctions. This figure was not cited as a national "estimate," nor was it widely acknowledged that it was arrived at through a geographically limited household survey that recorded 36 infant and 245 child deaths during the period. For some discussion of the controversy see Sarah Zaidi and Mary C. Smith Fawzi, "The Health of Baghdad's Children," *Lancet* 346 (2 December 1995): 1485–86; and various queries and replies in "Sanctions against Iraq," *Lancet* 347 (20 January 1996): 198–200. See also Kim Richard Nossal, Lori Buck, and Nicole Gallant, "Sanctions as a Gendered Instrument of Statecraft," paper presented to the British International Studies Association, Durham, England, 17 December 1996, esp. 17–20.

5. Richard Garfield, "The Impact of Economic Embargoes on Health," background document for Graça Machel, *Study on the Impact of Armed Conflict on Children*, A/51/306 (New York: United Nations. 1964).

6. Garfield, "The Impact of Economic Embargoes on Health," 14–18; Among those considered most vulnerable in sanctioned societies have been "women and children," to use the oft-cited phrase in the practitioner and scholarly literature. For a recent analysis of a plethora of issues dealing with women and sanctions, as well as the "gender" bias built into sanctions assessments that group victims like children and women together, see Nossal, Buck, and Gallant, "Sanctions as a Gendered Instrument," 24.

7. Eric Hoskins, "A Study of UNICEF's Perspective on Sanctions," draft consultant's report, January 1997, 1–10.

8. Hoskins, " UNICEF's Perspective," 17–20.

9. Claudia von Braunmühl and Manfred Kulessa, *The Impact of UN Sanctions on Humanitarian Assistance Activities*, report commissioned by the United Nations Department of Humanitarian Affairs (Berlin, December 1995), 31–33.

10. Lori Fisler Damrosch, epilogue to *Enforcing Restraint: Collective Intervention in Internal Conflicts*, ed. Lori Fisler Damrosch (New York: Council on Foreign Relations Press, 1994), 384.

11. Roger Normand, "Iraqi Sanctions, Human Rights, and Humanitarian Law," *Middle East Report* (July–September, 1996): 43.

12. See David Matthew Rowe, "Surviving Economic Coercion: Rhodesia's Responses to International Economic Sanctions" (Ph.D. diss., Duke University, 1993), 398–407.

13. For a fuller discussion of this effect, see *Economic Sanctions*, ed. Cortright and Lopez, 31–36, 204–5.

14. This section is influenced by Paul Humphreys, *The Chances of Explanation: Causal Explanation in the Social, Medical, and Physical Sciences* (Princeton: Princeton University Press, 1989); Gary King, Robert O. Keohane, and Sidney Verba, *Designing Social Inquiry: Scientific Inference in Qualitative Research* (Princeton: Princeton University Press, 1994), esp. 75–114; and Thomas Homer-Dixon, "Strategies for Studying Causation in Complex Ecological Political Systems," draft paper, University of Toronto, June 1995.

15. For a full discussion of the use of counterfactuals, see King, Keohane and Verba, *Designing Social Inquiry*, 10–11, 77–78, 88–89. See also James Fearon, "Counterfactuals and Hypothesis Testing in Political Science," *World Politics* 43, no. 2 (January 1991): 169–97.

16. For a discussion of this method, see Alexander George, "Case Studies and Theory Development: The Method of Structured-Focused Comparison," in *Diplomacy: New Approaches in History, Theory, and Policy*, ed. Paul Gordon Lauren (New York: Free Press, 1979), 43–68.

17. For discussions, see Thomas G. Weiss and Cindy Collins, *Humanitarian Challenges and Intervention: World Politics and the Dilemmas of Help* (Boulder, Colo.: Westview, 1996), 3–12; and Larry Minear and Thomas G. Weiss, *Humanitarian Action in Times of War: A Handbook for Practitioners* (Boulder, Colo.: Lynne Rienner, 1993), 7–11.

18. Because process tracing is especially sensitive to the role of expert opinion and sometimes even vacillating changes in outcomes over time, it may be particularly well suited to the type of investigation undertaken in these case studies. Thus, contributors were especially sensitive to the phases of sanctions and to the nuances of change that each sanction may have generated. For a discussion, see King, Keohane, and Verba, *Designing Social Inquiry*, 224–28; for thick description as understood here, see Clifford Geertz, *An Interpretation of Cultures* (New York: Basic Books, 1973).

19. For a helpful and fuller description of this phenomenon, see Ivan Eland, "Economic Sanctions as Tools of Foreign Policy," in *Economic Sanctions*, ed. Cortright and Lopez, 29–43.

Part II

Four Case Studies

3

The Humanitarian Consequences of Sanctioning South Africa: A Preliminary Assessment

Neta C. Crawford

Did sanctions against South Africa hurt those whom they were trying to help? South Africa under apartheid was widely sanctioned by governments, international organizations, business, and other institutions because of its policies of racial separation and discrimination; its brutal treatment of, and denial of the franchise to, the majority of the population; and its aggressive military behavior toward its neighbors in southern Africa. The first sanctions began with an embargo on exports to South Africa by India in July 1946 and were followed by a range of economic, social, and political sanctions that became most intense during the 1980s.

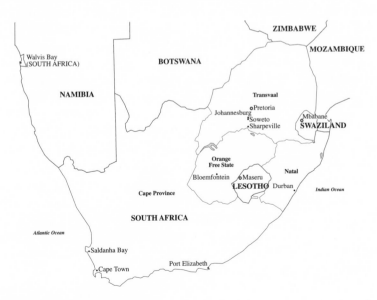

Figure 3.1 South Africa in the 1980s

The last sanctions were lifted in 1994 and 1995. During this nearly fifty-year period, there was intense debate about whether and how sanctions affected the apartheid government and the people of South Africa. Opponents of sanctions argued that sanctions would jeopardize economic growth, thereby hurting the black population—the very people sanctions were intended to help. This argument against sanctions included the belief that "it is only continued industrial growth and the widening of black economic empowerment, that such growth involves, which will make the desired and needed political change possible at all."[1]

What political effect did sanctions have on South Africa? Did they help or hinder efforts to bring about the end of apartheid and the relatively peaceful transition to democracy? Regardless of their political effect, did international sanctions hurt the majority population? Or did they, paradoxically, contribute to an improvement of their quality of life? To the extent that the international community came to the assistance of poor South Africans, was humanitarian assistance a help in redressing the effects of sanctions? I make four arguments in answer to these questions.

First, since the end of apartheid, there has been no systematic effort to understand the humanitarian impact of sanctions on South Africa or southern Africa. Even if such an effort were undertaken, the task of assessing the humanitarian impact of sanctions and differentiating this impact from the effects of other domestic and international factors is difficult, if not impossible. The next section discusses the analytical challenges posed by this problem and proposes a modest strategy to address them.

Second, the impact of sanctions on political change was complex. The many sanctions imposed from outside were only one of several forces at work in getting South Africa to end its international aggression, forcing a negotiated end to apartheid and creating the conditions for the construction of a democratic government. The determined resistance of those who fought South African aggression in South West Africa/Namibia and elsewhere in the region and the resistance of those who fought for a nonracial democratic society inside, along with long-term structural changes in the economy and society, probably had much more to do with the character and timing of the transition than sanctions. Still, sanctions played an important role. They directly helped to pressure the regime by increasing the costs of maintaining apartheid, and sanctions also helped to promote economic changes that undermined the economic structures of apartheid. In other words, rather than simply hurting the South African economy, which they certainly did, sanctions paradoxically also promoted economic growth in some sectors and nourished antiapartheid resistance.

Third, following from the previous two arguments, the humanitarian impact of sanctions in South Africa varied across economic sectors and population groups. To the extent that employment boomed or declined in a particular sector because of sanctions, there were welfare gains or losses. Overall, however, because the government resisted sanctions in part through import substitution, industrialization actually accelerated, with a concomitant increase in jobs and development of social infrastructure—not only for the already advantaged white minority, but also for the black majority. This is not to say that some people were not hurt by sanctions—some were hurt in both the short and the long term. But the humanitarian consequences were much more varied and complex over the short and long term than implied by the arguments of sanctions opponents.

Finally, humanitarian assistance to redress the possible harms of sanctions played a marginal role. Humanitarian assistance was initiated in response to the desperate poverty of South Africa's majority population and to aid the victims of apartheid policies. Little assistance was aimed specifically at redressing the impact of sanctions, and some aid was given to South Africans in lieu of imposing sanctions.

The Causal Challenge

Assessing the extent of humanitarian suffering in South Africa and distinguishing among its causes to determine the role of sanctions is an enormous analytical and empirical challenge, for three principal reasons: inadequate data, multiple causality, and feedback effects.

Data on the humanitarian status of South Africans before and during sanctions are incomplete. The Central Statistical Service of South Africa systematically undercounted black South Africans by excluding, from the mid-1970s onward, the so-called African homelands—Transkei, Bophuthatswana, Ciskei, and Venda—created to justify apartheid policies of separation. In addition, those black South Africans who were "officially" inside South Africa were also undercounted.[2] Official government figures thus were notoriously inaccurate. In discussing their own unemployment figures, the Central Statistical Service acknowledged that "It is known . . . that data on registered unemployment, especially among blacks, for various reasons do not reflect the true extent of unemployment."[3]

Nongovernmental efforts attempted to redress this lack of information about the status of South Africans. Perhaps the best single source on income and poverty in South Africa is the major study funded by the Carnegie Corporation and summarized by Francis Wilson and Mamphela

Ramphele in *Uprooting Poverty: The South African Challenge.*[4] Although this book was published in the late 1980s, much of the evidence in it is based on three hundred studies conducted nearly a decade earlier. Because of South African statistical practices and the dearth of research following the Carnegie study, there is little systematic data on poverty for the 1980s, the period when sanctions became most intense. The 1980s are also the period when, in addition to the possible impact of sanctions, several changes in the South African and regional economy—such as the reduced reliance on migrant labor from neighboring states, greater mechanization, and a downturn in the gold sector—may have had important effects on the overall health and welfare of South Africans.

Second, sanctions were just one of several stimuli at work in the domestic and international political economy of South Africa. Apartheid, drought, militarization, economic restructuring, urbanization, and global recession also affected the humanitarian status of people in South Africa. It is difficult to disentangle the effects of these stimuli.

Third, the problem of assessment is made more complicated by the fact that in some cases these stimuli reinforced and/or counteracted other processes and stimuli. In other words, there were feedback loops and countereffects. For example, rapid industrialization can mean more jobs and is also often accompanied by urbanization. Rapid urbanization can bring people in contact with better health and education infrastructure, but, especially if infrastructure development does not keep pace with urbanization, it may also lead to greater and different kinds of health and welfare problems. Any thorough assessment of the humanitarian and political impact of sanctions thus requires study of how sanctions fed into, exacerbated, or ran counter to other forces at work in the South African context. In other words, the difficulty of determining the humanitarian impact of sanctions is not only, or perhaps primarily, due to data problems, though more and better data would help to clarify the picture.

To come to grips with these problems, I use two strategies. The first traces the impact of specific sanctions policies. The second compares the humanitarian status of individuals before and after the major economic sanctions of the 1980s.[5]

The Context of Sanctions

Over the several decades that sanctions were imposed, South Africa's domestic political and economic situation changed significantly, as did the international context. When apartheid legislation began rolling out of the National Party–dominated government in 1948, the economy was primarily based on mining, heavily dependent on imports for capital equipment, and completely dependent on imports of refined oil. White South Africans dominated the economic and political institutions of South Africa to the almost complete exclusion of Asian, colored, and black South Africans. Over the decades, the economy also became increasingly militarized. In 1961, agriculture and mining accounted for just over 25 percent of South Africa's gross domestic product (GDP); by 1988 agriculture and mining's share of GDP was just over 19 percent. During the same period, the manufacturing sector grew from under 18 percent of GDP to 24.5 percent of GDP.[6] Thus, by the end of apartheid, manufacturing grew to become an important sector of the economy. By this time as well, military force was increasingly deployed within and outside South Africa to maintain the state and the apartheid system.

Apartheid South Africa came into being gradually over the centuries of white settlement. Legislated apartheid—whose cornerstones were the Mixed Marriages Act of 1949; the Population Registration Act and Group Areas Act, both of 1950; the Reservation of Separate Amenities and Bantu Education Bills, both of 1953—was designed to ensure that different racial categories were established, that racial groups were kept physically separate, and that black Africans, Asians, and colored people remained inferior politically and economically.[7] The practice of forced removals of black, Asian, and colored people so that white South Africans could obtain the most desirable areas for farming, residence, and business continued through the 1980s. Wealth was concentrated in white hands, and by 1970 the richest 20 percent of the population owned 75 percent of the wealth. In 1980, though whites were about 15 percent of the population, they earned almost two-thirds of the income and controlled over 80 percent of the land. In 1989, Wilson and Ramphele wrote:

> Thousands of South African babies are dying of malnutrition and associated diseases; two million children are growing up stunted for lack of sufficient calories in one of the few countries in the world that exports food; tens of thousands of men are spending their entire working years as lonely "labour units," in single sex hostels whilst their wives and children live generally in great poverty in the overcrowded reserves.[8]

In this context of inequality and poverty for the majority population, there was an intense debate within South Africa about the desirability and efficacy of sanctions. Most of the antiapartheid movement favored sanctions and endorsed the call in late 1958 by African National Congress (ANC) president Albert Lithuli for sanctions. The ANC saw sanctions as a tool of limited but important utility. Indeed, sanctions became one of the four pillars of the ANC struggle against apartheid—a supplement to mass action, armed struggle, and diplomatic isolation. Of the antiapartheid groups active in South Africa, only the Inkatha Freedom Party, founded in 1975, took a strong antisanctions position in the mid-1980s. Inkatha's leader, Mangosuthu Buthelezi, argued: "Without a means for survival—because blacks in South Africa are cash-dependent—their grinding poverty and degradation will continue unabated. . . . Divestment will not help the struggle for liberation; it will hinder it."[9] Despite the difficulties of polling a population on the question of sanctions in a context where advocating sanctions was sometimes a criminal offense (and unlike other sanctoned environments), there were several studies of the attitudes of South Africans toward sanctions. Surveys showed that black South Africans expressed qualified support for sanctions, though only a minority supported sanctions if "serious" unemployment would result.[10]

Sanctions were intended to change the behavior of white South Africans. Among them, opinion on the effects of sanctions was divided. In the late 1980s, a majority of white South Africans tended to see sanctions as a serious problem that would have a very harmful effect on the economy, though a somewhat smaller portion also tended to believe that the country could cope with sanctions.[11] Surveys of white South Africans in 1986, 1988, and 1990 showed that a majority thought the economy was not "strong enough" to prevent economic sanctions from hurting further. In a 1992 survey of white South Africans, 92 percent of respondents said the South African economy had been hurt by sanctions.[12] While sanctions were in effect, the apartheid power structure and the intellectuals who supported it persistently discounted sanctions and tended to argue that they would not work or would have limited effect on South Africa.[13] Those whites inside the National Party who led the long negotiations with the African National Congress, and other members of the establishment who sought to end apartheid, have had little reason to deviate from that position; to acknowledge any coercive effect of sanctions would diminish their claim to a benevolent and voluntary movement toward conciliation and democracy.

Outside South Africa a consensus slowly emerged that apartheid was wrong and ought to be eliminated.[14] Yet there was a sharp division of opinion regarding sanctions. Some governments, including members of the Organization of African Unity (OAU) and the majority of the United Nations General Assembly, believed that sanctions were essential and would probably be effective. Others, including the governments of the United States and the United Kingdom, felt that a policy of "constructive engagement," diplomatic persuasion accompanied by continued economic involvement, would bring about change.[15] To evade diplomatic pressure from members of the British Commonwealth, South Africa left the organization in 1961, though that did not stop the Commonwealth from eventually adopting sanctions against South Africa.

The UN General Assembly and later the Security Council gradually took a harder line against South Africa's practice of apartheid and its treatment of Namibia. The General Assembly established the Special Committee Against Apartheid in 1962 to monitor and report on the situation in South Africa. In July 1966, the International Court of Justice (ICJ) rejected a legal appeal by Ethiopia and Liberia to rule on the legality of South Africa's occupation of Namibia. The General Assembly in October 1966 declared an end to South Africa's mandate of South West Africa, established the UN Council for South West Africa (later Namibia), and provided funds for operations. In 1971, finally ruling on the issue, the ICJ declared South Africa's occupation illegal. In 1974, the General Assembly voted to reject South Africa's credentials, although the Security Council refused to expel the country. In 1977, the Security Council made the UN's 1963 voluntary arms embargo against South Africa mandatory. The UN also gradually increased the material resources devoted to monitoring events in the region, supported South African and Namibian exiles, and promoted negotiated solutions to conflict in the region. By the late 1980s, there was a near consensus in the international community that at least some sanctions against South Africa were warranted and that the alternative to apartheid was not reform but truly democratic government.

The Sanctions

International sanctions against South Africa were both long lasting and piecemeal, touching nearly every facet of society from sport to travel to technology transfers. In addition, sanctions were undertaken not only by national governments and international organizations but also by municipalities, small businesses, universities, religious organizations, international financial institutions, and multinational corporations. A complete accounting of the diplomatic, cultural, financial, trade, and military sanctions against South Africa would take dozens of pages. Table 3.1 lists some of the early and major sanctions against South Africa. It is based on more comprehensive

Table 3.1
Partial Summary of Sanctions against South Africa

Type of Sanction	Some of the Sanctioners	Year Sanction Initiated
Diplomatic	Individual countries	from the 1950s
	OAU exclusion	1963
	International organizations	from the 1960s
	UN General Assembly denied SA seat	1974
Arms embargoes	United Nations	1963 voluntary
exports		1977 mandatory
imports		1984 voluntary
Oil embargo	OPEC (not including Iran)	1973
	Iran joined embargo	1979
	Commonwealth Group and	
	European Union	1985
	U.S.	1986
Sport	Banned from Olympic competition	1964
	Commonwealth boycott	1977
Culture	Boycotts of South African artists	1970s
Finance	Individual banks	1970s
	Netherlands mid- and long-term	
	credit halted	1977
	Commonwealth Group	1985
	More and larger banks	1986
	U.S.	1986
Divestment and	University, corporate, municipal,	
disinvestment	and private	from the 1970s
Exports and	India—comprehensive	1946
imports	Jamaica—comprehensive	1959
	Denmark, France, U.S.—coal	1985
	U.S. Comprehensive Anti-Apartheid	
	Act	1986

lists of both voluntary and mandatory sanctions against the apartheid government drawn up by scholars in the late 1980s and early 1990s.[16]

Two principal policy aims underlay international sanctions against South Africa.[17] The primary goal was to force South Africa to end apartheid. The secondary goal, mentioned much less frequently by sanctioners, was to end South Africa's regional aggression, including its occupation of Namibia. In line with the primary goal, the conditions for lifting sanctions were actions by the government toward easing the harshest elements of apartheid and the initiation of negotiations for democratic reform. UN Security Council Resolution 182 of December 1963, which urged a voluntary arms embargo, called on South Africa to end discrimination and repression, release political prisoners, and move toward a peaceful transformation. In Resolution 418 of November 1977, the Security Council recalled the government's aggression in the region and its "massive violence against and killings of the African people" and called on it "urgently to end violence against the African people and to take urgent steps to eliminate apartheid and racial discrimination."

In 1985, the Commonwealth Group called on the apartheid government to declare that the system of apartheid would be dismantled, end the state of emergency in South Africa, release those imprisoned or detained for their opposition to apartheid, lift the bans against political parties, and initiate "a process of dialogue . . . with a view to establishing a nonracial and representative government."[18] The U.S. Comprehensive Anti-Apartheid Act, passed over President Ronald Reagan's veto in 1986, was "designed to bring about reforms in that system of government that will lead to the establishment of a nonracial democracy" and outlined six specific measures that it encouraged the government of South Africa to undertake. It called on the government to

(1) repeal the present state of emergency and respect the principle of equal justice under the law for citizens of all races;

(2) release Nelson Mandela, Govan Mbeki, Walter Sisulu, black trade union leaders, and all political prisoners;

(3) permit the free exercise by South Africans of all races of the right to form political parties, express political opinions, and otherwise participate in the political process;

(4) establish a timetable for the elimination of apartheid laws;

(5) negotiate with representatives of all racial groups in South Africa the future political system in South Africa; and

(6) end military and paramilitary activities aimed at neighboring states.[19]

The sanctions regime was, in addition to being a patchwork of voluntary and mandatory prohibitions, extremely "leaky." In other words, South Africa was able to circumvent even the strategic embargoes of arms and oil by purchasing oil and military equipment illegally. Hundreds of thousands of barrels of oil reached South Africa each year while military equipment, including tanks, was purchased through middlemen and arms merchants.[20] Similarly, although the United States, Denmark, and France prohibited imports of South African coal in 1985, coal exports grew overall, and the country became the major supplier of coal imports to the European Community (EC) in 1986.[21] This was also the case with regard to other commodities, such as gold. While sanctioned by some, South Africa was often able to find other buyers, though it was sometimes forced to sell at an "apartheid discount."

In sum, sanctions against South Africa may be characterized as long in coming, eventually comprehensive in their coverage, but simultaneously leaky. The end of sanctions was also gradual. Some were relaxed after the release of Nelson Mandela in February 1990. The UN Security Council ended sanctions, including the arms embargo, only in May 1994, a month after the successful completion of all-race multiparty elections in South Africa. Because the South African government and political elites often had warning before sanctions were imposed—in some cases years of discussion preceded the imposition of sanctions—they also had time to prepare for and react to sanctions. The length of time that sanctions were considered and imposed is an important factor in understanding their ultimate consequences.

The Consequences

Most scholars emphasize that sanctions do not work because of inadequate compliance. The argument is made, in a variant of Mancur Olson's collective-action maxim, that sanctions fail because others will supply the products sanctioned. It is also commonly argued that sanctions primarily provoke resistance and a "rally-round-the-flag" effect in the target state.[22] Sanctions against South Africa produced both the collective-action problem with regard to imposing sanctions and significant resistance by the government and the private sector. These are important issues for understanding the politics of getting sanctions imposed and enforcing compliance.[23] With regard to assessing the impact of sanctions—especially any humanitarian consequences—it is less important to know that sanctions were leaky than to understand the actual impact of the sanctions that were finally imposed.

The fact that the targets of sanctions are likely to resist them implies that understanding target resistance is essential for assessing the overall impact of sanctions on the economy, politics, and welfare. A theory of how sanctions work should therefore include a theory of both the direct effects on the reasoning and capabilities of the target and the indirect effects of sanctions—that is, the consequences of the target's resistance for sanctions.[24] Thus, this section traces the direct effect of some of the sanctions that were actually imposed, no matter how leaky, and the indirect or ripple effects that resulted from South African resistance.

Direct Effects

As emphasized above, there were many different types of sanctions, and not surprisingly their direct effects differed by sector. In general, the direct consequences of sanctions were to limit supplies of crucial imported commodities, to reduce access to international finance, and to increase the cost of imports. In the long term, South Africa's overall economic growth was probably stunted by sanctions, although as the section on indirect effects suggests, sanctions paradoxically led to some growth. The most outstanding direct consequences of sanctions are probably found in the oil, arms, capital equipment, and financial sectors, where South Africa was dependent on external sources and where access was substantially reduced by sanctions.

Oil. Both the antiapartheid movement and apartheid elites understood that oil was a critical vulnerability, since South Africa had no internal source of oil, nor even, until 1954, its own refineries. The Organization of Arab Petroleum Exporting Countries (OAPEC) called for a complete Arab oil embargo at the 1973 Algiers summit. Iraq, Saudi Arabia, and Qatar immediately halted shipments, which had amounted to nearly 50 percent of South Africa's crude oil supplies.[25] Iran did not join this embargo and became the largest supplier of crude oil to South Africa during the early years of the embargo, directly and indirectly supplying on average over 90 percent of needs from 1973 to 1978. After the political revolution in Iran in 1979, Iranian oil exports to South Africa ceased as well, and it became much more difficult for South Africa to import oil at market prices. South African oil imports dropped 40 percent in the first quarter of 1979 compared to the previous year.[26] In 1979, the Afrikaner-dominated Sanlam industrial group published an economic report on sanctions that said, "Without a doubt the Republic's Achilles' heel is *oil.*"[27]

Like much of the world, South Africa began oil conservation in earnest in the mid-1970s, following the first oil shocks. Conservation measures included increasing the pump price of gasoline, restricting the hours that filling stations were open, and lowering speed limits. From 1974 to 1978, conservation measures were somewhat successful at keeping gasoline consumption down to a 0.8 percent annual increase, though the consumption of diesel (used more in commercial and public transport sectors, the military, and agriculture) grew much more, 5 percent annually during that period.[28] Sasol (the coal to petroleum product industry) reported that gasoline consumption decreased 3 percent during 1985–1986 as prices increased, but that it increased in the late 1980s, growing, for example, 6.6

percent in 1988–1989 and 3.4 percent in 1989–1990.[29]

The costs of compensating for the oil embargo were substantial. While attempting to minimize the effects of the embargo at the time, the government has more recently admitted that "During 1979 the Republic of South Africa found itself in a situation where it could no longer obtain crude oil with out paying a price differential for delivery of crude oil to South Africa."[30] The Shipping Research Bureau, which monitored oil shipments to South Africa during the embargo, estimated that in 1979 South Africa had to pay a premium up to 50 percent above world oil prices.[31] In the early 1980s, the premium was about $8 per barrel.[32] While the embargo was in effect, the Shipping Research Bureau reported that "companies and middlemen are making profits in the tens of millions of dollars in the illegal oil trade to South Africa."[33] The Equalization Fund, a levy on liquid fuel consumption, was established in 1979 to help cover the extra costs of purchasing crude oil. White South Africans, who owned the vast majority of private and commercial automobiles, probably paid the most to the Equalization Fund. The oil sanctions had relatively little direct effect on the majority population.[34]

Arms. The only mandatory UN sanction against South Africa was the arms embargo that banned exports to South Africa in 1977 and placed a voluntary ban on imports in 1984. The direct consequences of the arms embargo were both a decrease from 1963 in the quantity and quality of armaments and military equipment purchased and an increase in the price paid for this equipment. South Africa still managed to purchase some weapons openly until the embargo became mandatory, and it also covertly bought military equipment through arms brokers and middlemen at a markup of between 20 and 100 percent.[35] Expenditures on importing military equipment showed a nearly fivefold decrease. Nonetheless South Africa continued to spend large sums importing weapons, averaging $452 million per year from 1973 to 1977 and $92 million per year from 1978 to 1992.[36] These figures are probably not correct. Like the oil embargo, the exact cost of these covert transactions has not yet been uncovered. Recent investigations by the new government suggest that the covert trade was not only substantial but also riddled with corruption.[37]

In addition, the quality of South Africa's military equipment gradually declined vis-à-vis the quality of military forces in Angola, where South Africa was engaged in a long-term war. The government complained in 1984: "A major problem is that some of the most reliable main armaments are obsolescent. More modern armaments available to our enemies contributed toward this process of obsolescence."[38] This decline is perhaps most evident in aviation. Because the Angolans had access to more sophisticated equipment and because South Africa was unable either to produce new aircraft or to provide enough spare parts to keep their sophisticated aircraft flying, South Africa gradually lost air superiority in Angola in the late 1980s.[39]

Finance. South Africa was quite dependent on external sources of finance for capital equipment, most of which was imported. Access to international finance declined in the beginning of the mid-1970s (after the Soweto uprising and massacre), at precisely the time when the country was attempting to modernize its capital equipment in primary production and manufacturing sectors.[40] Private banks and governments restricted lending to the government and to private borrowers. Long-term loans were especially affected.[41] By 1985, South Africa's debt was primarily— over 70 percent—short term. In July 1985, Chase Manhattan and other banks refused to renew short-term loans. The Commonwealth banned new government loans to South Africa in 1985. In 1986, the European Community and the United States halted new investments. In 1988, the Nordic Council prohibited investment and credits. These actions precipitated a debt crisis, and South Africa responded by placing a moratorium on the repayment of loan principal. New payment schedules were negotiated with international lenders.

Some observers have suggested that the international banks that halted new loans during the mid-1980s were not sanctioning apartheid policies but protecting their financial interests in the context of major recession and political instability in South Africa.[42] Even if the bankers' motivations were primarily economic rather than political, this does not diminish the powerful impact of decisions to withhold long-term financing. The accumulating sanctions contributed to the perception of risk instability. These sanctions not only had a negative effect on the economy, but they also probably pushed private lenders further along the path of withdrawal.

Whatever the reasons for the 1985 financial withdrawal by private banks, their action sent shock waves through the South African business community. Business executives appear to have been quite alarmed by the financial sanctions and the measures taken by the state to redress international financial concerns. One writer later explained in the *Financial Mail*, "In 1985 the severing of credit lines left us out on a financial limb, struggling with a huge debt burden as capital flight reached record proportions and the international value of the rand began a series of sharp descents."[43] Alan Hirsch has documented that South African business leaders lobbied for reforms in apartheid and government economic policy in order to ease the economic pressures due to sanctions and declining growth.[44]

In sum, the direct consequences of sanctions were to reduce South African access to certain commodities and technologies, and later to international finance. Sanctions also increased the costs that South Africa had to pay for goods, especially goods for which demand was relatively inelastic—for example, capital goods, oil, and arms. Although sanctions did not account for all of the change in South Africa's economy, growth rates declined steadily from the 1960s to the 1980s. Between 1946 and 1974, South Africa's real GDP (adjusted for inflation) grew at an annual average rate of 4.9 percent. In the subsequent decade, the annual growth rate dropped to 1.9 percent. During the 1980s as a whole, annual GDP growth was 1.5 per cent.[45] Many factors caused this decline in economic growth, but sanctions no doubt contributed at least to some degree to South Africa's economic difficulties.

Indirect Effects

South Africa resisted sanctions by procuring alternative sources of goods and finance, stockpiling commodities such as oil and arms, and engaging in massive restructuring of the economy for import substitution. Business leaders argued that "the real costs of apartheid have not been in the duplication of public facilities and services or the financing of the homelands and 'independent' states, but in attempts—perceived as strategic at the time—to make this economy self-sufficient."[46] The indirect effect of sanctions rippled through the entire economy, and while job creation and growth rates were certainly down throughout much of the sanctions era, some sectors of the economy actually experienced a boom.

The impact of financial sanctions was especially severe and became difficult to overcome. Financial sanctions meant that by the late 1980s, South Africa was essentially cut off from outside sources of long- and medium-term loans. To repay debt according to the schedules worked out with lenders, South Africa attempted to increase its exports of primary and secondary products. It also needed to restrain imports, and, as Hirsch has noted, this need "imposed a very severe constraint on growth since expansion of production in South Africa depends on the importation of capital and intermediate goods."[47] During this period, the country faced a growing number of bans on its exports of primary and secondary goods. For example, the Commonwealth, the Nordic Council, and the United States banned the purchase of Krugerrand gold coins in the mid- and late 1980s. Imports of other South African products were banned in many countries. At the same time, the price of gold, the largest foreign exchange earner, fell from over $600 per ounce in 1980 to just over $300 per ounce in 1985, and though the price recovered somewhat in the late 1980s, it fell to a seven-year low in 1992, averaging $344 per ounce.[48]

In other areas, South Africa pursued import substitution more successfully. This was especially so in two sectors that the state perceived as strategic: oil and arms. Oil import substitution consisted of a three-pronged effort: increased electrification run by coal power plants (converting some oil-run plants to coal); creation and subsidy of a synthetic fuels industry; and oil and natural gas exploration. Since oil and gas exploration yielded almost nothing of significance until the late 1980s, I will not discuss it here.[49] Coal electrification boosted domestic coal mining efforts, as did the synthetic fuel program that turned coal into oil at Sasol plants. Sasol was founded in 1950 and began production of oil from coal in 1955 at a plant in Sasolburg, south of Johannesburg. After solving some technical problems, Sasol produced 5,000 barrels of oil per day. In 1974, the government decided to build a second plant, and in 1975, levied two cents per liter on fuel consumption, which increased to four cents per liter in 1977, to finance the plant.[50] In February 1979, after the Iranian oil cutoff, the government decided to build Sasol III. The two additional Sasol plants were completed at Secunda in the Transvaal west of Johannesburg in 1980 and 1982, respectively. A fourth was considered but never constructed. Sasol II and III each produce 45,000 to 50,000 barrels of oil per day from coal, while Sasol I was gradually turned to producing other petroleum products.[51] The costs of coal-to-oil conversion were quite high. Though the cost per barrel of oil produced from coal was never released by Sasol, estimates range from $45 to $75 per barrel.[52]

The consequences of the drive to boost coal exports (which tied South Africa to multinational oil companies), to increase the use of coal inside the country for electricity production, and to develop the synthetic fuel program combined to increase demand for coal and led to a boom in the coal mining industry. Overall employment went up despite increased mechanization, and wages also rose. Whites received the more skilled jobs, but black workers' wages and working conditions also improved relative to the wages of white workers in the coal industry.[53] (In the gold mining industry, which intensified during the sanctions period, wages and working conditions for black workers also improved.)[54] In addition, Sasol employed thousands of workers and created demand in secondary industries.

South Africa also attempted to become increasingly self-sufficient in the production of armaments and military equipment. This drive began even before the 1963 UN arms embargo as the military anticipated an imminent embargo. Initially South Africa acquired licenses for the production of military equipment and armaments.[55] After the UN embargo began, South Africa established an Armaments Production Board in 1964, which evolved into Armscor, the giant network of state-owned corporations that produced many of the weapons needed by the South African Defence Force (SADF). Armscor also engaged in clandestine deals for the purchase of military equipment, technical expertise, and component upgrades for existing equipment. After 1978, Armscor also ran South Africa's nuclear weapons program.

Armscor consisted of companies directly owned and operated by the government.[56] It also worked with many "private" contractors and subcontractors who were wholly or in part dependent on government contracts. By 1990, in addition to companies directly owned by the state, South Africa had 975 private contractors directly engaged by Armscor.[57] Several thousand additional companies served as subcontractors, feeding components to contractors and Armscor subsidiaries. Official military spending grew from R23 million in 1967 to R4,845 million in 1989. The arms industry thus paradoxically became one of South Africa's largest employers. The scale of military industry is illustrated by the fact that, despite the UN embargo on purchasing South African–produced weapons, Armscor became the single largest exporter of manufactured goods, selling $900 million worth of arms in 1987.[58] In 1986 the South African Department of Defence argued that military spending, especially on the arms industry, was "one of the primary driving forces of the economy."[59] The 1986 Defence White Paper devoted several pages of discussion to the economic benefits of arms production, which it estimated at 5.42 percent of GDP in 1982.[60] South Africa's leading defense economist, Peter Batchelor, has estimated that "as a rule of thumb, 1 job in ARMSCOR supports approximately 5 jobs in the private sector defense industry. Therefore in the late 1980s about 150,000 people [were] employed in the defense industry."[61] Table 3.2 illustrates the rapid growth of arms industry employment.

The ripple effects of developing a large arms industry were substantial. They contributed to developments that undermined strict apartheid, brought liberal whites from private industry into contact with the government, and facilitated organizing efforts by Asian, colored, and black workers, especially in trade unions.[62] Far-reaching economic reforms were crucial for developing an arms industry large enough to support South Africa's use of military force in Angola and Namibia. Because white workers compose a relatively small number of total workers in South Africa, the government had to relax elements of apartheid that were barriers to the

Table 3.2
Armscor's Direct and Total Arms Industry Employment

Year	Armscor employment	Estimate of total employed in arms manufacture	Estimated % of all manufacturing jobs in arms manufacture*
1975	7,390	36,950	2.83
1976	7,919	39,595	2.92
1977	10,590	52,950	4.02
1978	16,870	84,350	6.43
1979	22,540	112,700	8.46
1980	24,560	122,800	8.64
1981	25890	129,450	8.58
1982	24,960	123,800	8.09
1983	23,180	115,900	7.91
1984	25,340	126,700	8.57
1985	23,310	116,550	8.16
1986	25,190	125,950	8.23
1987	27,610	138,050	9.02
1988	30,930	154,650	10.14
1989	31,150	155,750	10.17
1990	23,630	118,150	7.75
1991	18,280	91,400	6.16
1992	15,700	78,500	5.46
1993	15,200	76,000	5.41
1994	15,000	75,000	
1995	14,000	70,000	

Sources: Peter Batchelor, "History and Overview of the South African Arms Industry" (paper presented to the Group for Environmental Monitoring Workshop on the Future of the South African Arms Industry, Johannesburg, 7–8 February 1996); Financial Mail, "Public Sector Corporations," *Financial Mail Special Survey: Top Corporations* (Johannesburg, 30 June 1995), 248–52.

*Figures for percent of all manufacturing jobs devoted to full- and part-time arms manufacture are calculated from employment figures in Central Statistical Service, *South African Statistics, 1994* (Pretoria: Government Printing Office, 1994), 7.11.

use of black workers in order for economic mobilization to succeed.

To facilitate the labor of "non-white" workers in white areas, "influx control" laws limiting the number and location of Africans in urban areas were abandoned in the early 1980s.[63] This was particularly ironic because part of the original impetus behind the apartheid legislation of the late 1940s and early 1950s had been to halt and reverse the flow of Africans to urban areas that took place during the industrialization accompanying World War II. In the late 1970s, even as the demand for African workers grew in urban areas, the government strengthened the enforcement of influx control laws. By the mid-1980s, however, increased white emigration and the growth of industrial capacity made "non-white" workers a necessity.[64] "Gray areas" where people of all races could live together in urban areas were unofficially tolerated until influx control was finally officially abandoned in 1986.

Armscor also saw a value in treating all race groups well, since it feared that "the greatest threat to this sensitive industry is an inefficient and/or disloyal employee corps."[65] The strategy of military industrialization thus "meant blacks had to be trained for these skilled jobs, which in turn, meant upgrading their education and admitting them to previously Whites-only technical institutes and universities."[66] In the area of education alone, the changes were dramatic: from 1980 to 1988 the number of black students in technical colleges and technikons increased nearly 435 percent, while for the same period white enrollment grew less than 1 percent. During the same period there was also a 240 percent increase in the number of black students in teacher training and universities, compared to a 30 percent increase for whites.[67]

In sum, South Africa's attempt to overcome arms and oil embargoes through import substitution served as a stimulus to industrialization and the liberalization of labor markets. Even if whites took the most-skilled and best-paying jobs in the emerging high-technology arms industries, black workers gained the opportunity to fill in skilled and semiskilled jobs that white workers had left in other sectors. Many skilled black workers also worked in the industries that were created to feed military producers. In the process the black trade union movement grew to become one of the most powerful political forces in the country, and it remained so until the ban on political parties was lifted in early 1990. The increased education and employment opportunities stimulated by military industrialization and synthetic fuel production, along with black unionization, helped sustain the antiapartheid movement inside South Africa. Unionization in particular was crucial, since the labor movement was a central locus of antiapartheid organization and resistance.[68]

South Africa's industrialization strategy for import substitution had a major impact not only on labor markets but also on business management and the relationship between the business sector and the state. In the late 1970s, Prime Minister P. W. Botha moved to incorporate the business sector more fully into the total national strategy by meeting with important English and Afrikaner business leaders in South Africa and forming a Defence Advisory Board of leading businessmen.[69] In late 1979, the Carlton Conference of 250 leading South African businessmen was convened, and the prime minister asked private industry to continue to help implement the total strategy.

> The reformist wing of the NP [National Party] proposed the recognition of black trade unions, some form of political representation for blacks living outside the homelands, the establishment of homelands as viable economic and political units, the eroding of job reservation, the promotion of methods for training black workers, and the creation of a stable urban black population.[70]

Nationalist leaders were thus exposed to proposals for liberalization as they sought to enlist business executives in their strategy for resisting international sanctions. This is not to suggest that business managers as a whole were opposed to apartheid. Far from it. But corporate executives were primarily concerned with profitability and economic efficiency, and many saw the restrictions of apartheid and the international isolation of South Africa as obstacles to business growth. Over time, the concerns of business executives served as a moderating influence on elements of the National Party and generated pressure for reform and the eventual abandonment of apartheid.

Quantifying the Humanitarian Impact of Sanctions?

Returning to the question posed at the outset, whether sanctions hurt the poorest South Africans, some tentative conclusions are possible. William Carmichael—at the time a vice president of the Ford Foundation and a close observer of South Africa during the sanctions era—has observed that "sanctions did not have any really dramatic effect on the already miserable income levels of the poor in South Africa."[71] At the same time, already vulnerable populations may have been pushed over the edge into deeper suffering by sanctions. The evidence, subject to the problems of data and causality described above, shows that sanctions both helped and hurt the most vulnerable.

Employment

The South African economy probably would have grown more rapidly if sanctions had not been imposed, although the import substitution sectors benefited from more rapid industrialization. Some industrialists within South Africa believed that sanctions hurt the overall economy. As a writer in the *Financial Mail* observed in 1993, "Freed from trade sanctions and the need to counter or compensate for them, SA [South Africa] will be able to exploit its comparative advantages instead of pouring resources into unproductive industries spawned by the needs of what was an increasingly isolationist apartheid outlook."[72]

Estimates made inside South Africa during the sanctions era, based on economic modeling, predicted severe job losses due to sanctions, on the order of millions of workers. For example, in 1986 South Africa's Federated Chamber of Industries predicted that "medium intensity" sanctions would lead to an increase in unemployment of over 200,000 in the first eighteen months to two years and 685,000 over five years, while comprehensive sanctions could cost up to 1,135,013 jobs over five years.[73] In 1987, repeating his earlier analysis, Ronnie Bethlehem argued that intensified sanctions in the late 1980s would lead to an increase of 2 million unemployed workers by the year 2000, mostly in the category of unskilled labor (since import substitution industries would create higher skilled jobs).[74] However, Charles Meth suggests that most of these models were deficient partly because "the imponderables are too numerous, and the available data too inaccurate, to permit anything more than crude guesses."[75]

It is undeniable that unemployment grew in South Africa from the 1970s through the end of apartheid, but there were several reasons for this development. First, South Africa's population growth outstripped the rate of job creation. The economy could no longer absorb the growing number of potential entrants to the labor market.[76] Second, greater mechanization in mining, agriculture, and manufacturing reduced the demand for labor. In mining in particular, several waves of mechanization decreased the need for workers, in some cases by as much as 30 percent.[77] Third, export sanctions began to bite. As the government reported in 1986, "Employment creation was probably adversely affected by recent developments in the political sphere (such as the sanctions and divestment campaign against RSA [the Republic of South Africa] and the internal unrest) because of their effect on, among other things, business confidence and the investment climate."[78]

How many jobs were lost? In the period of most intense sanctions, between 1985 and 1989, Carolyn Jenkins estimated that employment fell by over 14,000 workers in coal mining, 20,000 in metal and engineering, 6,000 in electricity, and 39,000 in other manufacturing. In the agricultural sector, sugar and deciduous fruit producers also suffered job losses due to sanctions, totaling about 32,000 workers.[79] Assuming, improbably, that all the employment losses identified by Jenkins were due to sanctions rather than mechanization, the total figure for jobs lost because of sanctions between 1985 and 1989 comes to 111,000; most of these jobs were lost by black workers. Assuming conservatively that mechanization and rationalization account for 10 percent of the reduction, perhaps as many as 100,000 jobs were lost because of sanctions. Whites undoubtedly fared much better, but many gradually felt an economic pinch as well, as evidenced by growing rates of white emigration.[80]

On the other hand, some sectors saw employment increases. For example, the private services sector showed rapid growth, increasing by 25 percent in the 1980s. Government employment expanded 18 percent from 1980 to 1990. According to Jenkins, over 80 percent of all new jobs during this period came from the growth of government employment.[81] Moreover, as noted in table 3.2, employment in the arms industry alone grew by about 100,000 workers after the UN arms embargo became mandatory in 1977.

Thus, while sanctions undoubtedly resulted in a net loss of jobs, especially for black workers, the compensating increase in employment in certain sectors tempered these effects.

Health and Welfare

Any assessment of the health and welfare effects of sanctions must be placed in the context of the apartheid system.[82] Because of the persistent poverty and racial apartheid policies that have existed in South Africa, Asian, colored, and black populations have been denied the same access to water, health care, food, fuel, shelter, and education as white South Africans. This differential access to basic life necessities has resulted in marked differences in health among different population groups. Life expectancy, infant mortality, the types of diseases suffered, and the quality of medical treatment vary for different population groups. In general, white South Africans have been healthier and have tended to die from ailments such as cancer and heart disease. Black South Africans have been less healthy and have tended to die of infectious and respiratory diseases.[83]

Infant mortality and child mortality rates are among the most important indicators of a society's overall health. Table 3.3 gives figures for overall child and infant mortality rates in South Africa and in occupied Namibia.

Infant and child mortality rates vary significantly among different "race" groups in South Africa. Wilson and Ramphele have documented that infant mortality of blacks was many times greater than that of whites. Table 3.4 illustrates this wide disparity in infant mortality rates among

Table 3.3
Mortality of Infants and Children under Age 5

Years	South Africa infant mortality*	South Africa child mortality†	Namibia child mortality
1950–1955	152	217	284
1955–1960	140	199	269
1960–1965	130	184	254
1965–1970	120	168	240
1970–1975	110	153	226
1975–1980	95	129	212
1980–1985	83	112	194

Source: United Nations, *Mortality of Children under Age 5: World Estimates and Projections, 1950–2025* (New York: United Nations, 1988), 30.
*Deaths between birth and one year per 1,000 births
†Deaths between birth and age five per 1,000 births

categories employed by the government. Data for the so-called African homelands are not included.

Infant and child mortality rates have constantly decreased in South Africa in recent decades. Although infant mortality remained relatively high and the differences between white and black South Africans persisted, the downward trend continued after the imposition of the most intense economic sanctions in the late 1970s and 1980s, though the rate of decrease appears to have slowed.

A survey of other health indicators in South Africa paints a chilling picture of conditions for Asian, colored, and black residents, although there is little indication that these conditions were severely degraded by sanctions. As noted above, morbidity, disease type, and access to medical care in South Africa vary according to population group. Malnutrition rates averaging 15 to 25 percent were reported among black children in the 1980s, while black adults also suffered malnutrition. The incidence of some infectious diseases declined—notably cholera, diphtheria, and

Table 3.4
Average Infant Mortality, 1981–1985, by "Race" and Region

	White	Asian	Colored	African
National average	12	18	52	94–124
Ten major urban areas	12	17	26	39
Rural and peri-urban	12	20	66	100–135

Source: Francis Wilson and Mamphela Ramphele, *Uprooting Poverty: The South African Challenge* (Cape Town: David Philip, 1989), 107.

measles—but the rates of other diseases—notably tuberculosis and HIV—were on the increase during the late 1980s, especially among black South Africans. Life expectancy among blacks has been consistently ten to fifteen years shorter than for whites. Health care has also been less available for the majority population as measured by health insurance and the number of beds, doctors, and nurses per thousand of the population.[84]

Health is also affected by social, economic, and political instability, and during the 1970s and 1980s South Africa suffered from all of these. The 1976 government massacre of schoolchildren in Soweto was not repeated, but during the states of emergency in the 1980s, government violence toward antiapartheid activists—detentions, murder, and beatings—grew (for example, some twenty-five thousand were detained in 1986–1987). In addition, overall crime and in particular violent crime grew, a trend that continued after the transition to majority rule. These conditions—government-sponsored violence, increased military and police occupation of townships, and rising crime, combined with drought and grinding poverty—made life for many of South Africa's poor increasingly desperate. "For many households, the pressures . . . have driven many to lifestyles which are 'self-destructive' through drugs, prostitution, and alcoholism."[85]

The appalling conditions of health and welfare and the glaring disparities between whites and the majority black population were due to apartheid and long-term structural conditions. The precise contribution of sanctions to the ill health of the majority population, if any, is not clear. Indeed, most indicators of health continued to show some improvement in the status of black South Africans even after the imposition of the most biting economic sanctions of the mid-1980s. To the extent that sanctions prompted the recalcitrant government of South Africa to adopt an import substitution strategy, they may have indirectly promoted rapid urbanization, which put stress on already overcrowded and squalid townships. But sanctions were not responsible for the policies of the South African government that consistently denied the basic necessities for adequate health and welfare to the black, Asian, and colored populations.

Environment

The direct environmental effects of sanctions against South Africa were probably minimal. But there may be some long-term indirect effects resulting from South Africa's attempt to overcome the oil embargo by import substitution. Increased coal mining and consumption and synthetic fuels have created health and environmental effects that cannot be discounted.

Nearly 40 percent of South African coal is produced by the open-pit (strip-mining) method.[86] South African coal is primarily bituminous, which burns less cleanly and efficiently than anthracite. South African power stations emit half a million tons of smoke particles into the air each year.[87] During the 1980s, South Africa's most industrialized regions began to experience acid rain problems. "Highly acidic rainwater frequently falls in the industrial heartland of the eastern Transvaal Highveld. This pollution comes from the power stations and industries" of the area.[88] In January 1989, a study of sulfur dioxide emissions commissioned for South Africa's Council for Scientific and Industrial Research found that "emission densities are between five and just under ten times greater than those found in West Germany and the United States, and approximate the worst conditions found anywhere."[89]

The coal-to-liquid-fuel process was also a contributor to pollution. Though Sasol II and III were built to be cleaner, Sasol I, located south of Johannesburg, discharged toxic waste into the Vaal River: "Tests have identified twenty seven chemicals listed as priority pollutants in the United States in Sasol's effluent."[90]

Most coal consumption went to generate power for white-owned homes, manufacturing centers, and businesses. Most of the power used by township dwellers, until quite recently, was produced from the burning of wood or coal in large cans for cooking. In 1990, the head of Eskom noted that 70 percent of black South Africans did not have access to electricity in their households.[91] The majority population thus suffered air quality that was the same as, or perhaps worse than, the air quality endured by whites, while benefiting little from coal-fired power generation.[92] The studies that have been conducted on air quality in South Africa have traced negative health effects to air pollution. Respiratory disease was the second major killer of children under five in the Johannesburg-Soweto area. A study of two thousand children by Professor Saul Zwi of the University of the Witwatersrand in 1988 showed that children in polluted towns were shorter than those in cleaner areas.[93]

Humanitarian Assistance

The United Nations repeatedly called for humanitarian assistance to offset the effects of sanctions in South Africa and began as early as the 1950s to promote assistance to the victims of apartheid. From the 1960s onward, the UN also channeled money to antiapartheid movements in exile. In 1965 the UN coordinated contributions by twelve member governments totaling $300,000 to the International Defence and Aid Fund for Southern Africa based in London.[94] The General Assembly also established a UN Trust Fund for South Africa in 1965 that earmarked resources for legal assistance to victims of repressive laws and that also aided South African refugees. By June 1994 the trust fund had "spent $50 million on programmes of humanitarian, legal and educational assistance."[95] In addition, the UN established the Educational and Training Program for Southern Africa that provided funds to 7,216 South Africans who were studying abroad between 1965 and October 1993. Finally, the UN High Commission for Refugees provided over $5 million to assist student refugees who began leaving South Africa after the 1976 Soweto uprising.

Other forms of government and private assistance were also channeled to South Africa. The United States Agency for International Development initiated a program focusing on black South Africans that made grants totaling $66 million between 1984 and 1988. The European Community and Japan made grants to help victims of apartheid in the 1980s through the Kasigo Trust, a South African foundation that in turn supported community groups. Private assistance came to the South African Council of Churches from the Lutheran Office for World Concern, the World Council of Churches (Geneva), and the National Council of Churches (New York). Large amounts of private corporate and foundation assistance were also funneled into the country. For example, as part of their disinvestment, Ford Motor Company gave over $11.5 million to community trusts in South Africa in the late 1980s, and the Ford Foundation maintained an active foundation profile in southern Africa.[96]

Because of South Africa's overall diplomatic isolation, organizations of the UN system were not allowed to operate inside the country. However, private and government relief did make its way into South Africa. For example, the International Committee of the Red Cross, Operation Hunger, and World Vision attempted to provide humanitarian assistance. These organizations engaged in emergency feeding, water distribution, and well digging in South Africa.

Humanitarian assistance was primarily intended to meet the challenges and hardships created and exacerbated by apartheid. Tom Getman of World Vision argues that humanitarian assistance did help to save lives but that its contribution was "minimal" and that "relief agencies can't take credit for very much." Getman believes that "sanctions drove people to provide their own relief and development systems" and that over the long run "people became more self-sufficient and empowered because of sanctions."[97] Since the bulk of the humanitarian assistance that went to South and southern Africa was intended to redress the harms of apartheid, there is no substantial evidence that humanitarian assistance offset the hardships of sanctions. This arena, like many others, merits more detailed empirical inquiry.

Conclusions and Directions for Further Research

The direct and indirect political, economic, and humanitarian effects of sanctions against apartheid South Africa were highly complex and were mediated by other forces. Sanctions reduced South Africa's access to export markets, finance, and important commodities such as computers, oil, and arms. The price that the state paid to acquire embargoed items was higher than it would have been without sanctions. At the same time, because South Africa resisted sanctions with an import substitution strategy, sanctions indirectly promoted industrialization in certain sectors. The net effect of international sanctions was thus growth in import substitution sectors and stagnation or decline in others. It is likely that sanctions cost many thousands of jobs in South Africa and in this way led to increased poverty and insecurity, especially among the majority population. These job losses were compounded by the fact that the economy grew at a slower rate than the increase in population. Conversely, import substitution efforts led to a growth in some sectors that may have offset the job losses due to sanctions. The conclusion seems to be that, despite the claims of the opponents of sanctions, the unemployment consequences of sanctions for the majority population were probably much less than predicted. The fact that unemployment has continued to grow in South Africa since the end of sanctions suggests that many other factors are at work.

The direct health effects of sanctions seem to have been marginal. Although the majority of South Africans remained less healthy than the white population, overall health indicators continued to improve even after the most intense sanctions were instituted. On the other hand, the indirect effects of sanctions on the environment—due to South Africa's highly polluting coal and synthetic fuel industries—may be substantial and long lasting for all South Africans.

Governmental, intergovernmental, and nongovernmental agencies provided some assistance to South Africans to counter the effects of apartheid and to offset the impact of sanctions. More assistance aimed directly at the black population would perhaps have helped alleviate negative consequences of sanctions and also the humanitarian problems associated with apartheid economic structures.

Additional research is needed to draw more definitive conclusions about the effects of sanctions in South Africa. First, the discussion of the causes of unemployment outlined several potential explanations for job loss and showed that sanctions may have been only one of several contributing factors. An industry-by-industry study would undoubtedly help illuminate the precise role of sanctions versus, for instance, mechanization. Once evidence from these sectors is gathered, comparisons to nonsanctioned economies that are similar in most other respects may provide further insight. Similarly, the argument that South Africa's resistance to the oil embargo led indirectly to a growth in pollution requires more thorough investigation, as do the motivations, destinations, and quantities of humanitarian aid.

Notes

Dozens of people in South Africa and the United States shared their impressions, provided leads and made introductions for me while I did the research for this paper. Jacklyn Cock of the University of Witwatersrand stands out as the most enthusiastic supporter of this research while I was in South Africa. Jill Breitbarth, William Carmichael, David Cortright, Dennis Frado, George Lopez, Larry Minear, and Tom Weiss also made useful suggestions. Portions of this chapter are drawn from my contributions to Neta C. Crawford and Audie Klotz, *How Sanctions Work: South Africa* (London: Macmillan/St. Martin's, forthcoming).

1. Ronnie Bethlehem, "South Africa's Imperative for Growth," in *Sanctions and the Alternatives*, by Stanley Magoba, John Kane-Berman, and Ronnie Bethlehem (Johannesburg: South African Institute of Race Relations, 1988), 1–13, quote on 2.
2. The words "Asian," "black" or "African," "colored," and "white" denote racial categories that operated in South Africa through the mid- and late twentieth century. I use these terms as they were commonly used in South Africa, fully recognizing their historicity and acknowledging that none of these categories is homogeneous, nor their populations entirely like-minded.
3. Republic of South Africa (RSA), Central Statistical Service, *South African Labour Statistics* (Pretoria: RSA, 1986), xix.
4. Francis Wilson and Mamphela Ramphele, *Uprooting Poverty: The South African Challenge* (Cape Town: David Philip, 1989).
5. Other possible strategies are attempting to better the evidentiary base through more interviews and household surveys and comparing similar economies that faced similar external economic shocks and attempted similar mechanization programs.
6. Stuart Jones and André Mullen, *The South African Economy, 1910–1990* (New York: St. Martin's, 1992), 231.
7. Discrimination by Afrikaner and English-speaking whites against other

cultural groups, such as Jews, was rampant, just not legislated and enforced to the same degree.

8. Wilson and Ramphele, *Uprooting Poverty*, 4.

9. Mangosuthu Buthelezi, "Discerning the Divestment Debate," in *The South African Quagmire: In Search of a Peaceful Path to Democratic Pluralism*, ed. S. Prakash Sethi (Cambridge, Mass.: Ballinger, 1987), 165–69, quote on 165.

10. For a detailed review of several surveys of black South Africans done during the mid-1980s, see Meg Voorhes, *Black South Africans' Attitudes on Sanctions and Divestment* (Washington, D.C.: Investor Responsibility Research Center, 1988). Voorhes's comparison highlights the different results of the polls depending on the content of the question asked and the demographics of the survey population. Another excellent summary and analysis of these public opinion surveys, including his own polling, is Mark Orkin, "Politics, Social Change, and Black Attitudes on Sanctions," in *Sanctions against Apartheid*, ed. Mark Orkin (Cape Town: David Philip, 1989), 80–102.

11. Jan Hofmeyer, *The Impact of Sanctions on South Africa, Part II: Whites' Political Attitudes* (Washington, D.C.: Investor Responsibility Research Center, 1990).

12. Anthony van Nieuwkerk and Andre du Pisani, *What Do We Think? A Survey of White Opinion on Foreign Policy Issues*, no. 6 (Johannesburg: South African Institute of International Affairs, 1992): 32–34. This last version of the *What Do We Think?* series summarizes the results of the previous five surveys.

13. For examples of early articulations of this view, see South African Institute for International Affairs, *South Africa and Sanctions: Genesis and Prospects* (Johannesburg: South African Institute for International Affairs, 1979); Arnt Spandau, *Economic Boycott against South Africa: Normative and Factual Issues* (Cape Town: Juta, 1979); and Sanlam, "Sanctions and the South African Economy," *Sanlam's Economic Review*, February 1979, 1–12.

14. Richard E. Bissell, *Apartheid and International Organizations* (Boulder, Colo.: Westview, 1977); Audie Klotz, *Norms in International Relations: The Struggle against Apartheid* (Ithaca, N.Y.: Cornell University Press, 1995); United Nations, *The United Nations and Apartheid: 1948–1994* (New York: United Nations, 1994).

15. The Reagan administration coined the term "constructive engagement" and developed this policy in the early 1980s. See Chester A. Crocker, "South Africa: A Strategy for Change," *Foreign Affairs* 59 (Winter 1980/1981): 323–51.

16. More comprehensive lists of sports, cultural, diplomatic, military, and economic sanctions include Gary Clyde Hufbauer, Jeffrey J. Schott, and Kimberly Ann Elliott, *Economic Sanctions Reconsidered: History and Current Policy*, 2d ed. (Washington, D.C.: Institute for International Economics, 1990), cases 62–2 , 85-1; Timothy U. Moiza, "Chronology of Arms Embargoes against South Africa," in *Effective Sanctions on South Africa: The Cutting Edge of Economic Intervention*, ed. George W. Shepard Jr. (New York: Praeger, 1991), 97–108; Sandra Ferguson and Peter Sluiter, "Existing Sanctions," in *South Africa: The Sanctions Report Document and Statistics*, ed. Joseph Hanlon (London: Commonwealth Secretariat, 1990), 3–72; Merle Lipton, *Sanctions and South Africa: The Dynamics of Economic Isolation* (London: Economist Intelligence Unit, 1988). A discussion of early sanctions is included in D. G. Clarke, "Economic Sanctions on South Africa: Past Evidence and

Future Potential," in *Economic Sanctions against South Africa* (Geneva: International University Exchange Fund, 1980).

17. For the moment, this analysis leaves aside the possibilities that some sanctions were imposed simply to placate domestic constituencies or as symbolic expressions and punishment for apartheid.

18. "The Nassau Commonwealth Accord on Southern Africa, October 1985."

19. *Comprehensive Anti-Apartheid Act of 1986*, sec. 101.

20. For discussions of the leaks in the oil and arms embargoes, see Arthur Jay Klinghoffer, *Oiling the Wheels of Apartheid* (London: Lynne Rienner, 1989); R. Hengeveld and J. Rodenburg, eds., *Embargo: Apartheid's Oil Secrets Revealed* (Amsterdam: Amsterdam University Press, 1995), 206–21; Signe Landgren, *Embargo Disimplemented: South Africa's Military Industry* (New York: Oxford University Press, 1989).

21. Jean Leger, "Coal Mining: Past Profits, Current Crisis?" in *South Africa's Economic Crisis*, ed. Stephen Gelb (Cape Town: David Philip, 1991), 128–55, quote on 128.

22. Margaret P. Doxey, *Economic Sanctions and International Enforcement* (London: Oxford University Press/Royal Institute for International Affairs, 1971), 146.

23. On the politics of organizing sanctions and compliance with sanctions regimes, see Lisa L. Martin, *Coercive Cooperation: Explaining Multilateral Economic Sanctions* (Princeton: Princeton University Press, 1992).

24. For a review and discussion of sanctions theories and an elaboration of the idea of direct and indirect effects, see Neta C. Crawford and Audie Klotz, "How Sanctions Work: A Framework for Analysis," in *How Sanctions Work*, ed. Crawford and Klotz. See also Ivan Eland, "Economic Sanctions as Tools of Foreign Policy," in *Economic Sanctions: Panacea or Peacebuilding in a Post–Cold War World?* ed. David Cortright and George A. Lopez (Boulder, Colo.: Westview, 1995), 29–42; Hufbauer, Schott, and Elliott, *Economic Sanctions Reconsidered*; William H. Kaempfer and Anton D. Lowenberg, *International Economic Sanctions: A Public Choice Perspective* (Boulder, Colo.: Westview, 1992).

25. Martin Bailey, "Oil Sanctions: South Africa's Weak Link," in *Economic Sanctions against South Africa*, no. 5 (Geneva: International University Exchange Fund, 1980), 23.

26. Klinghoffer, *Oiling the Wheels*, 35–38.

27. Sanlam, "Sanctions and the South African Economy," 1.

28 Bailey, "Oil Sanctions," 13.

29. Sasol, *Annual Report 1989* (Johannesburg, 1989) and *Annual Report 1990* (Johannesburg, 1989).

30. RSA, *Report of the Auditor General on the Financial Statements for 1993–1994 of the Central Energy Fund* (Pretoria: RSA, 1995), 28.

31. Shipping Research Bureau, *Secret Oil Deliveries to South Africa, 1981–1982* (Amsterdam: Shipping Research Bureau, 1984), 29.

32. Peter A. G. Van Bergeijk, "The Oil Embargo and the Intellectual: The Academic Debate on Economic Sanctions against South Africa," in *Embargo*, ed. Hengeveld and Rodenburg, 338–45, quote on 343.

33. Shipping Research Bureau, *Secret Oil Deliveries*, 29.

34. There was a substantial increase in the number of cars in South Africa despite their rising cost and the sanctions on spare parts put in place by the United States and Japan in the 1980s. See RSA, Central Statistical Service, *South African Statistics 1994* (Pretoria: Government Printing Office, 1994) "Transport Vehicles–South Africa: Historical Summary," table 17.9.

35. *Washington Post*, 24 February 1985, A26. Cited in Hufbauer, Schott, and Elliot, *Economic Sanctions Reconsidered*, Supplemental Case Histories, 232.

36. Based on Stockholm International Peace Research Institute figures reported in Jonathan Cohen and Andrew Peach, *World Combat Aircraft Holdings, Production, and Trade* (Cambridge, Mass.: Institute for Defense and Disarmament Studies, 1994), 114–15.

37. Cameron Commission, "Commission of Inquiry into Alleged Arms Transactions between Armscor and One Eli Wazan and Related Matters," (Johannesburg: RSA, 15 June 1995), 23, 107.

38. RSA, *White Paper on Defence, 1984* (Pretoria, 1984), 22.

39. See Neta C. Crawford, "How Arms Embargoes Work: South Africa" (paper presented at the annual meeting of the International Studies Association, San Diego, April 1996); Thomas Ohlson, "The Cuito Cuanavale Syndrome: Revealing SADF Vulnerabilities," *South African Review 5* (Braamfontein: Ravan Press, 1989), 181–90, quote on 182; George Crown, "Success of the Arms Embargo," in *Sanctions Report*, 168–73.

40. See Richard C. Porter, "International Trade and Investment Sanctions: Potential Impact on the South African Economy," *Journal of Conflict Resolution*, no. 4 (December 1979); David Kaplan, "The South African Capital Goods Sector and the Economic Crisis," in *South Africa's Economic Crisis*, 175–97.

41. For a discussion of early financial restrictions, see Clarke, "Economic Sanctions on South Africa." A concise discussion of the mid- to late-1980s financial situation is Commonwealth Committee, *Banking on Apartheid: The Financial Links Report* (London: Commonwealth Secretariat, 1989).

42. E.g., see Lipton, *Sanctions and South Africa*, 59; Trevor Bell, "The Impact of Sanctions on South Africa," *Journal of Contemporary African Studies*, no. 1 (1993): 1–28, quote on 2–5.

43. "When Sanctions Go: Straining at the Leash," *Financial Mail*, no. 1 (2 July 1993): 24.

44. Alan Hirsch, "Sanctions, Loans, and the South African Economy," in *Sanctions against Apartheid*, 270–84.

45. Stephen Gelb, "South Africa's Economic Crisis: An Overview," in *South Africa's Economic Crisis*, ed. Gelb, 1–32, quote on 4.

46. "Oil and Oil Supports: Letting Go of the Obsolete," *Financial Mail*, no. 2 (10 April 1992): 23.

47. Hirsch, "Sanctions, Loans, and the South African Economy," 276.

48. "How Do South African Sanctions Work?" *Economist*, no. 7624 (14 October 1989): 53–54; RSA, Department of Mineral and Energy Affairs, *South Africa's Mineral Industry, 1992–1993* (Pretoria: RSA, 1993), 20.

49. For more on this, see Neta C. Crawford, "Oil Sanctions against South Africa," in *How Sanctions Work*, ed. Crawford and Klotz.

50. The levy was discontinued in 1988. RSA, *Report of the Auditor General on the Financial Statements for 1993–1994 of the Central Energy Fund* (Pretoria: RSA, 1995), 11.

51. The Sasol facilities were also the target of ANC sabotage in the 1980s. See Hengeveld and Rodenburg, *Embargo*, 25–55.

52. Kevin Davie, "Apartheid and the Cost of Energy Self-Sufficiency," in *Embargo*, ed. Hengeveld and Rodenburg, 242–53, quote on 243; Klinghoffer, *Oiling the Wheels*, 24.

53. Jean Leger, "Coal Mining: Past Profits, Current Crisis? " in *South Africa's Economic Crisis*, ed. Gelb, 129–55.

54. Bill Freund, "South African Gold Mining in Transformation," in *South Africa's Economic Crisis*, ed. Gelb, 110–28.

55. Landgren, *Embargo Disimplemented*, 41. See also Graeme Simpson, "The Politics and Economics of the Armaments Industry in South Africa," in *Society at War: The Militarization of South Africa*, ed. Jacklyn Cock and Laurie Nathan (New York: St. Martin's Press, 1989), 217–31, quote on 221.

56. RSA, *Briefing on the Organization and Functions of the South African Defence Force and the Armaments Corporation of South Africa, Limited, 1990* (Pretoria: RSA, 1990), 69; Landgren, *Embargo Disimplemented*; Gus Begg, "SAAF and the Arms Industry," *Ad Astra* 10, no. 2: 11–14.

57. RSA, *Organization and Functions of the South African Defence Force and the Armaments Corporation*.

58. *Washington Report on Africa* 6, no. 3 (1 March 1988): 11.

59. RSA, *White Paper on Defence and Armament Supply, 1986*, 38.

60. RSA, *White Paper on Defence and Armament Supply, 1986*, 36.

61. Peter Batchelor, personal communication with the author, 26 February 1996.

62. Other unanticipated ripple effects of the South African "total strategy" are discussed in Neta C. Crawford, "The Domestic Sources and Consequences of Aggressive Foreign Policies: The Folly of South Africa's 'Total Strategy,'" working paper no. 41 of the *Southern African Perspectives* series, University of the Western Cape, Bellville, South Africa, 1995.

63. "The modifications [of influx control] introduced were intended to improve the productivity of labour or comparable economic functions on the one hand, and to reduce the levels of opposition to the state on the other." Alf Stadler, *The Political Economy of Modern South Africa* (New York: St. Martin's Press, 1987), 96–101, quote on 97.

64. Armament production increased but overall manufacturing employment declined 1 percent from 1980 to 1985, while the entire South African economy suffered a recession. Anthony Black, "Manufacturing Development and Economic Crisis: A Reversion to Primary Production?" in *South Africa's Economic Crisis*, ed. Gelb, 156–74.

65. RSA, *Organization and Functions of the South African Defence Force and the Armaments Corporation*, 69.

66. Allister Sparks, *The Mind of South Africa* (New York: Alfred A. Knopf, 1990), 314.

67. Calculated from statistics given in RSA, *South Africa, 1989–1990, The Official Yearbook of the Republic of South Africa*, 15th ed. (Pretoria: RSA, 1990), 778.

68. For discussion of trade unions and sanctions, see Auret Van Heerden, "Trade Union Gains from Sanctions," in *South Africa*, 206–9. See also Gay W. Seidman, *Manufacturing Militance: Worker's Movements in Brazil and South Africa, 1970–1985* (Berkeley and Los Angeles: University of California Press, 1994).

69. Steven Metz, "Pretoria's 'Total Strategy' and Low-Intensity Warfare in Southern Africa," *Comparative Strategy* 6, no. 4, (1987): 437–69, quote on 446–47. James Barber and John Barratt, *South Africa's Foreign Policy: The Search for Status and Security,. 1945–1988* (Cambridge: Cambridge University Press, 1990), 257–58.

70. Gregory Huston, "Capital Accumulation, Influx Control, and the State in South Africa, 1970–1982," *Journal of Contemporary African Studies* 7, nos. 1/2 (April/October 1988): 111–31, quote on 125. These measures were implemented more or less successfully over the next several years.

71. William Carmichael, interview by author, 23 May 1996.

72. "When Sanctions Go," 26.

73. Federated Chamber of Industries, *The Effect of Sanctions on Unemployment and Production in South Africa* (Pretoria: FCI Information Services, 1986.) Cited in Charles Meth, "Sanctions and Unemployment," in *Sanctions against Apartheid*, 240–52, quote on 250.

74. Bethlehem, "South Africa's Imperative for Growth," 7–8.

75. Meth, "Sanctions and Unemployment," 252.

76. Carolyn Jenkins, "The Effects of Sanctions on Formal Sector Employment in South Africa," Institute of Development Studies Discussion Paper No. 320 (University of Sussex, March 1993), 2.

77. The total number of people working in the mines was 735,163 in 1985 and 718,384 in 1989, according to Department of Mineral and Energy Affairs, *South Africa's Mineral Industry, 1992* (Pretoria: RSA, 1993), 5. Leger ("Coal Mining," 134–36) and Freund ("South African Gold Mining in Transformation," 122) discuss the impact of increased mechanization on productivity and employment in the mines.

78. RSA, Central Statistical Service, *South African Labour Statistics*, 1986, xxi.

79. Jenkins, "Effects of Sanctions on Employment," 16–17.

80. The immediate economic costs of resisting sanctions were primarily shouldered by whites through government income and consumption taxes. On the other hand, there is no doubt that a few entrepreneurs were able to make their fortunes as sanctions busters and import substitution industrialists; their dealings are occasionally documented by South African tabloids.

81. Jenkins, "Effects of Sanctions on Employment," 16–17.

82. For an overview of health and environment issues in the context of apartheid, see Coleen H. Vogel and James H. Drummond, "Shades of 'Green' and 'Brown': Environmental Issues in South Africa," in *The Geography of Change in South Africa*, ed. Anthony Lemon (New York: John Wiley & Sons, 1995), 85–98; Garrett Nagle, "Trends in Health and Health Care in South Africa," in *The Geography of Change in South Africa*, ed. Lemon, 99–121; Wilson and Ramphele, *Uprooting Poverty*.

83. RSA, Central Statistical Service, *South African Statistics, 1994* data on principal causes of death.

84. Nagle, "Trends in Health."

85. Nagle, "Trends in Health," 101–2.

86. RSA, Department of Mineral and Energy Affairs, *South Africa's Mineral Industry, 1990,* 41.

87. Mark Gandar, "The Imbalance of Power," in *Going Green: People, Politics and the Environment in South Africa,* ed. Jacklyn Cock and Eddie Koch (Cape Town: Oxford University Press, 1991), 94–109, quote on 98.

88. Henk Coetzee and David Cooper, "Wasting Water," in *Going Green,* ed. Cock and Koch, 129–38, quote on 132.

89. Report quoted in James Clark, "The Insane Experiment: Tampering with the Atmosphere," in *Going Green,* ed. Cock and Koch, 139–57, quote on 144.

90. Coetzee and Cooper, "Wasting Water," 135.

91. Ian McRea quoted in Clark, "Insane Experiment," 149.

92. It would be a mistake to conclude that black townships were not electrified because of the oil embargo. Rather, apartheid policies included the denial of infrastructure to townships and other settlements populated by the majority of the population as part of the effort to discourage urbanization. Moreover, electricity itself was never in short supply; South Africa exported electricity to the region.

93. Clark, "Insane Experiment," 140–41.

94. United Nations, *The United Nations and Apartheid,* 80.

95. United Nations, *The United Nations and Apartheid,* 82.

96. Robert Price, *The Apartheid State in Crisis: Political Transformation in South Africa, 1975–1990* (Oxford: Oxford University Press, 1991), 233–35.

97. Tom Getman, interview by author, 23 February 1996.

4

The Humanitarian Impacts of Economic Sanctions and War in Iraq

Eric Hoskins

Prior to the Gulf War, Iraq was described by the United Nations as a high-middle-income country with a modern social infrastructure.[1] Since the early 1960s, Iraq has evolved from a largely rural, agricultural society to one where 70 percent of the country's 20 million citizens live in urban areas. Fifty-three percent of workers were employed in agriculture in 1960, but by 1990 this had been reduced to 12 percent.[2] Meanwhile, oil, which in 1990 accounted for more than 90 percent of export earnings and 62 percent of gross domestic product (GDP), has dominated all areas of the Iraqi economy since the early 1960s, if not earlier. It was this almost singular reliance on oil that, following the Iraqi invasion of Kuwait, made

Figure 4.1 Iraq

Iraq particularly vulnerable to the effects of economic sanctions that are analyzed here. This chapter examines the background of the sanctions, the sanctions regime, and the impact of the sanctions on the state, society, humanitarian assistance, war, and politics.

Background

Before 1991, Iraq's investment in its own economic and social development had a visible effect on the living conditions and health status of the civilian population. Iraq's medical facilities and public health system were well developed. There were more than 250 hospitals, with an extensive network of primary health care facilities. Since the 1960s, all health indices had shown dramatic improvement. Between 1960 and 1990, life expectancy climbed from forty-nine to sixty-seven years, a level comparable to many Latin American countries, including Brazil and Mexico.[3] By 1990, nearly all urban dwellers and 72 percent of rural residents had access to clean water, while 93 percent of Iraqis had access to health services.[4]

With the start of the Iran-Iraq war in 1980, military expenditures increased from roughly 10 percent of the country's gross national product (GNP) to more than 30 percent. Health expenditures, meanwhile, were reduced to just 0.8 percent of GNP, which is below the average for less developed countries.[5] Yet despite this decrease in health spending, the previous trend of improvement in health continued throughout the 1980s. Between 1977 and 1990, Iraq's infant mortality rate (IMR) declined by nearly 50 percent, from seventy to thirty-nine deaths per thousand live births.[6] During the 1985–1989 period, the proportion of fully immunized one-year-olds increased from 15 to 68 percent.[7]

Although dramatic improvements in health care occurred during (and despite) the Iran-Iraq war, Iraq's economy and labor force suffered. The eight-year war left Iraq in near financial ruin due to massive losses in oil revenue, a foreign debt of nearly $100 billion, and depletion of foreign currency reserves. Out of a total workforce of 5 million, approximately 1 million men were mobilized for the war, more than 100,000 died, and many tens of thousands were injured or captured. The resulting labor shortage contributed to even greater economic stagnation, forcing increasing numbers of women into the workplace and extending Iraq's reliance on foreign workers.

Although the Iran-Iraq war caused enormous economic damage, Iraq's health, education, and other social programs continued to advance throughout the 1980s. This has made it somewhat easier to separate the effects of the 1991 Gulf War, particularly in the area of health, from those of the earlier Iran-Iraq war. Observers familiar with Iraq agree that the 2 August 1990 Iraqi invasion of Kuwait unleashed a conflict far more devastating than anything ever before experienced in modern-day Iraq. In fact, the Gulf War erased many of Iraq's social and economic achievements of the previous two decades.

The Forty-Three-Day War

On 2 August 1990, Iraqi forces invaded and illegally occupied neighboring Kuwait. Iraq's refusal to withdraw from Kuwait, coupled with failed diplomatic efforts, quickly led to the largest mobilization of troops since the Vietnam War. On 17 January 1991, the Gulf War began with a relentless bombing campaign by the allied coalition that was aimed at eliminating Iraq's military capacity. Coalition forces were composed of military personnel and equipment from twenty-eight countries led by the United States and including, among others, Britain, France, Egypt, and Saudi Arabia. An estimated 25 percent of all sorties flown by coalition aircraft penetrated deep into Iraq's heartland, often targeting elements of the civilian infrastructure such as bridges, electric plants, and sites of other essential services.

Coalition forces dropped about 90,000 tons of explosives during the Gulf War. Despite claims that the war was fought "surgically" to minimize civilian casualties, only 8 percent of all bombs dropped on Iraq were so-called smart, or laser-guided, bombs, and, of these, more than 20 percent missed their targets. Overall, between 50 and 70 percent of all bombs dropped on Iraq missed their intended targets.[8] The coalition's overwhelming superiority in air power contributed to massive numbers of Iraqi wartime military deaths, estimated at between 30,000 and 120,000, compared with several hundred on the coalition side.[9]

Civilian wartime casualties were estimated by compiling data from hundreds of extensive interviews and direct eyewitness reports. Middle East Watch, an independent human rights agency, has estimated that between 2,500 and 3,000 Iraqi civilians were killed during the air campaign.[10] This estimate is further supported by a United Nations report of 20 March 1991 that estimated that 9,000 homes throughout the country were destroyed or damaged beyond repair during the war.[11]

The Sanctions Resolutions

When Iraqi troops invaded Kuwait, the United Nations Security Council immediately passed Resolution 660 condemning the invasion and calling for Iraq's immediate and unconditional withdrawal from Kuwait. Four days later, the council passed Resolution 661, which imposed military, financial, and comprehensive economic sanctions against Iraq. These sanctions required mandatory compliance by all UN member states. Punitive measures included a ban on all trade with Iraq, an arms embargo, suspension of international flights, and a ban on financial transactions, including the freezing of Iraqi assets abroad. Sea and air blockades were imposed on 25 August and 25 September 1990, respectively. Exempt from sanctions were "supplies intended strictly for medical purposes, and, in humanitarian circumstances, foodstuffs."

On 13 September, Resolution 666 sought to clarify what might constitute "humanitarian circumstances," thereby allowing the importation of foodstuffs. The UN secretary-general was asked to monitor civilian conditions in both Kuwait and Iraq and report circumstances of "human suffering" to the Security Council. The resolution emphasized that "it is for the Security Council, alone or acting through the [Sanctions] Committee to determine whether humanitarian circumstances have arisen." Such circumstances were not judged by the Security Council to have occurred in Iraq until 3 April 1991, at which time the prohibition of foodstuffs was lifted.

On 29 November, the Security Council issued Resolution 678 authorizing member states to use "all necessary means" to restore Kuwaiti sovereignty if Iraqi forces had not fully withdrawn on or before 15 January 1991. Further diplomatic efforts failed, and the Gulf War began one day after this deadline had expired. By 27 February, six weeks into the conflict, Iraq's occupying forces had been forced out of Kuwait. The following day, the United States ordered the immediate suspension of hostilities. On 3 March Iraq agreed to the terms of Resolution 686, which demanded implementation of all previous Security Council resolutions, the release of prisoners, and the return of stolen property. The Gulf War was officially over. One month later, on 3 April, the precise terms of Iraq's surrender were specified in Resolution 687:

- recognition of Kuwait's territorial integrity, with demarcation of international boundaries

- acceptance of a monitored, demilitarized zone between Iraq and Kuwait

- destruction of all chemical, biological, and long-range weapons, with ongoing United Nations monitoring of Iraq's weapons capability

- elimination of Iraq's nuclear weapons capability

- return of all stolen property

- acceptance of liability for all war-related losses and damage

- repatriation of all Kuwaiti and third-country nationals

- renunciation of all acts, methods, and practices of terrorism

In response to postwar reports of serious and worsening humanitarian circumstances within Iraq, Resolution 687 also made important changes to the existing sanctions legislation. The 20 March 1991 report of United Nations Under-Secretary-General Martti Ahtisaari described "near-apocalyptic" destruction, with Iraq "relegated to a pre-industrial age" where "most means of modern life support have been destroyed or rendered tenuous." The report concluded that "the Iraqi people may soon face a further imminent catastrophe, which could include epidemic and famine, if massive life-supporting needs are not rapidly met."[12] The report recommended the immediate lifting of sanctions with respect to food supplies and identified the urgent need for inputs of equipment and materials for agricultural production, water, sanitation, and health care. The list of supplies and materials provided by the report formed the basis for the "no objection" procedure in Resolution 687:

- Foodstuffs would no longer be prohibited, although suppliers were required to notify the sanctions committee of all shipments.

- A "no objection" procedure would be established, through which "materials and supplies for essential civilian needs," as identified in the 20 March 1991 Ahtisaari report, would be permitted.

- Any reduction or lifting of sanctions would depend upon "the policies and practices of the government of Iraq, including the implementation of all relevant resolutions."

- The export of Iraqi oil, as well as other commodities and products, would be permitted only after Iraq had complied with requirements concerning the destruction and monitoring of weapons of mass destruction and the establishment of a compensation fund.

- The arms embargo would include chemical, biological, nuclear, and long-range weapons and materials.

- An ongoing sixty-day sanctions review process would be undertaken to assess Iraqi government compliance with Security Council resolutions and determine whether to reduce or lift the prohibitions referred to therein.

Resolution 687 also opened the door for future discussions concerning the sale of oil as a means to finance the importation of commodities to meet the "essential civilian needs" of Iraq. The sanctions committee was "empowered to approve . . . exceptions to the prohibition against the import of commodities and products originating in Iraq" in order to provide financial resources for the provision of humanitarian supplies.

Humanitarian Intervention

On 5 April 1991, Resolution 688 was passed by the Security Council. The resolution condemned "the repression of the Iraqi civilian population," particularly in the Kurdish-populated areas. The council demanded an immediate end to this repression by Iraqi authorities and a guarantee of access "by international humanitarian organizations to all those in need of assistance in all parts of Iraq." There was no explicit linkage between Iraq's compliance with Resolution 688 and the continuation of comprehensive sanctions.

Resolution 688 was issued in response to an emerging humanitarian crisis involving Iraq's Kurdish population. Forced from their homes during a failed postwar uprising, approximately 2 million Kurds fled toward neighboring Iran and Turkey, where an estimated 10,000 to 30,000 civilians died of exposure, malnutrition, and disease in squalid refugee camps.[13] The resolution declared their repression and flight a threat to "international peace and security in the region" and insisted that Iraq "allow immediate access by international humanitarian organizations." This declaration provided the legal basis for United Nations activities in Iraq. In mid-April 1991, coalition forces declared the northern part of Iraq a "safe haven" and began providing relief assistance to the Kurds. By June 1991, most of the border camps had been emptied, and the relief effort was handed over to United Nations administration. Health and security conditions within northern Iraq, however, remained precarious. Coinciding with the Kurdish emergency, failed uprisings in Iraq's predominantly Shiite south also led to many thousands of deaths, human rights abuses, and worsening humanitarian circumstances. In contrast to northern Iraq, however, the south received no international protection and very little tangible humanitarian support.

Proposals for the Sale of Oil

From March until August 1991, successive United Nations interagency missions, as well as independent reports such as those issued by the Harvard Study Team, described deteriorating conditions among Iraq's civilian population.[14] On 15 August 1991, the Security Council passed Resolution 706, which permitted the restricted sale, within a six-month period, of up to $1.6 billion of Iraqi oil. The proceeds of the sale, closely supervised and monitored by the Security Council, would be deposited in a United Nations escrow account and used according to the formula specified in Resolution 712. The purchase and transport of humanitarian assistance (58 percent) and a war reparations fund (30 percent) accounted for the bulk, with modest sums for UN monitoring (6 percent) and destruction of weapons (6 percent).

Following the sale of Iraqi oil, the United Nations would closely monitor the purchase, transport, and distribution of approved humanitarian supplies. However, Iraq refused to accept Resolution 706 on the grounds that the mechanism for providing assistance was a violation of Iraqi sovereignty. Iraq also argued against linking any proposals for humanitarian assistance with payments for war reparations and other UN activities. Resolution 712 also allowed the transfer of Iraqi frozen assets and other funds into a subaccount of the UN escrow account, to be used exclusively for humanitarian purposes. However, this option was also refused by Iraq. Iraq's refusal to accept UN terms regarding the sale of oil has allowed the governments of the United States and the United Kingdom to blame the government in Baghdad rather than the economic sanctions per se for the humanitarian emergency in Iraq.[15]

The Sale of Oil, Revisited

On 14 April 1995, Resolution 986 offered a new proposal for the restricted sale of oil by Iraq. The proposed formula permitted the export and sale of up to $1 billion of Iraqi oil every three months. Funds generated are to be deposited in the United Nations escrow account, with 30 percent of the total deposit being transferred to the UN Compensation Fund. Resolution 986 contained important provisions aimed at reducing previous Iraqi opposition to the proposal. United Nations demands for its own involvement in the distribution and supervision of humanitarian supplies were reduced. Under Resolution 986, Iraq need only "effectively guarantee [the] equitable distribution" of humanitarian supplies, with this guarantee supported by periodic United Nations monitoring. Of each $1 billion generated, Iraq was supposed to provide the United Nations with $130 million to $150 million for the UN's own program of humanitarian assistance for the three predominantly Kurdish governorates in northern Iraq. Exemptions, considered on a case-by-case basis, were also to be permitted for the import to Iraq of equipment and spare parts necessary to maintain the Iraq-Turkey oil pipeline. Finally, to address earlier Iraqi opposition, Resolution 986 stated that "nothing in this resolution should be construed as infringing the sovereignty or territorial integrity of Iraq." In May 1996, Iraq accepted UN terms for the sale of oil contained in Resolution 986, leading to the partial resumption of Iraqi oil exports in December 1996.

Although news of the sale-of-oil agreement brought renewed hope to Iraq's suffering population, the arrangement will make only a limited contribution to humanitarian relief. Of the $4 billion in oil revenue potentially available on an annual basis, roughly $3 billion will be provided for basic human needs. This falls short of what is required to meet humanitarian needs. In 1991, Prince Sadruddin Aga Khan, executive delegate of the UN secretary-general, estimated that $22 billion was needed annually for "immediate requirements."[16] Prewar food imports alone amounted to approximately $3 billion.[17] Meanwhile, the cost of returning the civilian sector of Iraq to its prewar state has been estimated at more than $200 billion.[18] Iraq's debts are huge: destroyed infrastructure ($232 billion from Gulf War and $67 billion from Iran-Iraq war); reparations ($100 billion for Gulf War and $97 billion for Iran); and foreign debt ($86 billion).[19]

Under present circumstances, indeed even with the total lifting of sanctions, it is difficult to see how Iraq can begin to repair the damage done to its economy and infrastructure, let alone provide for the basic human needs of 20 million persons. Furthermore, it remains to be seen whether the sale-of-oil agreement will lead eventually to the total lifting of sanctions or whether the UN will argue that this supervised humanitarian exemption meets the needs of the poor while still permitting the use of sanctions as pressure against the Baghdad regime. The Iraqi government's gamble in accepting Resolution 986 undoubtedly was that the former scenario was more likely.

Kurdish "Double" Embargo

In October 1991, Iraqi authorities imposed their own "internal" embargo against the Kurdish areas of northern Iraq. With few exceptions—notably United Nations convoys—supplies and materials were not allowed to pass from government-controlled areas to the Kurdish-administered parts of Iraq. Following the withdrawal of Iraqi troops from Kurdish areas, salaries of government personnel were suspended and all food rations were cut off. Iraqi authorities defended this action by pointing out that they could only guarantee support to areas within their administrative control. Furthermore, Iraq argued, supplies were moving freely into Kurdish areas from neighboring Turkey and the majority of international assistance was directed to the Kurdish population.

Ongoing international concern regarding the poor nutritional and health status of civilians in all parts of Iraq, together with Iraq's continued refusal to accept the sale of oil according to Resolution 706, eventually led to the Security Council's passage of Resolution 778, on 2 October 1992. Member states were encouraged to transfer unilaterally up to $200 million of Iraqi frozen assets into the UN escrow account, as well as any proceeds from the sale of Iraqi oil currently in the possession of member states. The release of Iraqi frozen assets for the purchase of humanitarian supplies, permitted under cease-fire Resolution 687, was prohibited unless such funds were released directly to the escrow account. Several countries transferred funds to the escrow account, and these funds have been used for the stated purposes.

Iraqi Compliance and the Lifting of Sanctions

To what degree has Iraq complied with those paragraphs of Resolution 687 concerning the lifting of sanctions? Paragraph 21 of Resolution 687 refers to Iraq's importing goods, excluding food and medicine. The decision to "reduce or lift the prohibitions" depends on "the policies and practices of the government of Iraq, including the implementation of all relevant resolutions," to be reviewed every sixty days. Paragraph 22 of the resolution refers to the export of goods from Iraq (e.g., oil) and related financial transactions. Such prohibitions "shall have no further force or effect" once Iraq has complied with the requirements in Resolution 687 concerning the destruction and monitoring of Iraq's weapons of mass destruction and the establishment of a United Nations compensation fund. Although, according to United Nations special commission head Rolf Ekeus, Iraq has met requirements for the long-term monitoring of its weapons of mass destruction, it is generally believed that Iraq has been less than forthcoming in revealing all details of past weapons programs. Although the compensation fund has been established, arrangements for ensuring that payments are made to the fund are not yet complete. And while Iraq did recognize the newly demarcated Iraq-Kuwait border in

November 1994, threatening postwar Iraqi troop movements once again called into question Iraq's "policies and practices."

Meanwhile, some Security Council members, most notably the United States, maintain that Iraq must also comply with Resolution 688 and end "repression of the Iraqi civilian population," introducing yet another controversial and subjective requirement for lifting sanctions. Washington's argument stems from that portion of Resolution 687 requiring Iraq's "implementation of all relevant resolutions." Yet Resolution 688 offers no precise criteria for measuring compliance. Some member states have suggested that introducing new requirements, such as linking the lifting of sanctions to Iraq's compliance with Resolution 688, amounts to "moving the goalposts."

Ambiguous and conflicting interpretations of Resolutions 687 and 688 have therefore made it difficult to gauge Iraqi compliance objectively. Foreign and domestic policy considerations, inertia, and the lack of any consensus approach to postwar Iraq all further complicate Security Council policy and decisionmaking. Since any reduction or lifting of sanctions requires the unanimous agreement of all five permanent members of the Security Council, consensus may prove difficult to attain. Until late 1996, the Security Council repeatedly rejected Iraq's application to reduce or lift the sanctions. The chronology of sanctions resolutions is found in table 4.1.

Sanctions Regime

Foodstuffs

To monitor implementation of the embargo, the Security Council authorized the establishment of a sanctions committee, composed of all fifteen members of the Security Council. The committee's main task has been to ensure liaison with UN member states concerning action taken by them to implement the sanctions. Resolution 666 also charged the committee with monitoring the humanitarian situation within Iraq, particularly with regard to foodstuffs, requiring them to report to the Security Council any "urgent humanitarian need" and how it should be met. In the absence of any such committee report, it remained illegal and in violation of the United Nations sanctions to import any food into Iraq from 6 August 1990 until 3 April 1991, when foodstuff restrictions were finally lifted. Yet customary international law forbids the starvation of civilians. Iraq, a net food importer, was already showing signs of food shortage

Table 4.1
Chronology of Security Council Sanctions Resolutions

Resolution	Date Passed	Content of Resolution
661	6 August 1990	Military, financial, and comprehensive economic sanctions
665	25 August 1990	Sea blockade
666	13 September 1990	Clarification of what would constitute "humanitarian circumstances." Requirement that the UN monitor the Iraqi humanitarian situation
670	25 September 1990	Air blockade
687	3 April 1991	Cease-fire resolution Precise terms of Iraq's surrender, including conditions required for lifting sanctions. End of prohibition of foodstuffs. "No objection" procedure for approving humanitarian supplies
688	5 April 1991	Condemnation of Iraq's "repression of the Iraqi civilian population"
706	15 August 1991	Proposal for the sale of oil for food
712	19 September 1991	Precise terms of sale of oil, including distribution of revenue
778	2 October 1992	Member states encouraged to unilaterally transfer Iraqi frozen assets into UN escrow account for humanitarian purchases
986	14 April 1995	Revised proposal for the sale of oil for food

even before the war had begun, with malnutrition rates on the rise, food prices escalating, and, during the war itself, early signs of famine in evidence.[20] The Security Council's prohibition of foodstuffs is viewed by most legal scholars as being in breach of customary international law.[21]

Food should have been permitted from the outset, a requirement now widely recognized and indeed made part of all subsequent UN sanctions legislation (e.g., in the former Yugoslavia and in Haiti). The precise reason for its exclusion in the case of Iraq remains the subject of considerable debate. It is most likely that food was never intended to be fully prohibited but rather that the mechanism in place to identify an Iraqi humanitarian emergency and thus trigger an allowance for the importation of foodstuffs was overly bureaucratic and generally ineffective. Had an impartial, objective, and efficient assessment mechanism been in place early on during the sanctions regime, it is likely that any obstacles to the importation of food would have been overcome. Nonetheless, there is no justifiable reason to exclude any food to populations anywhere, and this component of the sanctions legislation is generally viewed as unethical, if not illegal.

The Nature and Focus of Sanctions

Sanctions against Iraq focused most directly on its oil economy. All Iraqi oil exports were banned. Oil pipelines traversing Turkey, Kuwait, and Saudi Arabia were cut off. Jordan, neutral during the war, was given special permission from the United Nations to import Iraqi oil after Saudi Arabia closed its pipeline to Jordan. The oil embargo alone resulted in a loss of more than 90 percent of Iraq's export earnings.[22] Some leakage has occurred, including covert shipments to Turkey and Iran, yet the overall revenue shortfall and its impact on the Iraqi economy have been devastating.

Shortly after the 25 August 1990 passage of Resolution 665, naval and air blockades were established to enforce Iraqi and international compliance with sanctions. Historically, Iraq's main ocean access was via the southern port of Basra and the Shatt-al-Arab waterway. Coalition forces effectively severed this access route by positioning warships in the Persian Gulf, off the coasts of Iraq and Kuwait. A second sea route, via the southern Jordanian port of Aqaba, was also rigorously policed by coalition ships. All vessels traveling to Aqaba were boarded and carefully searched and their manifests were scrutinized, and many vessels were turned back, all of which caused long queues and long delays. As a result, shipping costs soared, with many companies refusing to transport goods to the port of Aqaba. Vessels were required to provide access to every level and each compartment, forcing shippers to restrict their loads to roughly 75 percent capacity. A single bill of lading incompletely listing a container's destination was sufficient to result in the entire vessel cargo being refused entry and turned back. Rigorously implemented, the sea blockade was highly effective at preventing the entry of any questionable goods. It also prevented the entry of many legitimate shipments destined for local consumption in Jordan and delayed shipments of humanitarian supplies to Iraq. After numerous complaints and claims against the Multinational Inspections Force (MIF) enforcing the blockade, efforts were made to streamline operations. For example, Lloyds Insurance took control of the movement of containers through Aqaba's port, resulting in significantly faster movement of shipments.

Although naval blockades were implemented to enforce sanctions by sea, border policing remains the responsibility of those countries neighboring Iraq. This task has been made easier since, with the exception of Jordan, Iraq's neighbors remain unfriendly towards Baghdad. Even Jordan has openly expressed its dissatisfaction in recent years with the Iraqi leadership. Although leakage inevitably has occurred, for the most part border controls have been highly effective. On the long, relatively porous Jordanian-Iraqi border, ongoing diplomatic pressure from the UN, and particularly the United States, has resulted in greater Jordanian compliance with sanctions monitoring. Jordan's desire to regain its prewar, pro-West status, combined with its keen involvement in the Middle East peace process, has no doubt contributed to that country's greater compliance. Even with border leakage from Turkey, Iran, and Jordan, the dismal humanitarian situation within Iraq suggests that such leakage has not been sufficient to significantly alter the impact of sanctions on the civilian population.

Frozen Assets

Iraqi financial assets overseas, estimated in 1991 at over $4 billion, were frozen on 6 August 1990. UN member states were required to provide the sanctions committee with details of any Iraqi assets held within their territories. Kuwaiti assets were also frozen to protect them from Iraqi confiscation. No financial transactions involving Iraq were permitted except those concerning the provision of medicines and, after 3 April 1991, foodstuffs and other essential civilian needs as outlined in ceasefire Resolution 687. Indeed, more than a half-dozen countries released Iraqi frozen assets to private companies for the purchase of humanitarian supplies. This included more than $100 million by the United Kingdom and smaller amounts by Canada, Switzerland, and Greece, among others. This exemption was ended by Resolution 778 on 2 October 1992. Since that time, frozen Iraqi assets can only be released directly to United Nations relief programs or into the UN escrow account. Iraq claims that without access to their foreign currency reserves, it is unable to contract with overseas suppliers in contractual agreements to provide humanitarian supplies, including food and medicine. The Security Council counters that such purchases can be arranged through the transfer of Iraqi overseas assets into the UN escrow account, as stipulated in Resolutions 712 and 778.

Functioning of the Sanctions Committee: Shortcomings and Improvements

The Security Council originally intended that the implementation, and therefore policing, of sanctions would remain primarily the responsibility of member states. Individual countries would prohibit their nationals from trading with Iraq, freeze Iraqi assets, police borders, and inspect cargo. States were required to report to the sanctions committee about their enforcement efforts. In reality, however, few countries had the experience, let alone the legislation, to deal with the many complex legal and logistical matters concerning the imposition of comprehensive economic sanctions, and they looked instead to the sanctions committee for guidance. The lack of clear instructions and guidelines provided to states by the sanctions committee resulted in a rapid and unfortunate transformation of the committee's function.[23] Instead of reporting on the implementation of sanctions and providing liaison with member states, the sanctions committee was relegated to the role of license bureau, a point also made by the UN Department of Humanitarian Affairs (DHA) in its 1995 report *The Impact of UN Sanctions on Humanitarian Assistance Activities.*

From August 1990 until the end of the war, the role of the sanctions committee in approving requests for exemptions was relatively straightforward. Only "supplies intended strictly for medical purposes" were allowed. It wasn't until 3 April 1991, when foodstuffs and "essential civilian supplies" as detailed in the Ahtisaari report were permitted, that the committee's volume of work became substantial. The absence of any published lists of allowable items meant that states, nongovernmental organizations (NGOs), private firms, and even United Nations agencies themselves were forced to submit requests for nearly every item being considered for import into Iraq. The postwar mechanism of applying for "no objection" to items listed in the Ahtisaari Report, as well as the UN's insistence on "notification" of foodstuffs, greatly increased the workload of committee members while further slowing the humanitarian response.

Indeed, addition of the "no objection" procedure often led to even longer delays as, for example, blockade authorities and shipping management began refusing ocean passage to medicines that lacked the "appropriate" United Nations "no objection" documentation, even though no such documentation was required for medicines. Private companies were generally reluctant to conduct business with Iraq because of delays in receiving sanctions committee approval, pressure from their own governments, and concerns about their companies' public relations. Contractual agreements often did not allow the kind of flexibility required from the sanctions regime. Furthermore, many regional NGOs, concerned community groups, citizens, and the private sector lacked the basic means to negotiate with the sanctions committee. On most occasions, regional and local groups were unfamiliar with UN restrictions, let alone how and where to apply for required approvals. International NGOs were frustrated by long delays and narrow interpretations of the sanctions legislation and exemptions by committee members.

The absence of published lists, a lack of clear direction from the sanctions committee, and an understandable paranoia on the part of suppliers not wishing to incur the wrath of the Security Council resulted in a deluge of requests for committee approval and the subsequent, and predictable, long delays in turnaround time. Except for foodstuffs, medicines, and other materials clearly associated with health-related activities, all requests continued to be dealt with on a case-by-case basis. Furthermore, with decisions regarding approval made by consensus, each member of the committee had potential veto power over each and every request. The refusal by the sanctions committee to grant approval to certain items—for example, pencils, lightbulbs, window glass, and even some heart drugs—was not always easy to understand.

Despite these shortcomings, it is important to acknowledge that over time, considerable improvement was made in the committee's approval and enforcement procedures. Although delays remain lengthy, they have been shortened. UN organizations can now submit bulk requests for approval. Lists of approved items are on occasion published by the sanctions committee to guide member states and other applicants. The Iraqi authorities have not made the process any easier. Efforts to develop a list of humanitarian items requiring only committee notification were apparently scuttled by a lack of Iraqi support. And as mentioned before, efforts to permit the sale of oil to generate funds for humanitarian supplies did not receive the necessary Iraqi government approval until May 1996.

Impact on the State

The Gulf War and the imposition of economic sanctions have both disrupted and altered the day-to-day activities of the Iraqi state, its relationship to the Iraqi people, and its system of governance. The Iraqi economy is in a continuous state of decline affecting, to varying degrees, all levels of Iraqi society. This section will explore the impact of war-related damage and economic sanctions on the national economy, food production, governance, and the internal operations of the state. It will also review some of the coping mechanisms, both legal and illegal, adopted by different sectors of the population in an effort to protect themselves against the current state of affairs in Iraq.

Impact on Trade, Food Production, and Industry

Even before the war, the trade embargo against Iraq had resulted in hyperinflation, food rationing, and a deterioration in health care. Security Council Resolution 661 effectively eliminated any possibility that Iraq could generate sufficient trade revenue to sustain its domestic infrastructure and material needs. The economic embargo prevented, among other things, the unmonitored sale of Iraqi oil, which accounted for more than $10 billion in annual revenue (61 percent of GDP, and more than 90 percent of export earnings) during the presanctions period.[24]

Unfortunately, it will never be known whether the prewar deterioration in living conditions due to economic sanctions, together with the threat of military conflict, might have been sufficient to cause Iraq's withdrawal from Kuwait. Political analysts before the war had suggested that Iraq may have been planning a partial withdrawal from Kuwait, retaining a segment of Kuwait's coastline. But by January 1991, the allied coalition had grown weary of Iraqi intransigence and impatient with the slow progress of sanctions. Furthermore, preparations for war were nearing completion.

By this time, sanctions had so weakened the Iraqi economy that it had become highly vulnerable to the effects of the bombing campaign. The air bombardment caused extensive damage to Iraq's economic infrastructure. Eighteen of Iraq's twenty power-generating plants were rendered inoperable, reducing postwar electricity to just 4 percent of prewar levels.[25] Food storage facilities, industrial complexes, oil refineries, sewage pumping stations, telecommunications facilities, roads, railroads, and dozens of bridges were destroyed during the war. It took Iraq many decades, vast amounts of foreign currency, and considerable foreign expertise to build the estimated $232 billion worth of assets destroyed in the forty-three-day bombing campaign.[26]

Sanctions, meanwhile, seriously constrained postwar reconstruction. Imports were tightly restricted and controlled, while Iraqi exports were prohibited. Iraq's access to foreign currency, previously generated through its export earnings, was severely limited. It is estimated that Iraq has been able to generate only $800 million annually through the sale of small amounts of oil to Jordan and Turkey, by liquidating government gold reserves, and through smuggling.[27]

Iraq has used such funds to import food, medicine, and other basic supplies and to sustain the government and the armed forces. Baghdad's limited access to foreign currency, combined with cheap domestic labor and the cannibalization of spare parts from damaged facilities, has permitted some rudimentary postwar reconstruction, explaining the reported flurry of construction in Baghdad and other major cities. Iraq's agreement to Resolution 986 could generate approximately $3 billion per year for the purchase of humanitarian supplies.

Among the most critical issues facing the majority of the Iraqi population has been the availabiliy of food. Historically, Iraq relied heavily on imported food. Before the imposition of sanctions, approximately 70 percent of Iraq's food supply was imported. The United Nations Food and Agriculture Organization (FAO) estimates that more than 7 million metric tons of food must be imported each year, in addition to Iraq's domestic production of approximately 3 million metric tons—at a total cost of nearly $3 billion.[28] Food imports all but disappeared following the August 1990 imposition of sanctions; from then until 3 April 1991, it was illegal under existing sanctions legislation to import any food into Iraq.

After the war's end, although the importation of food was once again permitted, in practice it has remained problematic. Medicines, although in principle exempt from sanctions, are also in short supply. Before the war, Iraq imported an estimated $500 million in drugs and medical supplies, while roughly 25 percent of medicines were manufactured locally.[29] Most of Iraq's pharmaceutical capacity was destroyed during the war, while sanctions prevented the importation of raw materials for drug manufacturing. From 1991 to 1993, the amount of food and medicine imported by the United Nations and other aid agencies was estimated to be less than 5 percent of the total humanitarian needs of the civilian population.[30] Orders of millions of dollars worth of medicine, food, and water and sanitation equipment, paid for by Iraq before August 1990, have been canceled or delayed. Iraq also lacks, or claims to lack, the foreign currency required to purchase medicines and food.

As with food, most of Iraq's industrial base was heavily dependent on the import of sophisticated machinery, equipment, spare parts, and raw materials procured abroad. With the imposition of sanctions, these resources rapidly became unavailable and industrial production suffered. Widespread infrastructure damage due to the war made continued industrial activity difficult. Repair of most of these facilities has been slow and, in some cases, nonexistent. Consequently, postwar industrial production has decreased by more than 50 percent, resulting in high rates of unemployment and layoffs.[31]

Impact on Agriculture

Agricultural disruption was caused by both the embargo and the war. The embargo led, for example, to the lack of seeds, fertilizers, pesticides, replacement parts for irrigation, and harvesting and processing equipment. The war caused, among other things, damage to power stations, disruption of transportation and markets, and the displacement of populations, including migrant agricultural workers.

The combined impact of sanctions and war contributed to a reduction in the postwar 1991 crop harvest by an estimated 25 to 30 percent of the 1990 level.[32] Since then, harvests have still not reached prewar levels of production. Cereal production for 1994–1995 was 10 percent lower than the previous year and 16 percent lower than the average harvest for the previous five years, despite good rainfalls.[33] A lack of veterinary medicines has also contributed to a reduction in livestock, fish, and poultry. The lack of fuel for cooking has resulted in the collection of firewood, particularly in the northern governorates, leading to deforestation and environmental degradation ultimately affecting Iraq's agricultural base.

Impact on Governance

Harsh economic conditions in Iraq are believed to have contributed to increasing rates of crime, displacement, and human rights abuses. The Iraqi government, in an effort to retain control over the state, has resorted to abusive and often divisive social and legislative policies. Neither economic sanctions nor increasing numbers of opposition groups have been able to force Saddam Hussein from power.[34] The poorest sectors of the Iraqi population, which are also the most rapidly growing sectors, are largely preoccupied with collecting food and fuel necessary for their survival and have neither the financial nor the political will to force political change. The great majority of Iraqi people are also dependent on government food rations. The threat of withdrawal of these rations and the impact this would have on individual families or indeed whole communities is another effective way the government enforces compliance.

By comparison the rich, who consist largely of senior members of the Baath party and army officers close to Saddam Hussein, have been afforded protection by the government.[35] The government has extended preferential treatment to these and other privileged groups, including the upper strata of the civil services, the security forces, and those engaged in construction and the import trade business.[36] While the majority of Iraq's citizens have descended deeper into poverty, an elite few have been able, through their relationship with Saddam Hussein's regime, to maintain and in some instances increase their wealth, mainly through black market activities.

In Iraq, a parallel market has emerged for all items either in short supply or prohibited. Especially important has been the high price all imported commodities now exact. Those who control the importation of such goods—generally the privileged and loyal elite—have grown wealthy from sanctions. Access to foreign currency, required for commercial imports, has been tightly controlled by those in power. Import restrictions suspended after the war have gradually been reintroduced in a manner benefiting the Iraqi elite. In addition, a number of Iraqi companies operating in Jordan have been linked with key figures in the regime.[37]

Meanwhile, the Iraqi regime has continued to suppress the predominantly Shiite population in the south. Baghdad has cut off all government rations to the Kurdish majority in the north, who now rely entirely on support from the UN and nongovernmental organizations. In 1994, those who had moved into Baghdad after the Gulf War in search of employment were ordered to leave, and all further migration into Baghdad was prohibited. Since the Gulf War, tens of thousands of Iraqis have fled to Jordan and Iran. As many as 2 million Iraqis now live outside their country. The recent imposition of a $400 exit fee for Iraqi citizens has ended this large-scale flight.

Within Iraq, increasing poverty has led to a surge in theft, bribery, begging, and prostitution, despite the horrific punishments attached to these crimes. Prostitution, for example, is now punishable by death. Public executions and amputations have become more commonplace during the last few years. As an added deterrent, families frequently have been punished collectively for the crime of one of their members. Such policies have intimidated many Iraqis into submission and effectively discouraged public criticism of the regime for fear that family members or entire communities would suffer the repercussions. Furthermore, many leaders of opposition groups, particularly in the northern and southern governorates, feel that they have not received sufficient support from the international community.

As for the Iraqi regime itself, it has become increasingly concerned with self-protection and with assisting those who help it maintain power. According to Sarah Graham Brown, most postwar reconstruction efforts have been directed at increasing the control of the Iraqi regime.[38] Most of the financing for reconstruction, for example, has gone into initiatives aimed at rebuilding Iraq's communications system, conventional weapons projects, and some industrial projects. In addition, attempts to maintain a semblance of control and prosperity within government have led to the construction of several new palaces for Saddam Hussein and the erection of a grand mosque in Baghdad. It is difficult to defend such expenditures when civilian conditions are so desperate. Yet it must be acknowledged that the Iraqi regime has, almost single-handedly, prevented mass starvation through its provision of monthly food rations to the more than 15 million civilians residing in government-controlled areas.

In conclusion, the impact of sanctions has fallen predominantly on a growing number of the poor in Iraq. Threats to the health and welfare of Iraq's civilian majority have resulted in increasing rates of crime, prostitution, and displacement. Human rights violations have become increasingly common as the Iraqi regime attempts to exert its authority over a desperate populace. Responses to opposition have been harsh, and opposition efforts have not received much support from the international community, leading to the opposition's increasing disillusionment. If there were early expectations that sanctions might result in a change in the Iraqi leadership, this hope has proved to be an illusion.

Impact on Society

In 1996, the vast majority of Iraqi civilians subsisted in a state of extreme hardship and deprivation, with health care, nutrition, education, water, sanitation, and other basic services at minimal levels. The 1991 Gulf War and more than six years of economic sanctions erased most of Iraq's social and economic achievements of the previous two decades. According to the 1995 Department of Humanitarian Affairs Mid-Term Review for Iraq, some Iraqi hospitals had lost up to 75 percent of their pre-1990 staff, while wastewater facilities serving Baghdad's 5 million inhabitants were running at 30 percent capacity.[39] Among those hardest hit by the decline in health and social services in Iraq have been women, children, and the elderly. Rates of malnutrition, infectious and diarrheal diseases, miscarriages, psychological disorders, and anemia have increased significantly.[40]

This section will explore the impact of continued economic sanctions on Iraqi society. In particular, it will focus on the decline of health and social services and on the ways in which this continues to threaten the integrity and survival of Iraqi families. It is important to emphasize the difficulty in trying to separate the effects of sanctions from the consequences of military conflict. Although every effort will be made to draw this distinction, separation of the two effects is not always possible.

The authors of the 1995 report commissioned by the United Nations

Department of Humanitarian Affairs contend that there is "little value" in making a distinction between the impact of sanctions and the effects of war and other negative influences (including, for example, economic mismanagement and political decisions). Instead, they argue, it is only necessary to show that "sanctions substantially contribute to a serious degradation of the living conditions."[41] This approach may be adequate if one simply wishes to create a threshold for responding to human suffering, below which remedial action is taken. However, if the objective is to rethink or fine-tune the strategy and implementation of sanctions, then more reliable, sanctions-specific information is required. Although a complete separation of the effects of sanctions from other influences is probably impossible, it should nonetheless be the assessor's intended goal. Indeed, just as a physician attempts a specific diagnosis of the illness when a person falls ill in order to guide treatment, we will attempt to measure the humanitarian impact of economic sanctions to guide the analysis and reform of policy.

The Household Economy, Employment, and Wages

Since the end of the Gulf War, numerous United Nations assessment missions to Iraq have confirmed that the living conditions of the Iraqi population, particularly the poor and other vulnerable groups, have deteriorated.[42] Postwar industrial unemployment has been estimated at 70 percent. Agricultural production and employment have also declined, a drop generally attributed to the lack of seeds, pesticides, and spare parts. Underemployment has become commonplace, and the demand for trained technical and professional personnel has diminished. Engineers and technicians, for example, have resorted to selling vegetables and cigarettes on street corners and in markets. The demobilization of Iraq's army has added hundreds of thousands of potential workers to an already burgeoning workforce. Many women, children, and elderly people have entered the workforce in order to increase family incomes in the face of increasing hardship. Child labor has increased as sons and daughters drop out of public school to contribute to the family's income.

To compensate for the decline in Iraq's economy since the imposition of sanctions, average wages have increased. However, this increase has not been significant enough to keep pace with inflation. During 1993, average monthly salaries for civil servants ranged from 200 to 500 dinars, two to three times their August 1990 levels. Meanwhile, Iraq's food price index increased nearly 75-fold over the same period of time. In 1995, food prices were 4,000 to 5,000 times their August 1990 levels, while average monthly salaries were only 3,000 to 5,000 dinars. Consequently, families' real earnings have fallen to less than 5 percent of their presanctions level, as measured by their food-purchasing power. According to the Food and Agriculture Organization's 1995 report, the price of wheat flour in August 1995 was 11,667 times higher than in July 1990 and 33 times higher than in June 1993.[43]

Similarly, a monthly food basket for a family of six—providing 3,000 kilocalories per person per day—which cost only 100 dinars in July 1990, cost nearly 2,500 dinars in January 1993, and almost 200,000 dinars in July 1995. Figure 4.1 shows the rapid increase in price of an Iraqi food basket compared to the negligible rise in monthly salary levels. Even taking into account the provision of government food rations, providing approximately 1,100 kilocalories per person per day and roughly 37 percent of daily energy needs, a family of six would still need approximately 125,000 dinars monthly to purchase the shortfall in food. The average monthly salary in July 1995 was approximately 3,000 to 5,000 dinars.[44] Although life-sustaining, the government food ration is inadequate in terms of both quality of food (nutrients) and overall quantity (total caloric content). In addition, some families sell part of their ration on the free market as a means of earning dinars in order to purchase medicines or other essential goods. The dramatic change in the ability of Iraqis to purchase food is depicted in figure 4.2.

Even with its distribution shortfalls and the inadequate caloric and protein value of the food distributed, the government food rationing system remains the key to preventing widespread hunger and malnutrition among the civilian population.[45] Yet reductions in grain availability, and the cost of the food basket in foreign exchange have made it increasingly difficult for the government to maintain the rations. The Iraqi dinar, valued at 4 dinars to the dollar in 1990, has continued to depreciate and in April 1996 was valued at nearly 1,000 dinars to the dollar. The FAO has estimated that 270 billion dinars plus $258 million would be required to maintain rations in 1995–1996 at the previous level.[46] The lack of such funds would imperil the system of food rationing, which could have disastrous consequences for a significant majority of Iraqi families currently depending on it.

The damaging effects of sanctions have been most visible within Iraqi households. Many families were already suffering economically from the loss of one or more male wage earners, killed during the Iran-Iraq war or the Gulf War. Frequently, women were the single-parent heads of the households and the main generators of income. Annual per capita income was estimated at $335 in 1988 (using the free-market exchange rate) and

Figure 4.2
Increase in Price of Iraqi Food Basket Compared to Average Monthly Salary
(Food basket of approximately 3,000 kcal/person for a family of six)

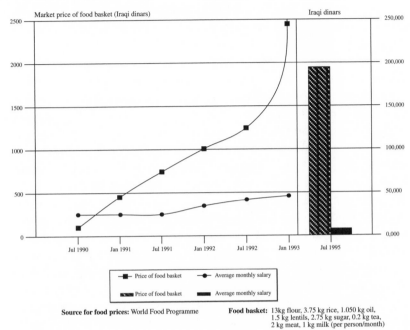

Source for food prices: World Food Programme   **Food basket:** 13kg flour, 3.75 kg rice, 1.050 kg oil, 1.5 kg lentils, 2.75 kg sugar, 0.2 kg tea, 2 kg meat, 1 kg milk (per person/month)

fell to $65 in 1991 and $44 in 1992.[47] These levels are far below the international poverty line of $100 established by the World Bank. Based on personal income and calorie-purchasing power, the prevalence of poverty has now become greater in Iraq than in India.[48] At such low incomes, even considering more than one wage earner per household, most Iraqi families have been unable to generate the funds necessary to meet their basic minimum requirements of food and other essential commodities. Most Iraqi families are living below the poverty line, often selling personal assets to make ends meet.

Nutrition

Following the imposition of sanctions in August 1990, food became increasingly scarce and costly. By early January 1991, supplies of many essential commodities (including wheat, rice, vegetable oil, and sugar) were scarce and very tightly controlled. Food prices were already five to twenty times their presanctions levels.[49] During the war, the lack of transport, communication, and electricity led to a collapse of the country's

Eric Hoskins

normal mechanisms for food distribution. The result was an acute food deficit that continued for the duration of the war and compelled most families to rely on hoarded food stocks.[50]

In the postwar period, limited food imports, decreased domestic production, and increasing food prices restricted the population's access to essential food. Malnutrition quickly emerged as one of the biggest threats to Iraqi children. In June 1991, UNICEF indicated an "alarming and rising incidence of severe and moderate malnutrition among the population of children under age five."[51] Their concern was echoed by the Food and Agriculture Organization report of July 1991 warning that Iraq was "approaching the threshold of extreme deprivation." In July 1993, two years after the war, the FAO warned that "a vast majority of the Iraqi population" was facing "persistent deprivation, severe hunger, and malnutrition" and that "large numbers of Iraqis now have food intakes lower than those of the populations in disaster-stricken African countries."[52] In August 1995, FAO reported that the level of child malnutrition in Baghdad was similar to that seen in Ghana and Mali. FAO wrote that "there is a strong possibility of outright collapse of the food and agricultural economy."[53]

Several nutritional surveys were carried out in postwar Iraq during 1991 and are summarized in table 4.2. The surveys differ in the methodology used, the location, and the characteristics of surveyed children. For these reasons, they should be viewed as individual case studies and not considered representative of the situation in Iraq as a whole. An exception to this may be the survey by the International Study Team, which was a representative national survey of nearly three thousand children in three hundred randomly selected locations throughout Iraq. Levels reported in table 4.2 are combined percentages for both moderate and severe malnutrition.

In 1995–1996, the financial challenge of sustaining the existing system of food rations, combined with elevated food market prices that are well beyond the means of most Iraqi families, has resulted in even higher rates of malnutrition than those seen during the immediate postwar period. According to the 1995 FAO report on the nutritional situation in Iraq, when compared to similar surveys in 1991, the percentage of children under five with wasting (< -2 standard deviations below the median reference value, weight-for-height) had quadrupled to 12 percent, while stunting (< -2 standard deviations below the reference median, height-for-age) had more than doubled to 28 percent.[54] The prevalence of both undernutrition and micronutrient deficiencies have increased in hospitals and in the general population. The monthly average number of cases of kwashiorkor and marasmus has reportedly increased fiftyfold since 1989,

Table 4.2
Early Postwar Nutritional Studies*a*

Study Authors	Survey Date	Survey Location	Number of Children	Weight-for-Age Group Surveyed	Height-for-age*b* (percent)	Weight-for-age*c* (percent)	height*d* (percent)
Helen Keller, Save the Children, UNICEF	May 1991	Basra	231	<6 years	40	18	19
Tufts University	June 1991	Basra/Amara	680	<5 years	26	39	4
UNICEF Basra	July/August 1991	Basra	742	<5 years	22	21	7
International Study Team	August 1991	National (300 sites)	2,902	<5 years	12	22	3
Catholic Relief Services	December 1991	Baghdad	315	<5 years	17	9	11
UNICEF Tehran	May 1991	Kurdish camps in Iran	900	<5 years	32	29	not measured

Source: See Eric Hoskins, "Public Health and the Persian Gulf War," in *War and Public Health*, ed. Barry Levy and Victor Sidel (Oxford: Oxford University Press, 1996). Reprinted with permission.

*a*Percent malnutrition indicated is moderate and severe (< -2 standard deviations from the reference median). Although not reported here, most of the above studies also found mild malnutrition (< -1 standard deviations) in an additional 25% of children measured.

*b*Weight-for-age = underweight = an indicator of acute and/or chronic malnutrition reflecting either stunting, wasting, or a combination of both.

*c*Height-for-age = stunting = an indicator of chronic or long-standing malnutrition reflecting skeletal growth.

*d*Height-for-age = wasting = an indicator of acute malnutrition reflecting weight loss or short-term growth failure.

while the monthly average number of deaths due to malnutrition for children under five years has increased nearly eightfold.[55] Other nutritional surveys have also confirmed a high prevalence of anemia in children and pregnant women, along with an increased incidence of iodine deficiency (goiter) and rickets (vitamin D deficiency).

The postwar nutritional status of the country as a whole can be characterized by an overall nutritional deficit. Most people have, for many years, been consuming a diet deficient in calories, protein, and essential vitamins and nutrients. Although the caloric intake has been adequate to prevent overt starvation, it has led to a chronic state of nutritional deficiency, making both adults and children more susceptible to illness and death.

Nutritional status is determined by a combination of one's access to nutritious foods, the ability to care for oneself—or, in the case of children, a mother's ability to spend time caring for the physical well-being of her child—and access to health care. War and sanctions have compromised all three of these determinants of nutritional status. The result has been an overall reduction in the level of nutrition of most Iraqi civilians, greatly increasing morbidity and mortality. Recovery from these high levels of malnutrition, even with the 1996 agreement for the sale of oil, will be slow.

Water

Before the Gulf War, nearly all urban dwellers and 72 percent of rural residents had access to clean water.[56] From the early hours of the war, the supply of water to Iraqi households either stopped or was greatly reduced. The destruction of the electrical generating system resulted in total paralysis of the water purification and supply networks. In addition, a number of water supply and treatment facilities were directly damaged by air bombardment. During a WHO/UNICEF mission in February 1991, the available piped water supply was reported to be between zero and fifteen liters per person per day in Baghdad, less than 5 percent of the prewar supply.[57] Throughout Iraq, most people were forced to obtain untreated water from rivers and stagnant ponds.

Even with the gradual postwar restoration of electricity, most water-pumping and water-treatment facilities remained inoperable or functioned on a very irregular basis. Fluctuations in returning power burned out many pump motors. Imported spare parts were not available, nor permitted, until late March 1991—and then only on a slow case-by-case basis if approved by the sanctions committee.

The low pressure within the gradually recuperating system prevented water from entering many homes. In response, civilians frequently dug their way down to street water mains, broke into the pipes, and inserted plastic hosing to withdraw water. These practices not only further reduced the overall pressure in the system but also facilitated the entry of impurities and raw sewage, contaminating the entire water system downstream from the break. Breakage of pipes in this way occurred on almost every street in southern Iraq.

Further damage to the water supply system in both the north and south of the country was caused by the destruction and looting that took place during the civil uprisings of March and April 1991. Tanker trucks used for the distribution of water were often stolen or destroyed. Water testing laboratories were looted of equipment and reagents. Pumping and purification stations were vandalized and burned.

The damage to the water infrastructure has been so vast that it will probably take years and hundreds of millions of dollars before the water supply network can be rehabilitated to prewar levels. Without proper reconstruction and repair, it is expected that ad hoc repairs made with substandard or cannibalized spare parts will eventually break down and that the water supply will slowly deteriorate. In 1995, national water production was estimated at only 50 percent of prewar levels.[58] Most families continued to consume contaminated water from damaged systems or from untreated local sources. An August 1995 UNICEF survey found that 50 percent of rural people in Iraq had no access to potable water.[59] By comparison, the survey also found that the "treated water" assumed to be available to 77 percent of the total population, largely in urban areas, may not be safe for public consumption.

Sewage and Sanitation

Sewage collecting systems in Iraq have suffered from many of the same difficulties as the water sector. Prior to 1990, major urban centers and most cities on the Tigris and Euphrates Rivers had modern sewage treatment systems, while smaller towns and cities relied on older systems consisting of open sewers and septic tanks. Iraq's flat topography means that sewage-lifting stations are essential to move sewage to plants for treatment and eventual discharge into rivers. With the war-related loss of electricity, sewage-lifting stations could no longer function. This has caused lakes of sewage to pool in residential areas, contributing to the spread of infectious diseases.

During 1995, approximately half of all sewage produced by Baghdad's

4 million people was still being discharged untreated into the Tigris, which downstream becomes the principal source of drinking water for most of the densely populated governorates in southern Iraq. Other treatment facilities around the country were in a similar state or not functioning at all due to a shortage of spare parts or a lack of sufficient electricity. Spare parts could not be purchased without foreign exchange and specific approval from the sanctions committee. Even in 1995, wastewater facilities in Baghdad continued to function at only 30 percent capacity, while in the southern areas water-sample tests showed up to 50 percent contamination.[60]

As a result of a breakdown in the system of garbage collection, huge piles of garbage accumulated in streets and residential areas throughout Iraq. During 1993, it was estimated that Iraq's solid-waste collection and disposal system was operating at less than 25 percent of prewar capacity. At that time, only 18 out of 152 garbage-collection vehicles remained in service in the three northern governorates of Dohuk, Erbil, and Sulaimaniyah.[61]

The weakened water and sanitation infrastructures caused by wartime bombing and years of economic sanctions have become a major health risk to the civilian population. Postwar Iraq has experienced an increase in infectious diseases associated with poor sanitation, including cholera, polio, and typhoid.

Health

The breakdown of health, water and sanitation, and other essential social services that followed the Gulf War and economic sanctions has led to a dramatic upsurge in infectious disease and malnutrition. Shortages of medicines and health services have made treatment difficult, contributing to high rates of "delayed mortality." Indeed, the number of deaths that have occurred as a result of war-related damage and the continued application of sanctions against Iraq has greatly surpassed the number of civilian casualties occurring during the war itself.[62] The gulf crisis has therefore become a "bomb now, die later" conflict, owing to the drawn-out, delayed impact of the aerial bombardment.

Medical Services and Medicines

Both during and after the war, physical damage was sustained by many health facilities. The Iraqi Ministry of Health in Baghdad was badly damaged following a direct hit by a cruise missile. Several hospitals were hit by poorly targeted free-falling bombs, while many facilities had windows shattered during near misses. During the postwar unrest, both government and rebel troops often occupied hospitals because of their strategic worth and because they were generally modern, well-equipped facilities. Such occupation frequently led to violent exchange of gunfire and artillery between government and rebel troops and hence massive damage to health facilities.

In the immediate postwar period, hospital personnel were unable to find transportation to work. Medicines stored in Baghdad could not reach outlying areas owing to the lack of fuel for transport. Hospitals lacked electricity, water, and sanitation, further limiting their usefulness. Hundreds of community-level health centers were closed. Hospitals effectively became empty shells, unable to provide even basic medical or surgical care. In postwar, sanctioned Iraq, all but the most rudimentary diagnostic and therapeutic capabilities of the prewar health care system were eliminated.

Despite exemptions for "supplies intended strictly for medical purposes" as mentioned in Resolution 661, basic medicines were in short supply even before the onset of war.[63] Iraq historically imported nearly $500 million worth of medicines and medical supplies each year.[64] With the onset of the embargo, many suppliers refused to ship orders to Iraq, fearing legal or political repercussions from their governments. With Iraqi overseas assets frozen, the uncertainty of payment also made suppliers reluctant to ship medicines and diagnostic equipment.

Sanctions have resulted in shortages of medicines, vaccines, syringes, anesthetics, and materials used for surgery, radiology, and laboratory and diagnostic tests. As early as February 1991, medical stocks were estimated at one-sixth of normal levels, with the supplies of many essential medicines completely exhausted.[65] During the first days of the war, the collapse of the electrical generating system destroyed all refrigerated and frozen vaccines, medicines, and laboratory reagents. A shortage of insulin has led to deaths of children and adults with insulin-dependent diabetes. Children with treatable cancers, including leukemia, have been unable to find anti-cancer drugs. X-ray films, laboratory reagents, sutures, intravenous fluids, and antibiotics have been in short supply. Screening of transfused blood for the human immunodeficiency virus (HIV) and hepatitis B virus was suspended after the war because of a lack of laboratory supplies and reagents. Disposable syringes, needles, and surgical gloves became scarce and were reused. A shortage of anesthetics has led to the deferral of most nonemergency surgery. The setting of bones and leg amputations have sometimes been performed without anesthesia.

International organizations, overwhelmed by the acute need for drugs and medical supplies after the war, have focused on medicines and supplies for children with infectious diseases. However, this has meant that chronic diseases, as well as illnesses specific to the adult population, including the elderly, have not received adequate attention. As a result, an increase in deaths due to stroke and heart attack has been observed, with antihypertensive and antianginal medicines no longer readily available.[66]

Infant and Child Mortality

In August 1991, the Harvard-based international study team conducted a comprehensive assessment of child deaths due to the Gulf War and its aftermath.[67] The team surveyed more than 9,000 households in nearly 300 population centers throughout Iraq. According to their data, there were an estimated 47,000 excess deaths (a threefold increase) among children under five years of age during the first eight months of 1991. Of these deaths, 33,000 occurred among infants less than a year old. The infant mortality rate rose from 33 deaths per 1,000 live births prewar to 93 deaths postwar (1991). There has been considerable discussion concerning Iraq's prewar infant and under-five mortality rates. An in-depth analysis of several prewar demographic surveys conducted by UNICEF estimated a 1990 infant mortality rate of 39 (compared to the international study team's 33).[68] Even if this higher prewar figure is used, the 1991 postwar infant mortality rate would still be 2.4 times prewar levels.

In her review of civilian casualties due to the war, Beth Osborne Daponte, a statistician with the United States Census Bureau, estimated that 111,000 civilians died in 1991 from the health effects of the Gulf War. Of these deaths, 70,000 were children under fifteen years of age, while another 8,500 were people more than sixty-five years old. In addition, she estimated that 56,000 military personnel and 3,500 civilians died during the war itself, while postwar violence accounted for another 35,000 deaths. Therefore, according to Osborne Daponte, a total of 205,500 Iraqis died during 1991 as a consequence of the Gulf War (table 4.3). Seventy percent of these deaths were among civilians. Life expectancy at birth was reduced from sixty-eight years prewar to forty-seven years by late 1991. Thirty times more civilians died after the war than during the military conflict itself.[69]

The 1995 study conducted by FAO found a further deterioration of health conditions in postwar Iraq.[70] The death rate for children under five was estimated by FAO to be five times higher than during the immediate prewar (1990) period. Death rates from diarrheal disease had tripled since

Table 4.3
Excess Deaths Due to the Gulf War, 1991

Cause of Death	Estimated Casualties
Wartime violence/bombing	56,000 military 3,500 civilians
Postwar violence/unrest	50,000 military 30,000 civilian
Postwar health effects	70,000 children (0–15 years) 32,500 adults (16–65 years) 8,500 elderly (over 65 years)
TOTAL	205,500

Source: Beth Osborne Daponte, "A Case Study in Estimating Casualties from War and Its Aftermath: The 1991 Persian Gulf War," *PSR Quarterly* 3, no. 2 (1993): 57–66.

1990. Infants were dying at twice the prewar rate. The death rate of under-five children of illiterate mothers was nearly nine times estimated prewar levels for the same group. In absolute terms, members of the FAO team estimated that approximately 500,000 more children than expected died in the five year period following the Gulf War (1991–1995).[71] In arriving at this estimate, the survey team extrapolated nationally from mortality data gathered in Baghdad, leading to questions regarding the reliability of this figure.

Infectious Diseases

The breakdown in water and sanitation that occurred during the Gulf War, and the Iraqi government's inability to effectively repair these services, have been responsible for outbreaks of cholera, typhoid, gastroenteritis, malaria, meningitis, brucellosis, measles, polio, hepatitis, and other infectious diseases. Contaminated water supplies and poor sanitation have created health conditions enabling diarrhea to emerge as the leading child killer during the postwar period. During both 1991 and 1992, mortality due to diarrhea was estimated at more than three times the 1990 levels.[72]

Cholera, which during the 1980s was scarcely detected, reached epidemic levels in 1991 with more than 1,200 confirmed cases.[73] Typhoid also spread rapidly, and during 1991 the number of cases was more than ten times the number of cases reported during 1990. In Sulaimaniyah, monthly reported typhoid cases increased from 426 cases in January 1992 to 2,180 cases in January 1993.[74]

Postwar environmental hazards, including poor hygiene and contaminated water, resulted in outbreaks of hepatitis A, especially in urban areas. Hepatitis B became more prevalent owing to the reuse of disposable syringes and needles and the lack of testing of blood supplies for the hepatitis B virus. Poor hygiene also led to increases in the prevalence of intestinal parasites.

An upsurge in acute respiratory infections occurred because of the poor postwar living conditions, crowding, and increased exposure to harsh climates. The lack of meaningful medical treatment and the higher prevalence of malnutrition increased the proportion of such infections resulting in death. The incidence of malaria increased more than tenfold owing to the lack of aerial and ground spraying, while large areas of stagnant water became breeding grounds for mosquitoes.[75]

Vaccination Services

Before the Gulf War, Iraq's Expanded Program on Immunization (EPI) had made significant progress. The Ministry of Health and UNICEF reported high levels of immunization for all vaccines. The proportion of Iraqi children who were fully immunized increased from 15 percent in 1985 to 68 percent in 1989.[76]

Within a few days of the start of the Gulf War, a collapse of the primary health care system brought Iraq's vaccination services to a halt. Refrigerated and frozen vaccines were destroyed by the breakdown in electricity that occurred with the onset of war. Iraq's only syringe factory was destroyed during coalition bombardment. With the gradual postwar restoration of electricity, unstable electric current and frequent electricity cuts damaged many refrigeration units. In all parts of the country, vaccine services were suspended until March 1991. This suspension of services led to a massive backlog of hundreds of thousands of unvaccinated children and women who were left susceptible to infection. It was not until late 1991 that vaccine programs were again established at near prewar levels.

The reduction in vaccine coverage, combined with the contaminated postwar water supply and poor sanitation, led to a resurgence of vaccine-preventable diseases. For polio, previously in sharp decline with only 10 cases reported in 1989, there were 186 cases in 1991 and 120 in 1992. Diphtheria increased from 96 reported cases during 1989 to 369 cases in 1992. In 1992, a measles epidemic swept through Iraq with almost 20,000 reported cases. Recent vaccination campaigns have reduced the risks of full-scale epidemics. However, the EPI has been weakened because of the war and continued sanctions. Considerable material assistance will be required to restore the program to its prewar status and capacity.

Maternal Health and Prenatal Care

More than 750,000 babies are born each year in Iraq. Both maternal and perinatal mortality have increased since the Gulf War.[77] The health care system has been unable to provide mothers with adequate prenatal care and delivery services, leading to an increased incidence of severe complications.

The prevalence of anemia during pregnancy has increased because women's diets have become deficient in iron and folic acid. Anemia, reported to affect nearly 70 percent of Iraqi women, has put them at higher risk of both pregnancy-related complications and of delivering low-birthweight infants. The percentage of low-birthweight babies (less than 2.5 kilograms) quadrupled from 4 percent in August 1990 to 17 percent by late 1992 and 22 percent in 1995.[78]

Even if hospital delivery services can be restored to prewar levels, the underlying socioeconomic conditions, poverty, and malnutrition have increased the risks of childbirth. It is likely that the recent prevalence of nutrient-deficient mothers, low-birthweight infants, and malnourished children will result in the retarded mental and physical development of thousands of Iraqi children.

Education

Hundreds of primary schools were destroyed during the Gulf War and in the uprisings that followed. Schools fortunate enough to remain intact during the onslaught often had all their desks, blackboards, textbooks, equipment, and other movable objects removed or destroyed.

Although in most cases schools have undergone structural rehabilitation and repair, the inner workings of such facilities have remained in desperate need of restoration and restocking. The overall caliber of education has been reduced to such an extent that, in many parts of the country, teachers have virtually no resources or teaching aids. Teacher training has come to a near standstill. Children, especially female children, who are often required to assume greater responsibilities at home, have been dropping out of school in greater and greater numbers.[79]

School supplies have dwindled drastically. Paper and pencils have become almost impossible to obtain. A dozen pencils, which cost less than one dinar prior to August 1990, cost more than fifty dinars in 1993. A shipment of newsprint for the local production of school exercise books was stalled for more than two years because of a lack of funds and questions about the "humanitarian need" for such an item. In September 1992, the sanctions committee refused a request from the International Baghdad School for authorization to import four school buses. A request to import thirty-six tons of pencils was refused in October 1992 on the grounds that the graphite in the pencils could be used to manufacture casings for missile warheads.

The quality of education in Iraqi schools has deteriorated in the face of economic sanctions. Students in many governorates have lost years of education. Because of the link between quality education and both personal and national development, the educational impact of the Gulf War and sanctions in the years to come is likely to be greater illiteracy and impeded socioeconomic development.

Women

Iraqi women have shouldered a considerable burden as a result of the Gulf War.[80] More than 10 percent of married Iraqi women are widows. Many more have become single parents and sole wage earners, having to cope with severe economic hardships. Work for them has become more difficult to find, and more women have had to join the informal working sector, selling such items as vegetables and tea. Satisfying the needs of children and families and performing household chores have become more demanding. Women's health has suffered because of nutritional problems, a lack of prenatal care, and a shortage of medicines.

During the Iran-Iraq war, women were often left solely responsible for the household and cared for elderly relatives and young children. After the 1991 Gulf War, hundreds of thousands of men were decommissioned from the military and returned home. As a consequence of economic sanctions, most have remained unemployed and without income, increasing the burden on women's ability to provide for their families.

Securing adequate quantities of food has become a major preoccupation for Iraqi women. Many families have become totally dependent on government rations and charity. As early as August 1991, many Iraqi families indicated that they had used up their savings and sold most of their personal belongings. Forty-eight percent of families surveyed by the International Study Team in 1991 already had incurred heavy debts.[81] This has increased the dependency and vulnerability of many women and their families, sometimes leading to begging or, in more extreme cases, prostitution. Furthermore, 60 percent of women interviewed during the same study indicated that they suffered from psychological problems, including depression, anxiety, headache, and insomnia. Anxieties often manifested themselves as physical problems, including weight loss, menstrual irregularity, difficulty in breast-feeding, and other ailments.

Daily chores, such as purchasing and preparing food, have become more time-consuming. New chores such as waiting in line, often for hours, for water, medicines, and medical consultations and collecting firewood (especially in northern governorates) have added to women's household burdens. Men's frustration at their own inability to find employment has led to a rise in family conflicts. Marital breakups reportedly have increased during the postwar period.

Yet despite these threats to their health and well-being, Iraqi women have been credited, according to the international study team, with "experiencing this whole crisis not only as victims, but also as crucial actors who have sustained the family and the society. The basis of the Iraqi society, the home, has been held together by their ingenuity and strength—despite their own economic, social, emotional and psychological deprivation."[82]

Children in Especially Difficult Circumstances

For many Iraqi children, the war and the continued deprivation caused by the economic embargo have taken away their hope for the future and have left them feeling anxious, fearful, and uncertain. Many thousands of children in the northern governorates of Dohuk, Erbil, and Sulaimaniyah have been displaced from their homes. Others have been left mentally or physically disabled by war-related violence, malnutrition, and inadequate health care.

In August 1991, and again during 1992, 214 children of primary school age were interviewed by child psychologists expert in the impact of conflict on children. Two-thirds of the children interviewed did not even believe they would survive to become adults. The study revealed the level of psychological stress and pathological behavior to be the highest ever recorded by the psychologists in over ten years of experience in conflict-affected areas. Their findings led the researchers to conclude that postwar Iraqi children were "the most traumatized children of war ever described."[83]

Disabled Children

The Iran-Iraq war and the 1991 Gulf War have added thousands to the number of physically handicapped children in Iraq, especially amputees. Unexploded ordnance, land mines, and the use of antipersonnel bombs have in particular affected Iraqi children. It is estimated that thousands of children, many in the northern governorates, have lost their limbs because of exploding land mines and other ordnance.

Apart from death, there is no other effect of war upon children more profound or long lasting than being maimed or incapacitated. Such injuries affect not only the physical and emotional development of the child but also adult prospects for work, marriage, social life, self-support, and dignity. The wounded, permanently damaged child becomes a burden not only for the family but also for society as a whole.[84] The economic embargo has further compounded the problems associated with disability by delaying and even preventing the procurement of supportive and rehabilitative materials.

Kurdish-Administered Regions of Northern Iraq

Generally speaking, humanitarian conditions in the three Kurdish northern governorates have been similar to those observed in the rest of Iraq. There are, however, several important differences. As mentioned earlier, roughly 2 million Kurds were brutally displaced from their homes during the civil disturbances that followed the Gulf War. Many thousands died from exposure and disease in refugee camps in Turkey and Iran.[85] Following the creation of the United Nations "safe haven" in northern Iraq, most Kurds returned home, but to squalid conditions fostering ill-health, malnutrition, and disease. Despite a massive international humanitarian response, conditions have remained precarious for the Kurdish population, and their health has suffered. An internal embargo, imposed by Iraq in October 1991, has further increased Kurdish isolation and led to shortages of foodstuffs, medicines, and fuel for both cooking and heating, as well as shortages of other basic commodities.

The relatively porous borders of northern Iraq, Turkey, and Iran have permitted passage of humanitarian aid and other basic supplies. This movement of goods has helped to counterbalance the inflationary effects of the "double embargo" imposed by Iraq. Yet restrictions on public services such as electricity, access to medical care, subsidized food, and inexpensive fuel have severely aggravated conditions in the Kurdish regions.

Political infighting among the two main Kurdish factions, together with a drastic reduction in the amount of funding available from international sources, has threatened to drive the Kurdish population to the brink of disaster. Internal armed conflict between warring Kurdish factions contributed to a worsening humanitarian situation and threatened the postwar recovery. A high percentage of locally generated revenue, as well as human resources, was channeled into the internal military conflict.

International food assistance decreased in 1995 to less than one-half of what was available a year earlier.[86] A lack of agricultural inputs, including seeds, fertilizers, and spare parts, has compromised local production of basic foodstuffs. A December 1995 NGO survey of Kurdish children under five years of age found only 3 percent with acute malnutrition (less than -2 standard deviations weight-for-height) and 5 percent chronically malnourished (less than -2 standard deviations height-for-age).[87] These figures were dramatically below (that is, better than) the levels of malnutrition found in the rest of Iraq. For example, the August 1995 FAO survey of children under five found 12 percent acute malnutrition (weight-for-height) and 28 percent chronic malnutrition (height-for-age) in Baghdad.

Nonetheless, conditions within the Kurdish region remain bleak. Waning foreign interest has threatened a deterioration of conditions. More important, a political resolution will be necessary both within the Kurdish-administered parts of northern Iraq and in relation to the rest of Iraq before stability and personal security can be restored to the civilian population.

The Environment

The environmental impact of the Gulf War was enormous. Burning oil wells, the deliberate spillage of oil into fragile gulf waters, the use of environmentally damaging weaponry, and the release of a host of toxins and contaminants into the region's ecosystem caused widespread environmental damage.

The first oil spill reportedly occurred on 22 January 1991, when oil was discharged into the ecologically fragile northern gulf waters. At least three other spills followed, in total covering hundreds of square kilometers of gulf water, as well as more than five hundred kilometers of coastline. An estimated 4 million barrels of oil were spilled. The oil has severely affected the gulf's wildlife and marine biology, which includes many fragile and endangered species. Human populations were also put directly at risk when their source of water, desalination plants along the gulf coast, was directly affected.

More than five hundred burning oil fires blackened skies and released thousands of tons of contaminants into the atmosphere, delivering unquantifiable health risks to human and wildlife populations. While they burned, oil fires in Kuwait were creating approximately ten times as much air pollution as all industrial and power plants in the United States. Levels of carcinogenic gases tens of times higher than World Health Organization safety levels were found in the region. Soot from burning oil fires was detected in the air of places as distant from the gulf as Hawaii and the Himalayas.[88] Tons of sulfur dioxide and nitrogen oxide released by the burning oil wells came into contact with water droplets, turning into sulfuric and nitric acids and falling to the earth as acid rain. Other toxic chemicals, including benzene (a known carcinogen), toluene, and xylene were dispersed into the atmosphere. Fortunately, the oil fires were all extinguished by November 1991, but by then, fumes from burning more than 1 billion barrels of oil had been discharged into the atmosphere. Between 35 and 150 million barrels of oil were spilled over as much as 60 percent of Kuwait's surface area, forming shallow black lakes of crude.[89]

Before the Gulf War, Iraq possessed a formidable stockpile of chemical and biological weapons as well as a growing covert nuclear weapons program. During the war, coalition forces admitted to destroying more than twenty of Iraq's chemical and biological production or storage facilities. On 22 January 1991, chemical protection units along the Saudi-Kuwaiti border detected chemical agents in the air, assumed to be the result of coalition bombardment of chemical factories or weapons stockpiles.[90] Similar reports of chemical releases came from other military and anti-chemical units in the region. Sites identified by coalition forces as being part of Iraq's nuclear weapons program were also specifically targeted and destroyed during the Gulf War.

Tens of thousands of tons of bombs were dropped on Iraq during the Gulf War. Many were cluster bombs, which dispersed into hundreds of smaller bomblets. Unexploded bombs still litter the landscape of the gulf region. In addition, thousands of land mines were scattered in southern Iraq, Kuwait, and the northern Kurdish regions. Unexploded ordnance has caused numerous civilian deaths and injuries since the end of the war.

Coalition forces also used radioactive, depleted uranium in many shells and armor-piercing projectiles. Depleted uranium is a radioactive byproduct of the enrichment process used to make atomic bombs and nuclear fuel rods. Used because of its exceedingly high density and hence its effective penetrating capability, between forty and three hundred tons of uranium remain scattered throughout much of southern Iraq and Kuwait. Toxic like lead, the depleted uranium can become airborne and can be both inhaled and ingested. It can concentrate in the kidneys, lungs, and bones, causing illness. Although low in radioactivity, internalized particles remain for life, constantly emitting low-level radiation to the surrounding tissues. In addition to the direct health risks, it is possible that the depleted uranium may have contaminated soil and drinking water in Iraq and Kuwait, resulting in exposure to the radioactive and toxic effects of depleted uranium for generations to come.

These and other environmental impacts were not caused by economic sanctions, but the continuing embargo and political dispute between Iraq and the UN have delayed the amelioration of these effects. The absence of export earnings, shortages of spare parts, and a lack of international cooperation resulting from continued sanctions have slowed or prevented progress in addressing many of the environmental impacts identified here. In addition, as noted earlier, continued sanctions have prolonged the environmental and health effects of contaminated water and crippled sanitation systems.

Long-Term Impact of War and Economic Sanctions

The above-mentioned effects of war and economic sanctions will have measurable effects for years to come. Infrastructural damage due to air bombardment will cost tens of billions of dollars to repair after sanctions have been lifted and revenue is available. The Arab Monetary Fund has estimated the value of destroyed infrastructure and economic assets attributable to the Gulf War at $232 billion.[91] Add to this the destruction from the Iran-Iraq war ($67 billion), Iraq's foreign debt ($86 billion), and war reparations of $97 billion to Iran and $100 billion to Kuwait, and the total is in excess of $500 billion.[92] Even after the lifting of sanctions and Iraq's generation of export earnings through the sale of oil, it will take many decades to overcome these burdens. These staggering economic costs have resulted from the effects of war, not international sanctions, although the continued embargo has compounded the hardships and postponed the process of redevelopment.

The social costs have been immeasurable. The long-term effects of postwar repression, ethnic division, economic crisis and stagnation, intense poverty, social disintegration, and violence will be felt for many generations to come. The very fabric of Iraqi society has been torn to pieces. The health of Iraqis has also suffered greatly. Physical health has deteriorated, with disease rife and malnutrition epidemic. Measured in terms of mortality, postwar death rates of children in 1996 were similar to those experienced in Iraq during the early 1960s. Diseases associated with poverty have become resurgent. Although invisible to the naked eye, the mental health of Iraqis has also suffered. Most households have experienced the loss of a family member. Many children, witnesses to death and human misery and raised in a culture of militarism, have no doubt been scarred for life. The toll of this mental impact is incalculable, and its sociopolitical impact on future generations is unknown. In summary, the gulf crisis has had a devastating impact on the people of Iraq.

Impact on Humanitarian Assistance Activities

Background

Prior to the Gulf War, very few humanitarian organizations were operating within Iraq. Apart from the various United Nations agencies, there were no international NGOs functioning on a regular basis. Following the imposition of sanctions, UN activities in Iraq became subject to the same restrictions as those that apply to the rest of the international community. Programs requiring the delivery of supplies and equipment were either suspended or scaled down. For example, routine vaccination services were suspended in September 1990 because of a shortage of syringes and needles.

Meanwhile, a growing number of immigrant workers, displaced persons, and refugees began fleeing Iraq and Kuwait. From August to October 1990, more than a million migrants were accepted into Jordan alone. Although the most critical and substantial humanitarian contributions came from within Jordan itself, many international NGOs also responded with emergency relief activities. By the time the Gulf War erupted, most refugees and third-country nationals had already been repatriated to their countries of origin or absorbed locally.

In Iraq, as the deadline for military conflict grew closer, and in light of Iraq's hostage-taking activities, United Nations personnel were withdrawn from all agencies. Only UNICEF maintained a handful of national staff active throughout the military conflict. On 16 February 1991, a joint mission by UNICEF and WHO delivered sixty tons of emergency medical supplies by overland convoy from Tehran to Baghdad.[93] Several international staff members accompanying the convoy remained in Baghdad for the remainder of the war. At the same time, the Jordanian Red Crescent, a number of Middle Eastern NGOs, and many committed volunteers risked their lives delivering emergency medical supplies to Iraq during the conflict.

Once an end to the war was declared on 28 February, a growing number of international NGOs began to express interest in assisting civilians in postwar Iraq. None of them had recent experience within the country, and most began their efforts by transporting medicine and conducting assessment missions. As the situation in Iraq grew more stable, NGO and UN personnel established themselves in Baghdad, eventually moving to the more outlying areas once regional uprisings had been put down. International personnel required travel authorizations and were accompanied by Iraqi "minders" during their travel outside of Baghdad. As

Iraqi authorities reestablished their control over the country, they also demanded greater accountability from NGOs. According to most NGOs, Iraq also demanded greater control and attempted to limit NGO activities.

Meanwhile, emergency relief activities were also under way along Iraq's northern borders. By mid-April 1991, more than 2 million Kurds had fled the advancing Iraqi army and were residing in camps along the Turkish border (.5 million) and in Iran (1.5 million). More than one hundred international NGOs, compared to perhaps one dozen in Iraq, provided assistance to the refugees. Many thousands of Kurds, mostly children, died of exposure and disease.[94] As the surviving Kurds returned to northern Iraq under the protection of coalition forces, the NGOs moved with them. Since October 1991, Iraqi authorities have provided no assistance or services to the Kurdish-administered parts of northern Iraq. In 1996, the Kurdish population, still very much in need, continued to rely heavily on United Nations and NGO support.

As conditions throughout the country grew more stable, the United Nations adopted a more substantial coordinating role. In April 1991, the United Nations Inter-Agency Program was formed to oversee UN and NGO activities and to ensure liaison with the Iraqi government. Coordination was entrusted to the Department of Humanitarian Affairs through its representative in Baghdad. The Iraq Relief Coordination Unit (IRCU), headed by the DHA representative, was charged with overseeing the humanitarian program.

Memoranda of understanding (MOU), first signed in April 1991, specified the nature of international assistance to Iraq as well as the precise conditions of cooperation. The main objective of the memoranda was "to provide humanitarian assistance to the vulnerable groups and to help the country move from the emergency relief situation which has affected most of the population since the Gulf war."[95] Subsequent MOUs became more restrictive, limiting UN/NGO access as well as their freedom to operate. No further MOUs have been signed since the last six-month agreement in October 1992. The October 1992 MOU remains the working basis for today's continuing humanitarian assistance.

During the following four years, international interest and funding for humanitarian efforts in Iraq diminished. This, combined with Baghdad's refusal—until May 1996—to accept UN terms for the sale of oil for food, greatly reduced activities throughout all parts of Iraq. By 1996 only three international NGOs—CARE, the International Federation of Red Cross and Red Crescent Societies, and the Middle East Council of Churches—were functioning in central and southern Iraq, a reflection of the lack of international interest in non-Kurdish Iraq and stringent Iraqi government control over NGO operations. In northern (Kurdish) Iraq, the number of NGOs declined from more than one hundred in January 1995 to approximately twenty-five in April 1996. This distribution of NGOs does not in any real sense reflect human need but is more likely the result of donor bias towards the northern Kurdish areas. Furthermore, NGOs have been reluctant to operate under the restrictive controls imposed by the central authorities in Baghdad, preferring instead to function with relative autonomy in the Kurdish-administered northern governorates. Meanwhile, UN programs throughout Iraq were operating on a shoestring budget. At the same time, Iraqi government and local NGO efforts to provide humanitarian assistance continued to suffer from a lack of foreign currency, the ongoing sanctions restrictions, and domestic political interference.

Humanitarian Assistance Activities in Iraq

With few exceptions, notably in the northern Kurdish-administered areas, humanitarian assistance provided to Iraq has been limited to relief activities. UN, NGO, and government efforts have focused everywhere on the supply of food, medicines, potable water, sanitation, and the delivery of health care. In the north, relief to displaced populations, resettlement assistance, shelter, and the distribution of kerosene have also been provided through international assistance.

The United Nations has targeted vulnerable households for supplementary food rations. In earlier years, despite increased need, funding shortages forced the World Food Program (WFP) to reduce its target beneficiaries from 2 million (1993) to 1.3 million (1994) and most recently to 1 million (1995).[96] A documented increase in malnutrition, together with a harvest shortfall, occurred in 1995, prompting the World Food Program to double its 1996 target population from 1 million to 2.15 million. This larger figure represented only 10 percent of Iraq's total population.

Sanctions-Related Constraints on Humanitarian Assistance

The 1995 DHA report on sanctions reported that some of the past obstacles encountered by humanitarian agencies working in sanctioned countries have been overcome in the course of time.

> No longer are UN food convoys kept waiting at borders for considerable lengths of time or are ships queuing in long lines. Enforcement inspection procedures have been streamlined and so have exemption procedures. Bulk waivers, global exemptions and drawing down notifications, priority treatment for UN and other humanitarian agencies have greatly simplified get-

ting humanitarian supplies in the country. Over the years, agencies have developed smooth working relationships with the sanctions committees, at times complemented by regular quasi monitoring meetings.[97]

The DHA report focuses mainly, however, on the larger, more-established international NGOs. Yet the majority of the humanitarian response, at least in the case of Iraq, has come from local and regional NGOs, the private sector, and concerned individuals and communities, among other entities. These groups have not enjoyed the same access or relationship to the sanctions committee as do the UN agencies and the ICRC. Their work generally has been more adversely affected and made more complicated by Security Council restrictions.

Member states have also constrained the work of humanitarian organizations. Political influence often dictates the manner and ease through which humanitarian items negotiate national regulations. Companies are often pressured and risk negative publicity if they continue to engage in business with sanctioned countries. Shipping companies may not wish to become involved in the red tape required to negotiate the sanctions bureaucracy. A lack of clarity or understanding concerning the interpretation of existing sanctions legislation can also hinder humanitarian efforts.

Restrictions concerning the transport of goods and personnel have also caused delays, slowing the humanitarian response. After years of queuing at the port of Aqaba, ships gradually were able to move somewhat more quickly through the Red Sea blockade, yet the overall process of shipment to Iraq remained slow. Layers of paperwork complicated the preparation of shipping manifests. Higher transport costs and fewer available shipping companies affected the delivery of supplies. With few exceptions, relief personnel were unable to find passage on scheduled United Nations flights from Amman and instead traveled by car the nearly one-thousand-kilometer (twelve- to eighteen-hour) journey across the desert to Baghdad.

Sanctions greatly increased the amount of administrative work required for planned activities. Every spare part required by a UN agency or NGO has had to go before the sanctions committee for approval. Apart from the added paperwork, the long delays before receiving sanctions committee approval have required considerable patience and forward planning. Lengthy delays have occurred despite the fact that humanitarian agency applications are given priority. The uncertainty of when, and if, approval will be granted has required great flexibility in program planning, good timing, and often the capacity to rapidly mobilize staff once such approvals have been secured. The uncertainty surrounding approval has increased the need for rigorous contingency planning. Sanctions demand extraordinary amounts of time from all those concerned—agencies, suppliers, and shippers, as well as sanctions committee members. Small or local NGOs generally face considerable difficulties meeting the demands of sanctions application. Their lack of precise knowledge regarding the sanctions bureaucracy, as well as their generally poor access and variable credibility in front of the sanctions committee, may also negatively influence the length and outcome of the approval process.

Generally speaking, humanitarian agencies have found working within the confines of the sanctions process cumbersome, unpredictable, and time consuming. NGO mandates became secondary to "what was permitted under sanctions." Programs were defined, not according to humanitarian need, but rather according to the sanctions committee's definition of acceptable need. Uncertainty regarding whether requests would be approved by the UN has resulted in poor planning and many failed projects. The international humanitarian community—almost without exception—has felt constrained and incapacitated by the sanctions regime.

Funding for Activities

In recent years, funding for humanitarian activities in Iraq has greatly diminished. A lack of global interest, political considerations, and pressing needs elsewhere have contributed to this decline. Since 1991, the major source of funding for humanitarian activities in Iraq has been the Consolidated Appeal launched jointly by United Nations agencies operating in Iraq. For the period from January 1992 to March 1993, over 80 percent of the resources required were mobilized; in the subsequent two-year-long period, however, only 26 percent and 32 percent were mobilized.

In recent years, less than one-third of appeal funds requested by the UN have been received from donors.[98] More recently, Iraqi frozen assets transferred to the United Nations escrow account have been used for humanitarian activities, although this mechanism has not met earlier expectations.

Diminished funding has forced agencies to scale back relief efforts while retaining those programs they consider most likely to receive funding. Funding generally has come earmarked for specific agencies, governorates, and programs. This has greatly reduced the flexibility of agencies to respond effectively to the greatest needs. Approximately 70 percent of assistance provided thus far has targeted the Kurdish-administered north, although this population represents less than one-quarter of Iraq's total.[99]

This emphasis on the north has been due partly to Iraq's embargo against the Kurds, which increased their dependence on foreign aid. However, as noted earlier, it may also reflect donor bias and other motives. The Harvard Study Team and others consistently demonstrated that the humanitarian situation in the country as a whole was roughly uniform, suggesting that aid should be dispersed on an equal per capita basis, without regard to region. Instead, donors have preferred to allocate funding to the pro-West Kurdish areas, administered by international NGOs and the United Nations.

Philosophical Concerns of Humanitarian Agencies

Humanitarian agencies, particularly those within the UN system, have felt uneasy being so closely associated with both the implementation and the enforcement of sanctions. Indeed, many of the system's humanitarian personnel have misgivings about the role of the world organization as both sanctioner and caregiver to Iraq. Furthermore, agencies have often been uncomfortable serving as sanctions enforcers. They have often been asked to interpose themselves between the Iraqi government and the sanctions committee, making requests for spare parts and monitoring the distribution of dual-purpose items (e.g., chlorine gas for water purification is distributed and supervised by UNICEF). Some agency personnel, pointing to international humanitarian law, have questioned whether agencies providing legitimate humanitarian aid should be bound by sanctions legislation at all.

In his 1994 report to the United Nations General Assembly, the secretary-general stressed "the importance of shielding humanitarian assistance against the effects of sanctions."[100] Security Council Resolution 771 also stated that "access to humanitarian assistance should be facilitated and not delayed or complicated." Nonetheless, many of the humanitarian agencies operating in Iraq have encountered serious limitations in their ability to provide assistance.

Impact of Sanctions versus War

That Iraq has suffered severe humanitarian consequences from the gulf crisis is undeniable. Much less clear is the relative weight to be given to war versus economic sanctions. It is extremely difficult to separate the effects of sanctions from those of the forty-three-day bombing campaign and subsequent ground war. The war itself reduced Iraq to a very low socioeconomic baseline and set in motion severe human vulnerability. This makes it even more difficult to talk about the impact of sanctions after the war, when so much of the economic devastation was caused by the war itself. As time has passed, however, the effects of sanctions have increased and have come to outweigh the lingering effects of the war.

A nonsanctioned country could reasonably be expected to achieve at least partial recovery from wartime damage within two to three years of the end of a conflict. Yet this would require billions of dollars in revenue, access to foreign markets, and massive imports of spare parts, machinery, and foreign technical expertise. As mentioned earlier, Prince Sadruddin Aga Khan's report of July 1991 estimated that perhaps $20 billion would be required to restore power, oil, water, sanitation, food, and agriculture to their prewar levels.[101] This alone is equivalent to roughly two years of Iraqi oil revenue that was not available because of sanctions. Indeed, recovery in all sectors of Iraqi society has been minimal. Sanctions have prevented Iraq from earning income, making reconstruction all but impossible. That is not to deny that some progress has been made, although this has generally been in areas where raw materials, spare parts, technical expertise, and foreign currency were not needed. The repairs that have been made have been limited and generally makeshift. Cannibalization of spare parts from one facility to another has been commonplace as prewar stockpiles of spare parts have become exhausted.

The water sector may provide an illustration of how the effects of sanctions can be separated from those of war. In the water sector, there were some early postwar gains. These were mostly the result of Iraq's use of its prewar stockpiles and cannibalization from damaged facilities. Yet, the condition of the water sector began to deteriorate again after the initial restoration effort.[102] Makeshift repairs started to break down and water quality declined. Prior to the war, approximately $100 million per year was spent on water and sanitation equipment, spare parts, and consumables. Now sanctions committee permission is required for the importation of every water-related item. The total of aid for water and sanitation was estimated by the FAO team at approximately $10 million for the entire five-year period following the war. According to FAO, water quality and sanitation in Basra deteriorated from 1993 to 1995. Water quality has also suffered from the lack of domestically produced chlorine. Production facilities were destroyed by wartime aerial bombardment. The annual shortage of chlorine, which must be imported by the United Nations, has been estimated at two thousand tons per year. As a result of these difficulties, most Iraqi water has remained either inadequately chlorinated or not treated at all.

These developments in the water sector show how postwar rehabilitation has been hindered by UN restrictions on imports and Iraq's lack of foreign currency to purchase spare parts and consumables. Poor water quality has been responsible for many tens of thousands of deaths due to diarrheal disease, including cholera, typhoid, and dysentery. In the case of the water sector, the observed effects have been the result of sanctions preventing postwar recovery. This has been the case in other sectors as well, including health, education, and agriculture. In these cases it has been the impact of sanctions, not war-related damage, that has been most responsible for the continued hardship and suffering of the Iraqi population. Although it may not be entirely possible to separate the effects of sanctions from those resulting from the war itself—and even more difficult to apportion blame for the observed humanitarian impact—it does appear that, with the passage of time, sanctions have become increasingly responsible for sustaining the Iraqi emergency.

A number of factors have exacerbated the effects of sanctions. The Iraqi government has, until recently, been intransigent in the face of United Nations offers to provide revenue for humanitarian purposes, primarily through the sale of oil (Resolutions 706, 712, 986). At the same time, Iraq has chosen to use the limited resources at its disposal to strengthen its military, maintain party loyalty, and undertake showcase construction efforts. On the other hand, leading members of the UN Security Council, through the sanctions committee, have often placed unreasonable demands and insurmountable administrative hurdles in front of Iraq's legitimate efforts to provide humanitarian aid. A deepening of sanctions' effects has therefore been due to political decisions taken by the parties themselves, both the government in Baghdad and the leading members of the UN Security Council.

Political Impact

The debate over sanctions against Iraq ultimately centers on the question of their political effectiveness. Yet profound methodological difficulties stand in the way of such analysis, making any assessment of political impact highly subjective and open to varying interpretations. Only the Iraqi leadership itself can tell us whether its decisionmaking process was significantly influenced by the hardships imposed by comprehensive sanctions.

As a first step to examining the political impact of sanctions, it is necessary to consider the original reasons for the imposition of sanctions and the conditions set for their eventual lifting. Sanctions were initially imposed on 6 August 1990 to force Iraqi withdrawal from Kuwait. It will never be known whether sanctions on their own might have been sufficient to force Iraqi withdrawal. As mentioned earlier, there were suggestions before the war that Iraq may have been hoping for Washington's acceptance of a partial withdrawal, with Iraq perhaps retaining a segment of Kuwaiti coastline. There was evidence prior to January 1991 that sanctions were indeed causing hardship among the Iraqi population. Yet, the postwar intransigence of the Iraqi regime has put political survival ahead of human suffering. Baghdad might well have continued the occupation of Kuwait, ignoring the suffering of its own civilian population caused by the sanctions. Furthermore, stockpiles of spare parts and other basic supplies in place before the military conflict likely gave Iraq the means to withstand the effects of sanctions (without war) for some time.

After the war, the Security Council imposed new preconditions for the lifting of sanctions. Two days later, the council also demanded that Iraq end repression of its civilian population, although there have been questions among some members whether compliance with this resolution is a further prerequisite to the lifting of sanctions. Table 4.4 summarizes these postwar preconditions and assesses the degree of Iraqi compliance.

Despite Iraq's compliance with a number of the cease-fire terms, considerable gaps remain. Foremost is the legitimate concern that Iraq has not yet fully disclosed its nuclear, chemical, and biological weapons programs. Iraq has also not yet been sufficiently forthcoming regarding the whereabouts of missing Kuwaitis. The biggest obstacle to compliance may be the demand by the UN that Iraq end repression of its civilian population. Compliance with this condition is not only difficult to verify, it is sufficiently subjective as to permit any one member of the Security Council to argue indefinitely that compliance remains unsatisfactory.

Apart from measuring Iraqi compliance with the cease-fire resolution—the standard imposed by the United Nations in order to determine whether sanctions should be lifted—there is a second fundamental issue. How much of Iraq's compliance has been due to the effects of economic sanctions and how much has been in response to some other form of coercion? For example, just one month after the United States threatened to use military force against Iraqi troops massing along the Kuwaiti border, Iraq recognized Kuwait with its international borders. Similarly, after the 1995 defection of Saddam Hussein's son-in-law, Hussein Kamal, and his sharing of nuclear and other military secrets with the West, Iraq provided further disclosures regarding its nuclear program. On the other hand, a bankrupt Iraqi regime faced with increasing civilian suffering

Table 4.4
Iraqi Compliance with United Nations Security Council Cease-Fire Resolution 687

Term of Cease-fire Resolution	Compliance?	Comments
1. Recognition of Kuwait's territorial integrity, with demarcation of international boundaries	Yes	Declaration of Iraqi parliament recognizing Kuwait, November 1994
2. Acceptance of a monitored, demilitarized zone between Iraq and Kuwait	Yes	
3. Destruction of all chemical, biological, and long-range weapons, with ongoing UN monitoring of Iraq's weapons capability	Mostly yes, but also no	UNSCOM head Rolf Ekeus stated (September 1994) that monitoring mechanisms are in place, but he has questioned the completeness and veracity of Iraq's response to inquiries on past programs, particularly on biological and chemical weapons.
4. Elimination of Iraq's nuclear weapons capability	Mostly yes	Most nuclear weapons facilities destroyed, but questions regarding disclosure remain.
5. Return of all stolen property	Mostly yes	Most state-owned property returned. Military equipment still not returned. Most privately owned assets stolen.
6. Acceptance of liability for all war-related losses and damage	No	But by agreeing to the sale of oil for food, Iraq will contribute 30% of export revenue to a UN compensation fund for war reparations.
7. Repatriation of all Kuwaiti and third-country nationals	Most	Iraq claims to have repatriated all prisoners, while the U.S. wants to know whereabouts of 600 missing Kuwaitis.
8. Renunciation of all acts, methods, and practices of terrorism	No	
9. End of repression of the civilian population (Resolution 688 (5 April 1991)	No	This condition is unlikely to be fulfilled as long as Saddam Hussein remains in power.

and hardship—the result of sanctions—had no choice but to acknowledge wartime liability implicitly by accepting Resolution 986 and agree-
ing to deposit 30 percent of oil sales earnings into the UN Compensation
Fund for war reparations. Furthermore, Rolf Ekeus asserts his belief that
sanctions have been essential to the UN's weapons dismantlement and
inspection process.

Sanctions have also been promoted as a means to ensure Iraq's containment—that is, to weaken the country sufficiently to prevent its
reemergence as a significant Middle Eastern power. Indeed, the military
and economic role of Iraq among the gulf states has been greatly reduced,
at least in the short term. Yet while Iraq's external role has been frozen,
sanctions have unleashed great turmoil within the country—socially, economically, and politically. The destabilizing impact of these changes both
in terms of national stability and, once Iraq has rejoined the global community, internationally, cannot be predicted. It is possible that the short-
term gain of incapacitating Iraq's regional influence may be superseded
by the future negative consequences of political and economic instability
within Iraq spilling out into the region.

Many political observers expected that the hardship created by sanctions would both weaken the Iraqi regime and incite Iraqi citizens to rebel
against their government. There is no evidence that sanctions have had
any such effect. If sanctions were intended to hurt those elements of the
population responsible for war and repression—the Iraqi government
and Baath party members—they have clearly failed to do so. On the contrary, the Iraqi regime has continued to appear well entrenched and in
firm control. Sanctions instead have weakened the general population
while putting scarce resources in the hands of the Iraqi leadership. This
impact has not only made the privileged sectors of Iraqi society rich at the
expense of the general population but also has handed the Iraqi regime a
valuable propaganda tool. The imposition of sanctions—perceived by
most Iraqis to be targeted against their children and the poor—has in
many ways enabled the regime to mobilize the population against an
external aggressor, thereby deflecting attention from the regime's own
shortcomings.

A third rationale for the use of sanctions has been to force Saddam
Hussein into respecting the human rights of Iraqi citizens, particularly
after Baghdad's abuses of Iraq's Kurdish and Shiite populations. Ironically, the hardship caused by economic sanctions has made Iraq's civilian
population even more dependent on the regime for survival—for example, through reliance on government-provided monthly food rations—
and has provided Baghdad with even greater opportunities for control,

repression, and abuse. There is little or no evidence that Iraq's disregard for human rights has changed.

Meanwhile, sanctions have taken on a life of their own. The mere fact that so many justifications for the continuation of sanctions have been put forward—compliance with UNSC resolutions, the containment of Iraq, inciting civil rebellion, forcing an end to repression, even the statements by U.S. leaders that "Saddam must go"—suggests a lack of coherent policy. This "moving the goalposts" has almost certainly been a disincentive to Iraqi compliance, thereby undermining the fundamental goal of economic sanctions: encouraging positive change. Critics of UN policy toward Iraq have suggested that sanctions have been used as a broad cover for a variety of political agendas, many of them U.S.-driven.

Any determination about the political impact of sanctions against Iraq must be placed in the wider context of international standards of justice and human rights. Assuming that the aim of sanctions against Iraq was to enhance security, human rights, and justice, the question becomes: at what cost? Collective punishment leading to great human suffering, including the deaths of hundreds of thousands of children, is a strategy difficult to defend regardless of the motivation. This is particularly true in the case of Iraq, where it could have been predicted that the regime would give priority to its own survival at the expense of its citizens, thereby aggravating even more the damaging effects of sanctions. Does a regime's refusal to help its own citizens give the international community ethical license to exact punishment on an entire civilian population, particularly the poor and the young? It may not be acceptable to impose economic sanctions—a form of collective punishment—and defend our actions simply by demonstrating political impact. Some have argued that the United Nations overstepped the boundaries of international humanitarian law in its implementation of comprehensive economic sanctions against the people of Iraq.

Sarah Graham-Brown highlights these concerns:

> It is difficult to avoid concluding that the humanitarian needs and even the human rights of the Iraqi people have been subordinated to other policy priorities of the Security Council states. The Iraqi regime had the support of the Western powers throughout the 1980s, despite its transparently awful record on human rights. The people of Iraq still endure this abusive regime, but over the last four years gross infringements of human rights have been compounded for the vast majority by severe curtailment of their fundamental right to life and livelihood.[103]

Yet if the goal of UN policy has been to contain or perhaps even reform the Iraqi regime, a number of alternative coercive measures were available. "Targeted" punitive measures might have served the West's objectives better while at the same time sparing the Iraqi civilian population. The DHA report on the humanitarian impact of sanctions recommends the use of partial and targeted sanctions and argues for the avoidance of comprehensive economic sanctions due to their "very negative humanitarian impact and their lack of target-specific focus." The DHA report states that "there is little reason to believe that their (comprehensive economic sanctions) chance to succeed in terms of compliance is superior to other forms of sanctions."[104] If one accepts that targeted sanctions can be an effective instrument of coercion, then one might prescribe a combination of measures.

The above measures are punitive by design, yet they spare civilian populations the hardships caused by the bluntness of comprehensive economic sanctions. The DHA report suggests that the choice of sanctions should be dictated by a number of criteria:

- arms embargo: punitive measures against both importing and exporting countries

- financial sanctions: freezing of government foreign assets

- diplomatic sanctions: cultural boycotts, etc., but no measures that might reduce a country's capacity for dialogue

- traffic and communications restrictions: air, sea, etc.

- partial or comprehensive trade boycott: voluntary

- partial economic sanctions: for example, high-technology items and/or luxury goods

- proportionality between the peace-threatening misbehavior of the country and the anticipated impact of sanctions

- chance of success: reasonable prospects for the desired policy change in the target country

- target specificity: intention to hit the wrongdoers first and hardest

- humanitarian concerns: protection of the innocent and vulnerable

Whatever the international community decides regarding the future imposition of sanctions, there are elements of the gulf crisis that require additional emphasis before concluding. By invading Kuwait in August

1990, Iraq unleashed a series of events resulting in unparalleled suffering and great destitution for both the Kuwaiti and the Iraqi people. Iraq's refusal to accept, as early as August 1991, UN terms for the monitored sale of oil for food contributed to many tens of thousands of civilian deaths. The Iraqi regime put its own political survival ahead of the livelihood of its citizens. At the same time, the nature of the air campaign waged by the allied coalition during the forty-three-day conflict resulted in a devastation wholly out of balance with Iraqi transgressions, causing countless human casualties and immeasurable suffering. The extreme hardships caused by more than six years of comprehensive economic sanctions have violated Iraqi citizens' fundamental right to life and livelihood. The intransigence, repression, and cruel disregard of the Iraqi regime for the well-being of its citizens does not diminish the moral responsibility of Western nations toward the people of Iraq. The punitive economic sanctions imposed by the UN Security Council have brutally touched the lives of nearly every Iraqi citizen, with tragic consequences for the most vulnerable, the poor, and the innocent.

Notes

1. Elements of this chapter were adapted from earlier material published by the author in *War and Public Health*, ed. Barry Levy, and Victor Sidel (Oxford: Oxford University Press, 1996).
2. See Jean Drèze and Haris Gazdar, "Hunger and Poverty in Iraq, 1991," *World Development* 20, no. 7 (1992): 921–45.
3. See Beth Osborne Daponte, "A Case Study in Estimating Casualties from War and Its Aftermath: The 1991 Persian Gulf War," *PSR Quarterly* 3, no. 2 (1993): 57–66.
4. United Nations Children's Fund, *The State of the World's Children 1993* (Oxford: Oxford University Press, 1993), 72.
5. Andrew Haines and Ian Lee Doucet, "Persian Gulf War: The Human Tragedy," in *Medical and Health Annual* (London: Encyclopedia Britannica, 1993), 20–42.
6. See Daponte, "Estimating Casualties."
7. Judith Sayegh, *Child Survival in Wartime: A Case Study from Iraq, 1983–1989* (Baltimore: Department of Population Dynamics, Johns Hopkins School of Hygiene and Public Health, 1992), 46.
8. See Haines and Doucet, "Persian Gulf War."
9. See Daponte, "Estimating Casualties," and Haines and Doucet, "Persian Gulf War," 7. See also William Arkin, Damian Durrant, and Marianne Cherni, *On Impact: Modern Warfare and the Environment: A Case Study of the Gulf War* (Washington, D.C.: Greenpeace, 1991), 8; Medical Educational Trust, *Continuing Health*

Costs of the Gulf War (London: Medical Educational Trust, 1992), 3–4; and Beth Osborne Daponte, "Iraqi War Deaths," in *Hidden Casualties: Environmental, Health, and Political Consequences of the Persian Gulf War*, ed. Saul Bloom et al. (Berkeley: North Atlantic Books, 1993), 189–93. For a lower estimate, based on analysis of the actual number of Iraqi troops in the Kuwaiti theater of operations, see John Mueller, "The Perfect Enemy: Addressing the Gulf War," *Gulf Studies* 5, no. 1 (Autumn 1995): 77–117.

10. Middle East Watch, *Needless Deaths in the Gulf War* (New York: Human Rights Watch, 1991).

11. United Nations, *Report to the Secretary-General on Humanitarian Needs in Kuwait and Iraq in the Immediate Post-crisis Environment by a Mission to the Area led by Mr. Martti Ahtisaari, Under-Secretary-General for Administration and Management, dated 20 March 1991* (New York: United Nations, 1991), 11 (hereafter *Ahtisaari Report*).

12. *Ahtisaari Report*, 5, 13.

13. Arkin, Durrant, and Cherni, *On Impact*, 8, 9. See also Centers for Disease Control, "Public Health Consequences of Acute Displacement of Iraqi Citizens, March–May 1991," *Mobidity and Mortality Weekly Report* 40 (1991): 443–46; Richard Sandler et al., "Initial Medical Assessment of Kurdish Refugees in the Turkey-Iraq Border Region," *Journal of the American Medical Association* 266, no. 5 (1991): 638–40; and Ray Yip and Truman Sharp, "Acute Malnutrition and High Childhood Mortality Related to Diarrhea: Lessons from the 1991 Kurdish Refugee Crisis," *Journal of the American Medical Association* 270, no. 5 (1993): 587–90.

14. See *Ahtisaari Report*; Ahmed Al-Hadi and Omer Obeid, "Report on the Nutritional Status of Iraqi Children: One Year following the Gulf War and Sustained Sanctions," United Nations Children's Fund, June 1991; and United Nations, *Report to the Secretary-General on Humanitarian Needs in Iraq by a Mission Led by Sadruddin Aga Khan, Executive Delegate of the Secretary-General, dated 15 July 1991* (Geneva: Office of the Executive Delegate of the Secretary-General for a United Nations Inter-agency Humanitarian Programme for Iraq, Kuwait and the Iraq/Turkey and Iraq/Iran Border Areas, 1991) (hereafter *Khan Report*).

15. See Sarah Graham-Brown, "Intervention, Sovereignty, and Responsibility," *Middle East Report* (March/April 1995): 2–12.

16. *Khan Report*, 19.

17. *Khan Report*, 37.

18. Arab Monetary Fund et al., *Joint Arab Economic Report 1992* (Abu Dhabi: Arab Monetary Fund, 1993), 18.

19. Abbas Alnasrawi, "Does Iraq Have an Economic Future?" *Middle East Executive Reports* 19, no. 3 (March 1996): 8–19.

20. See Drèze and Gazdar, "Hunger and Poverty."

21. Claudia von Braunmühl and Manfred Kulessa, *The Impact of UN Sanctions on Humanitarian Assistance Activities: Report on a Study Commissioned by the United Nations Department of Humanitarian Affairs* (Berlin: Gesellschaft für Communication Management Interkultur Training mbH—COMIT, December 1995), 11–19.

22. See Drèze and Gazdar, "Hunger and Poverty."

23. See von Braunmühl and Kulessa, *Impact of UN Sanctions*.

24. Economist Intelligence Unit, *Iraq: EIU Country Report, 3rd quarter, 1994* (London: Economist Intelligence Unit, 1994), 3.

25. Harvard Study Team, "The Effect of the Gulf Crisis on the Children of Iraq," *New England Journal of Medicine* 325, no. 13 (1991): 977–80.

26. Alnasrawi, "Does Iraq Have an Economic Future?" 13.

27. See Graham-Brown, "Intervention," 9.

28. Food and Agriculture Organization (FAO), *Basic Food Requirements of Iraq for One Year, 1991–1992* (Baghdad: FAO, 1992); and Congressional Research Service, *CRS Report for Congress: Iraq's Food and Agricultural Situation during the Embargo and the War* (Washington, D.C.: Library of Congress, 1991), (hereafter *CRS Report*).

29. Ian Lee and Andy Haines, "Health Costs of the Gulf War," *British Medical Journal* 303 (1991): 303–6.

30. Lee and Haines, "Health Costs," 305.

31. *Ahtisaari Report*, 5.

32. FAO, *Evaluation of Food and Nutrition Situation in Iraq* (Rome: FAO, 1995), 60.

33. FAO, *Evaluation of Food*, 14.

34. See Rend Rahim Francke, "The Iraqi Opposition and the Sanctions Debate," *Middle East Report* (March/April 1995): 14–25.

35. Graham-Brown, "Intervention."

36. Alnasrawi, "Does Iraq Have an Economic Future?"

37. Graham-Brown, "Intervention," 11.

38. Graham-Brown, "Intervention," 9.

39. UN Department of Humanitarian Affairs, *United Nations Consolidated Inter-Agency Humanitarian Cooperation Programme for Iraq: Mid-Term Review, 21 September 1995* (Geneva: Department of Humanitarian Affairs, 1995), 5.

40. See Medical Educational Trust, *Continuing Health Costs*, and Alberto Ascherio et al., "Effect of the Gulf War on Infant and Child Mortality in Iraq," *New England Journal of Medicine* 327, no. 13 (1992): 931–36.

41. von Braunmühl and Kulessa, *The Impact of UN Sanctions*, 32.

42. *Ahtisaari Report*; *Khan Report*; and FAO, *Evaluation of Food*; also World Health Organization (WHO), "The Health Conditions of the Population in Iraq since the Gulf Crisis," document WHO/EHA/96.1, March 1996.

43. FAO, *Evaluation of Food*, 14.

44. FAO, *Evaluation of Food*, 64.

45. See Drèze and Gazdar, "Hunger and Poverty."

46. See FAO, *Evaluation of Food*.

47. United Nations Children's Fund, *Children and Women in Iraq: A Situation Analysis* (Baghdad: UNICEF, 1993), 27.

48. See Drèze and Gazdar, "Hunger and Poverty," 934.

49. *CRS Report*, 10.

50. Drèze and Gazdar, "Hunger and Poverty," 933–34.

51. UNICEF, *Children and Women*, 40.

52. FAO, *Special Feature: Food Supply Situation and Crop Outlook in Iraq* (Rome: FAO, July 1993), 22.

53. See FAO, *Evaluation of Food*.

54. FAO, *Evaluation of Food*, 71.

55. FAO, *Evaluation of Food*, 16.

56. UNICEF, *State of the World's Children 1993*, 72.

57. "Joint WHO/UNICEF Team Report: A Visit to Iraq," 16–21 February 1991, 3.

58. von Braunmühl and Kulessa, *Impact of UN Sanctions*, 99.

59. von Braunmühl and Kulessa, *Impact of UN Sanctions*, 99.

60. Department of Humanitarian Affairs, *Inter-Agency Humanitarian Cooperation Programme*, 5.

61. UNICEF, *Children and Women*, 68.

62. See Daponte, "Case Study;" World Health Organization, "Health Conditions"; and Sarah Zaidi, "War, Sanctions, and Humanitarian Assistance: The Case of Iraq, 1990–1993," *Medicine and Global Survival* 1, no. 3 (1994): 147–55.

63. See Haines and Doucet, "Persian Gulf War"; Lee and Haines, "Health Costs"; and Harvard Study Team, "Effect of the Gulf Crisis."

64. Lee and Haines, "Health Costs," 305.

65. See Carl Taylor and Richard Reid, "Children as Victims of War," United Nations Children's Fund, 1991.

66. See Haines and Doucet, "Persian Gulf War."

67. See Ascherio et al., "Effect of the Gulf War"; International Study Team, *Health and Welfare*; and Zaidi, *War, Sanctions*.

68. Statistics and Monitoring Unit, UNICEF, New York, May 1992.

69. See Daponte, "Case Study."

70. See FAO, *Evaluation of Food*.

71. Zaidi and Fawzi, "Health of Baghdad's Children," 1485.

72. See UNICEF, *Children and Women*.

73. WHO, "Health Conditions," 12.

74. WHO, "Health Report: Northern Governorate," Baghdad, January 1993, 8.

75. WHO, "Health Conditions," 9–10.

76. See UNICEF and WHO, "National Cluster Surveys," Baghdad, 1985–1989; and UNICEF et al., *Iraq Immunization, Diarrheal Disease, Maternal and Childhood Mortality Survey, 1990* (Amman: UNICEF, 1990).

77. WHO, "Health Conditions," 7–8.

78. WHO, "Health Conditions," 7.

79. See H. Sholkamy, *The Prospects and Problems for Peace Education in the MENA Region: A Report on the Situation of Children in Armed Conflict* (Amman: UNICEF, 1992).

80. See Bela Bhatia, Mary Kawar, and Mariam Shahin, *Unheard Voices: Iraq Women on War and Sanctions* (London: CHANGE, 1992).

81. Bhatia, Kawar, and Shahin, *Unheard Voices*, 39.

82. Bhatia, Kawar, and Shahin, *Unheard Voices*, 52.

83. See Magne Raundalen and Atle Dyregrov, *The Long-Term Impact of the Gulf War on the Children of Iraq* (Bergen, Norway: Research for Children, February 1992).

84. See Consultative Group on Early Childhood Care and Development, *Protecting Children from the Scourge of War* (New York: UNICEF, October 1991).

85. See Arkin, Durrant, and Cherni, *On Impact*; Centers for Disease Control, "Public Health Consequences"; Sandler et al., "Initial Medical Assessment"; and Yip and Sharp, "Acute Malnutrition."

86. UN Department of Humanitarian Affairs, Iraq Relief Coordination Unit, "Regional Implementation Report, January 1996," Dohuk, Iraq, January 1996, 3.

87. Northwest Medical Teams, "Report on 30 Cluster Nutrition Survey Conducted in Northern Iraq: 20 December 1995–4 January 1996," Zakho, Iraq, February 1996, 7, 11.

88. Medical Educational Trust, *Continuing Health Costs*, 16.

89. Arkin, Durrant, and Cherni, *On Impact*, 10.

90. Arkin, Durrant, and Cherni, *On Impact*, 10.

91. Alnasrawi, "Does Iraq Have an Economic Future?" 13.

92. Alnasrawi, "Does Iraq Have an Economic Future?" 13.

93. See "Joint WHO/UNICEF Team Report."

94. See Centers for Disease Control, "Public Health Consequences"; Sandler et al., "Initial Medical Assessment"; and Yip and Sharp, "Acute Malnutrition."

95. United Nations and the Government of Iraq, "Memorandum of Understanding," Baghdad, April 1991.

96. FAO, *Evaluation of Food*, 30–31.

97. von Braunmühl and Kulessa, *Impact of UN Sanctions*, 55.

98. von Braunmühl and Kulessa, *Impact of UN Sanctions*, 104.

99. von Braunmühl and Kulessa, *Impact of UN Sanctions*, 103.

100. See Boutros Boutros-Ghali, *Report on the Work of the Organization*, A/49/177, 21 June 1994.

101. *Khan Report*, 19.

102. See FAO, *Evaluation of Food*.

103. Graham-Brown, "Intervention," 32.

104. von Braunmühl and Kulessa, *Impact of UN Sanctions*, 60.

5

Sanctions in the Former Yugoslavia: Convoluted Goals and Complicated Consequences

Julia Devin and Jaleh Dashti-Gibson

For numerous reasons, the disintegration of, and wars within, the former Yugoslavia (June 1991–November 1995) present a complicated
case of economic sanctions and their impact on the quality of civilian life.
First, according to most observers, there were four distinct internal wars
of varying intensity and duration, each of which generated its own set of
international responses, among which economic sanctions were prominent.[1] To speak of the impact of sanctions is to analyze a wide range of
embargo policies, aimed at a diversity of actors (primarily Serbia and
Montenegro) and imposed in an attempt to change a set of unacceptable
behaviors that were themselves in motion.

Figure 5.1 The Former Yugoslavia

149

Second, this sanctions episode poses a major conceptual and policy irony regarding the meaning of humanitarianism. For the former Yugoslavia, each of the sanctions was imposed in order to prompt one or more of the conflicting parties to eschew violence as a means of settling differences. As the violence against "noncombatants" increased in frequency and cruelty, especially—but not exclusively—as perpetrated by the Bosnian Serbs against Bosnian Muslims, it became clear that the highest humanitarian goal should be to end the bloodshed. Closely related to this primary objective was the imperative to bring humanitarian relief to people denied such aid by the violent (again, primarily Serb) factions. Thus, there would appear to be a prima facie case that if sanctions were successful in coercing the antagonists to end the war, they would have had a significant and positive humanitarian impact, most especially for besieged Bosnian Muslims. However, a variety of other measures were also required to bring Belgrade and Bosnian Serbs to the bargaining table, and this occurred only after massive suffering, ethnic cleansing, and the demise of United Nations capacity to forestall these situations.[2] On the way to accomplishing this humane goal for Bosnian Muslims (in ways that many observers would note were too little and much too late), sanctions also combined with other economic realities to make life harsh for many civilians, especially the predominantly Serbian population of what remained of the former Yugoslavia.

Third, this case exemplifies the dilemma of precise identification of the causal dynamic of sanctions impact that was described in depth in chapter 2. In this instance, there exists a clear but indirect relationship between sanctions and a host of other factors, including the humanitarian situation within the target state. Given the Bosnian Serbs' subnational status and their connections with Belgrade, the council understood that sanctions imposed on them would be impossible to administer and would have little impact. But imposing such measures on their most visible supporters—that is, on the Belgrade government and the society led by Slobodan Milosevic—was the most viable means of applying pressure, albeit indirectly, on Bosnian Serbs.

As this chapter illustrates, sanctions, by interacting in a dynamic manner with other economic factors, produced an abysmal socioeconomic situation for many civilians, especially in Serbia and Montenegro. This harsh economic reality seems to have contributed, both directly and indirectly, to decisions made in Belgrade in 1994 and 1995 that lessened Milosevic's material and political support for the Bosnian Serbs' war effort and ultimately led them to negotiate an end to the conflict in the Dayton accords. A UN report on the Yugoslav sanctions, based on a July 1996 roundtable in

Copenhagen hosted by the Organization for Security and Cooperation in Europe (OSCE), asserted that the sanctions against Yugoslavia were "remarkably effective" and may have been "the single-most important reason for the government in Belgrade changing its policies and accepting a negotiated peace agreement."[3] Military analyst Edward Luttwak expressed a similar view in a 1995 article in *Foreign Affairs* arguing that sanctions "moderated the conduct of Belgrade's most immoderate leadership" and "induced whatever slight propensity has been shown to negotiate."[4] At the same time, however, sanctions generally led the Serb citizenry neither to reject aggressive nationalism nor to reject Milosevic as leader, both articulated as goals of sanctions by the imposers from 1991 through 1993. Definitive judgments about the political effectiveness of the sanctions against Yugoslavia are thus difficult to make.

This chapter analyzes the phases of sanctions and their relative impacts across a host of socioeconomic indicators. It also examines the deteriorating social and economic situation that faced most residents of Serbia and Montenegro, the primary targets of the multilateral sanctions. Finally, the political context of sanctions is discussed, especially the effect that these international measures had on the likelihood that forces for peace might be strengthened to provide an alternative to war among the contending groups in the former Yugoslavia.

Historical Context

At the time of the outbreak of war in June 1991, Yugoslavia was a state with a parliamentary form of government with power vested in citizens who exercised it themselves or through representatives elected in multiparty elections.[5] Although various officials had held the post of president throughout the 1990s, the recognized leader at the time of the breakup and throughout the war was Slobodan Milosevic. It was widely acknowledged early in the war that Milosevic not only provided military support and materials to the Bosnian Serbs in their struggle to remain part of Serbia but also directed much of the war. His involvement was the primary factor behind both the war in Bosnia and the international community's ostracism. Moreover, Milosevic's vision of a "greater Serbia," his skilled use of the media, and his tight grasp on power played a large role in the disintegration of the former Yugoslavia. Despite growing economic problems, UN sanctions, international ostracism, and the war in Bosnia, Milosevic was overwhelmingly reelected in December 1992, further consolidating his power.

Yugoslavia is situated in the southern part of central Europe in the north central portion of the Balkan Peninsula. It shares borders with Bosnia, Croatia, Hungary, Romania, Bulgaria, Macedonia, and Albania. The northern region contains fertile lowlands rich in agricultural production. The central and southern regions are mountainous; the southwestern area borders the Adriatic coast. Its major rivers empty into the Black Sea; some smaller rivers head to the Adriatic. The Danube is a major international waterway. Most of the country is marked by long, sharp, and dry winters; long, hot summers; and short springs and autumns.

Traditionally, Serbia has had plenty of food, producing enough to meet the needs of its population with a large surplus for export. Montenegro, however, is mostly mountainous and has never been self-sufficient in food or agricultural production. Both republics rely on imports of oil and fuel, although their hydroelectric power is more than adequate. Food production and water both sustained the country during the sanctions and cushioned the blow of many of their worst humanitarian consequences.

As the wars began, Yugoslavia had a population of approximately 10.5 million from a variety of ethnic groups including, in descending order, Serbs (62.5 percent), Albanians (16.5 percent), Montenegrins (5.0 percent), Yugoslavs (people of mixed ethnic origin, mainly Slavs, 3.4 percent), Hungarians (3.3 percent), and other nationalities including Muslims, Romanies (Gypsies), and Croats (9.2 percent). There were also a small number of other ethnic groups such as Macedonians, Romanians, Bulgarians, Ruthenians, Vlachs, and Slovaks. Montenegro, the smallest of the former republics with a population of about 600,000, had 13 percent ethnic Muslims and 7 percent Albanians. In a March 1992 referendum, Montenegro voted to remain in a federation with Serbia. Bosnia-Herzegovina was the most complex of these diverse entities, with Muslims comprising 44 percent of the population, Serbs constituting 31 percent, and Albanians more than 17 percent. Almost one in four Bosnians, but especially those in the multiethnic cities, self-described their identity as "Yugoslav."[6]

Kosovo and Metohija (hereafter Kosovo)[7] in the south have a population of about 2 million people, of whom 90 percent are Albanian. While under full Serbian control, the Albanians in Kosovo declared their independence in September 1991 and elected a president. However, Kosovo was not recognized as an independent state. In spite of measures limiting the rights of Albanians, they have established their own parallel system of government, including schools, hospitals, and social services. The situation continued to be tense as of this writing, in spite of the presence of the United Nations Preventive Deployment Force (UNPREDEP) in neighboring Macedonia.

The war that erupted in Yugoslavia has been widely cast in terms of ethnic conflict. At the dawn of the post–Cold War era, a cascading series of events in Yugoslavia began one of the most vexing sets of armed conflicts in recent history. To most observers, the first crisis and war began with declarations of independence from both Slovenia and Croatia on 25 June 1991. In both cases the Yugoslav People's Army (JNA), based in Serbia, attempted to intervene in order to prevent secession. Although fighting in Slovenia lasted only a few days, military conflict spread throughout Croatia in the succeeding two months. In response to these events, the Security Council passed Resolution 713 and imposed an arms embargo on Yugoslavia on 25 September 1991. This was to be the first of a long line of Security Council resolutions concerning the former Yugoslavia, many of which were to involve sanctions imposed solely on Serbia and Montenegro.

By the time a cease-fire was brokered by the United Nations in January 1992 for this particular phase of the conflict, Serbian forces had gained control over approximately one-third of Croatian territory in the Krajina, an area along the Croatian border with Bosnia-Herzegovina. Human rights observers reported the brutal killing of thousands of Croatians by Serbian troops as they took over towns and villages, including one of the worst incidents in the war, the "ethnic cleansing" of the town of Vukovar.[8] This served as a prelude to widespread atrocities as armed conflict spread next into Bosnia-Herzegovina after the European Community (EC; now the European Union [EU]) and the United States recognized its independence in April 1992. As a result of Western recognition of declarations of independence by various components of Yugoslavia, the republics of Serbia and Montenegro formed the Federal Republic of Yugoslavia (FRY) on 27 April 1992.

An understanding of changes in internal social and economic conditions over time, rather than easy explanations based on ancient ethnic hatreds, helps provide insights. The best-recognized expert on this situation, Susan Woodward of the Brookings Institution, places the origins of the road to war a decade before the fall of the Berlin Wall. At that time, Yugoslavia faced a foreign-debt crisis that necessitated a program of economic austerity and reforms that led, in turn, to political disintegration. Among the main causes of the conflict, Woodward includes "the collapse of states, the problematic meaning of self-determination in relation to human rights and borders, and the process of incorporating (or excluding) former socialist states to the West."[9] Ethnic animosity is notably absent from her list.

In addition to dramatic internal changes occurring long before the wars in Yugoslavia, the changing international context also contributed to the outbreak of violence. Yugoslavia found itself in a new situation, different from the Cold War world in which it had been a leader of the Non-Aligned Movement (NAM). Woodward claims that the very viability of the Yugoslav regime depended on its policies of national independence, policies that were intimately linked with a world defined by the Cold War. When the external environment changed, Yugoslavia faced the daunting task of transforming a socialist state into a market economy; domestic institutions created to preserve a delicate internal balance of power needed transformation into a democracy. The task proved too difficult.

The changing geopolitical role of Yugoslavia was not the only contributor to the political disintegration that resulted in war; the response of the major powers to this disintegration also exacerbated matters. At one level, the major powers misunderstood the causes of the conflict and disagreed about the desired outcome and acceptable solutions. Their disagreement impeded effective intervention at various stages, especially early on. Concurrent attempts at negotiating an end to the conflict undermined each other, emboldening intransigent parties to continue the war as they gambled that the major powers had no desire to stop it. When the major powers were inclined to take action, it was more a response to domestic pressures than to a particular strategy for ending the conflict. Furthermore, disagreements about Bosnia took the form of a crisis of confidence in the very regional and international security organizations that should have dealt effectively with the deteriorating situation in the former Yugoslavia.

The Evolution of Sanctions in the FRY

As Yugoslavia's wars erupted, the world's political and humanitarian systems were engaged in their first major post–Cold War test: cooperation in dealing with Iraq's invasion of Kuwait and the associated humanitarian challenges. As the war progressed, UN and U.S. attention also moved to Operation Restore Hope in Somalia. In light of the high costs of handling these crises, both in terms of obtaining cooperation for action and in organizing armed forces to intervene in new forms of operations, the major powers were less than enthusiastic about intervening decisively in Yugoslavia. As a result of increasing dismay at the situation in Yugoslavia and a desire "to do something," the major powers turned to sanctions as the tool of choice against the FRY.

Sanctions provided a type of mini-max strategy to Europe and the world while sending a clear message to the Serbs (both in Bosnia and in

Belgrade) that the costs of their aggression would increase over time. As the war progressed, images of atrocities and refugees and media reports of rape, detention camps, and ethnic cleansing multiplied. Western governments consequently turned to sanctions policy as one way to appease domestic pressure created by their morally outraged publics.[10]

The initial decision to impose sanctions was only the first of many such decisions. It is helpful to distinguish five phases of sanctions against Yugoslavia between May 1991 and April 1993; these are listed in table 5.1. During the first phase in May 1991, the United States and Europe were on alternative, if not counterproductive, paths of sticks and carrots. Washington withdrew aid in order to force the parties to negotiate and resolve the conflict peacefully, while Brussels offered additional aid as an incentive for Yugoslavia to remain intact.[11] The second phase began in response to the wars in Slovenia and Croatia and resulted in a comprehensive arms embargo imposed by the Security Council on all parties to the Yugoslav conflict. The third phase of sanctions was marked by lifting trade sanctions on all parts of the former Yugoslavia except Serbia and Montenegro and imposing a "universal, binding economic blockade under Articles 41 and 42 of the UN Charter" against the FRY in May 1992.

The fourth phase, representing a classic economic embargo, included measures from November 1992 through 1993 to tighten the sanctions by improving monitoring and freezing assets in the hope of forcing Serbia to

Table 5.1
Phases of Sanctions

Phase	Dates	Content
I	April–July 1991	U.S. and EC differential approaches to violence after independence declarations of Slovenia and Croatia
II	July 1991–April 1992	Arms embargo on all parties in response to violence; economic embargoes begin
III	May–October 1992	Sanctions increasingly focused on Serbia and Montenegro as aggressor parties in the war
IV	November 1992– December 1993	Sanctions tightened; improved monitoring under the plan to force Belgrade to force the Bosnian Serbs to accept the Vance-Owen plan
V	September 1994	Partial lifting of sanctions on Belgrade; full sanctions extended to territories controlled by Bosnian Serbs

pressure the Bosnian Serbs to accept the Vance-Owen peace plan. A fifth phase was added as the major powers induced Serbia in August 1994 to sanction the Bosnian Serbs by essentially cutting them off from Serb trade and support. Although not all of the phases affected humanitarian conditions in the FRY, a closer consideration of the evolution of sanctions helps to provide the context for actions against Serbia and Montenegro; it is particularly important to consider this context when trying to develop policies that might be politically effective but less harmful to humanitarian objectives.

The active involvement of the United Nations in the conflicts in the former Yugoslavia began in September 1991, with Security Council Resolution 713, which imposed an arms embargo on the entire region (see table 5.2). The council applied the embargo more clearly to all parts of the former Yugoslavia in Resolution 727, passed in January 1992, the same month that the EC recognized Slovenia and Croatia as independent states. The conditions for lifting the arms embargo were ambiguous; the embargo was to remain in effect "until the Security Council decides otherwise."[12] Despite frequent calls from the United States to lift the embargo on Muslim-controlled areas of Bosnia, it was not formally lifted until 22 November 1995, when the Security Council passed Resolution 1021 after the peace agreement between the parties.

Although intended to prevent long-term conflict escalation, or at least limit the fighting in the region, the arms embargo effectively helped to maintain the balance of military power largely in favor of the Serbs and, to a lesser extent, the Croats. The latter were able to take advantage of geography and regional trade patterns to acquire weapons from various Eastern European sources as they declared independence. At the point of the embargo and for the duration of the war, the FRY was better armed than the Bosnian Muslims, was geographically situated to make contraband trade in arms easier than for landlocked Bosnian Muslims, and was able to offset some of the constraints of the arms embargo with its own weapons production.

Owing to the nature of the former Yugoslav federation, individual republics did not maintain active military forces, or even police. Serbia controlled the JNA, although many of its troops had come from Bosnia. Thus, the Bosnian Serbs were often well trained and well fortified. Many sections of Muslim Bosnia had to create armies from local militia. As the war was drawing to a close, Western observers noted both that the United States might have been channeling weapons to the Bosnians and that arms shipments and various "freedom fighters" from other Muslim nations had flowed readily into Bosnia.

Table 5.2
Major Sanctions Imposed against Actors in the Former Yugoslavia

Date	Resolution	Purpose	Sanctioners
5 May 1991*	Nickles amendment	Suspends U.S. economic aid to Yugoslav government until human rights violations against ethnic Albanians end. OPIC insurance also rescinded	U.S. Congress
11 July 1991	EU–U.S. joint declaration	Suspends all arms sales and transfers to all parties in emerging Yugoslav conflict owing to JNA and local militia use of force against Slovenia and Croatia	EU, U.S.
25 September 1991	UN SC 713	Imposes mandatory arms embargo on all identifiable parties in the internal fighting in the FRY	UN Sec. Council
6 December 1991	U.S. Congress	Ends trade preferences and economic aid as a response to continued fighting and the unwillingness to negotiate terms of disengagement	U.S. Congress
January 1992	UN SC 727	Extends the arms embargo as a penalty on all parties for continued fighting	UN Sec. Council
May 1992	U.S. executive branch action	Freezes all Serbian property assets held singly or jointly in the U.S. or under U.S. jurisdiction	U.S. executive
30 May 1992	UN SC 757	Imposes sanctions in support of UN SC Resolution 752, which on 15 May called upon the FRY government in Belgrade to end its military role in the Bosnian conflict, to withdraw the JNA, and to disarm the "irregular forces" it was supporting within Bosnia. These are comprehensive trade sanctions; interdiction of air transportation except for humanitarian aid; a ban on all financial transactions; suspension of scientific, cultural, and other exchanges	UN Sec. Council
16 November 1992	UN SC 787	Closes all borders and ends the transshipment of all embargoed goods across soil of the FRY	UN Sec. Council
17 April 1993	UN SC 820	Further tightens sanctions, puts in place SAMCOM monitoring system to improve effectiveness of sanctions and delivery of humanitarian assistance	UN Sec. Council
September 1994	UN SC 942	Extends all existing sanctions to Bosnian Serbs and territory they hold	UN Sec. Council

*The Nickles amendment was actually passed by Congress in late 1990, setting the 5 May 1991 date as the point at which aid would automatically be suspended unless improvements were observed. The force of the amendment lasted less than three weeks, as Secretary of State James Baker granted a waiver to the government of Yugoslavia by certifying that the Belgrade leadership was carrying out its pledges under the human rights provisions of the Helsinki accords.

The arms embargo was the least strictly enforced of all the sanctions against the former Yugoslavia. All parties had access to some types of arms, ranging from light weapons through the very large 152mm howitzers used by Serb shellers of Bosnian towns and cities.[13] Thus, the arms embargo had no identifiable impact on the level of violence during the war, save constraining, for 1992 and portions of 1993, the ability of Bosnians fully to defend themselves. The arms embargo had a limited effect on bringing the war to a close. At best, sanctions may have increased the cost of obtaining these weapons, thereby increasing the economic impact of the war on postwar recovery.

An attack that killed as many as twenty-two people waiting in a bread line in Sarajevo prompted the Security Council to impose comprehensive international sanctions against the FRY in May 1992. The UN's involvement followed the withdrawal of economic and financial aid to the region by the EC and the United States in May and June of 1991 in an attempt to prevent the disintegration of the former Yugoslavia. The EC had also imposed trade sanctions against the entire region after fighting broke out in Slovenia and Croatia in July 1991. Following the UN's action in May, the EC lifted its trade embargo on all of the republics except the FRY in November 1992.

On 15 May 1992, the Security Council passed Resolution 752, which requested that the FRY end its military interference, withdraw the JNA, and disband and disarm the irregular forces operating in Bosnia-Herzegovina. This resolution provided the foundation for all the sanctions resolutions that followed and set out the framework for lifting subsequent sanctions measures. Resolution 757, passed on 30 May 1992—only two weeks after Resolution 752—established comprehensive sanctions against the FRY. Its provisions included a boycott on all goods from the FRY; an embargo on all imports into the FRY; the interdiction of air traffic and related services; a ban on all financial transactions; the reduction of staff at diplomatic missions; a ban on the FRY's representation at sports and cultural events; the suspension of scientific and technical cooperation and cultural exchanges; and a provision that no legal claims could result from the consequences of implementing sanctions. This resolution did not prohibit the transshipment of goods through the FRY, mainly out of concern for neighboring countries that stood to lose revenue. Moreover, Resolution 757 exempted humanitarian activities and supplies including "supplies strictly used for medical purposes and foodstuffs," payment transfers "exclusively for strictly medical purposes and foodstuffs," and flights for humanitarian purposes, all subject to the approval of the Security Council. Instead of setting forth specific requirements, Resolution 757 merely stated that the sanctions "might be suspended or terminated following compliance with the requirements of Resolution 752." The conditions in Resolution 752 included a complete end to the military interference of the Serbian military in Bosnia.

Six months later, the sanctions were reportedly having little effect because of numerous violations and the porous borders with neighboring states. On 16 November 1992, Security Council Resolution 787 tightened sanctions by prohibiting transshipments of certain strategic items through the FRY unless specifically authorized by the council. Its provisions prohibited the transshipment of crude oil and petroleum products; coal and energy-related equipment; iron, steel, and other metals; chemicals; and rubber tires, vehicles, aircraft, and motors of all types. By 17 April 1993, almost one year after the initial imposition of the sanctions, Resolution 820 confirmed, partly restructured, and tightened the existing sanctions. Specifically, the Security Council strengthened monitoring and control mechanisms; asserted Bosnia's and Croatia's right to move goods on their respective territories; and reaffirmed the council's previous decision to freeze all FRY funds, prohibit all transport to and from the FRY, impound transport vehicles and cargoes used to export goods from the FRY, prohibit the provision of services (with exceptions for telecommunication, post, and humanitarian assistance), and strictly limit the transshipment of goods to cases authorized by the Security Council. As in previous resolutions, the Security Council exempted medical supplies and foodstuffs, subject to approval by the sanctions committee, including "other essential humanitarian supplies" and "services whose supply may be necessary for humanitarian and other exceptional purposes."

The council entertained the possibility of gradually lifting sanctions, linked to Bosnian Serb acceptance of a peace plan and cooperation in its implementation. This link underscored the assumption that the FRY exercised a decisive influence in the actions and decisions of the Bosnian Serbs. Moreover, Resolution 820 offered a carrot to the FRY by expressing the council's interest in the "full readmittance" of the FRY into the community of states "once it has fully implemented the relevant resolutions of the council." As the authors of a report commissioned by the Department of Humanitarian Affairs (DHA) on the impact of sanctions on humanitarian assistance activities point out, these provisions substantiate the claim that the ostracism of the FRY from the international community is a "hidden sanction," but nonetheless part of the UN's sanction package.[14]

After the breakup of the former Yugoslavia, the FRY was excluded from many international bodies, including the Conference on Security and Cooperation in Europe (CSCE, now the Organization for Security and

Cooperation in Europe, or OSCE), the UN, the EC, the World Bank, the International Monetary Fund (IMF), and even the World Health Organization (WHO). This was primarily in response to the FRY's active military support of Bosnian Serbs and their aggression in the war in Bosnia. However, rather than permitting it to retain automatically the seat previously occupied by the former Yugoslav Federation, many organizations required the FRY, like the other republics, to reapply for membership, often suspending the FRY's participation in the interim. On 10 July 1992, the FRY was suspended from the CSCE for its role in the war in Bosnia. On 19 September 1992, the Security Council in Resolution 777, and later the General Assembly, decided that the FRY could not automatically retain the seat previously occupied by the former Yugoslavia but would have to reapply for membership like all the other former republics. Although not formally part of the sanctions package, each of these resolutions—and the resulting international ostracism of the FRY—clearly reflected the belief that the FRY was the main threat to peace in the former Yugoslavia.[15]

In August 1994, President Milosevic finally agreed to enforce an embargo against the Bosnian Serbs after they again rejected a U.S.-backed peace plan. By this time, Serbs occupied almost 70 percent of Bosnia, as well as about one-third of Croatia. Sanctions against the FRY had been in place for almost a year and a half and had firmly taken hold. The economy of the FRY had nearly collapsed in late 1993. Although it had stabilized somewhat since internal economic reforms in January 1994, the gains were tentative. Milosevic had seemingly had a change of heart and had begun to work with the international community to establish peace in the region.

In September 1994, Security Council Resolution 942 extended the UN sanctions to Bosnian-Serb territory in eastern Bosnia bordering Serbia. Milosevic permitted UN observers to monitor the border and verify his compliance with the blockade. His action against the Bosnian Serbs met with fierce opposition from right-wing nationalists within Serbia. Yet, according to some observers, Milosevic bet "that most Serbs would care more about the collapsing economy and international isolation."[16] Other observers point out that the real reason for Milosevic's complete turnaround and blockade of the Bosnian Serbs was his decision to consolidate gains. Apparently he believed that nothing else would be achieved by continuing the war in Bosnia. Cutting off Bosnian Serbs was the first step in undercutting the Bosnian-Serb leader, Radovan Karadzic, whose power had come to rival that of Milosevic himself.

One of the sanctions that apparently had the greatest impact for ordinary Serbs in Bosnia was severing all telephone lines to Serbia and the rest of the world. The sanctions imposed by the FRY included a ban on all trucks going from Serbia to the Krajina. Such actions again signaled a turning point in the war and bolstered efforts to bring peace. They also marked one of the first times that Milosevic had complied with the conditions set forth in previous resolutions and paved the way for the gradual lifting of economic sanctions against the FRY.

On 5 October 1994, after receiving the first report from the 135 UN observers monitoring the 375-mile-long border between Serbia-Montenegro and the Serb-held sections of Bosnia, the UN Security Council ordered the easing of sanctions against the FRY. Based on the "effective closure of the border" between the FRY and Bosnia, Security Council Resolution 943, adopted 23 September 1994, suspended the sanctions prohibiting international air traffic and ferry service between Montenegro and Italy (for transport of persons and personal effects only) and the embargo on sporting and cultural events for a hundred days (later extended).[17] The Security Council also welcomed the FRY's expressed support for the proposed territorial settlement in Bosnia.

It should be noted that while this partial suspension of the sanctions rewarded the change in attitude of the Serbian government and gave a tremendous psychological boost to most Yugoslavs, it had little impact on the wider economy or the provision of social and health services. As one Serbian physician noted one hundred days after the partial lifting, "It was shameful of the world to lift sports and cultural sanctions while doctors have to wait three months for permission to obtain anesthetics for patients."[18]

Economic Decline under Sanctions

The war in the former Yugoslavia began at a time when the country was experiencing extreme economic pressure, both internally and externally. Although by no means the sole cause of the economic and social disintegration in the FRY, sanctions appear to have hastened and intensified the crisis by adding to a vicious cycle of increasing needs and decreasing resources for an economy caught in transition to a post–Cold War world and with leaders bent on maintaining the autocratic control of an economy that held in the old order. The UN Children's Fund (UNICEF) 1995 Situation Analysis attributed much of the crisis in the FRY to the relatively inefficient economic system characteristic of all former socialist countries.[19] It argued that Yugoslavia's economic and development strategies are riddled with long-term, chronic, and deep-rooted tensions and that its economic decline began in 1979 and continued over the following ten years as the former Yugoslavia transitioned to a market economy.[20] Whatever impact these tensions may have had, the economic and social crises in the FRY also were caused by several acute factors including the breakup of the former Yugoslavia, the resulting war, and the government's own inappropriate economic policies. Although it is impossible to disaggregate the effects of each factor, a brief description of some of the more salient consequences of each for humanitarian conditions may help to isolate the humanitarian impacts attributable to sanctions themselves.

Before the war, the former Yugoslav republics accounted for 40 percent of trade with Serbia and Montenegro. With the breakup of the former Yugoslavia, this trade almost disappeared. Because the economies of the republics were so highly interdependent, the loss of these markets probably had a greater impact on the economy of the FRY than the loss of foreign trade that resulted from sanctions. The combination helped render large parts of the FRY's industry idle because of a lack of materials, spare parts, and machinery. Sanctions exacerbated this problem by stopping the flow of goods that were either formerly imported from abroad or otherwise could have been, to help fill gaps left by the breakup and loss of interrepublic markets. In either case, the loss of trade caused by the breakup of the former Yugoslavia had both macroeconomic and microeconomic consequences that affected humanitarian conditions. These included a significant loss of income for many families and the loss of important markets that were relied on for humanitarian purposes.

The war in Croatia and Bosnia also played a major role in the collapse of the FRY's economic and social structure. Although the precise impact is difficult to measure, the war exacted a high toll on the populations of both Serbia and Montenegro not only in economic costs but also in terms of lost lives; ruined families; casualties; material destruction; decreased social product; economic, social, and cultural regression; and involuntary mass migrations.

The most vivid humanitarian consequence of the war was the influx of over 700,000 refugees, whose need for food, shelter, education, and health care placed a heavy burden on an economic and social system already stretched well beyond its capacity and suffering from sanctions.[21] Over 90 percent of the refugees were housed in private homes, stretching the dwindling resources of individual families and in some cases creating tension with the local population.

Economic policies implemented by the FRY government, particularly after the breakup of the former Yugoslavia in 1991 and the imposition of sanctions in 1992, contributed significantly to the economic crisis and growing humanitarian needs throughout the FRY. The UNICEF reports, along with Woodward and others, note that the government failed to respond appropriately to the country's changed economic and social circumstances, changes that were already under way before the outbreak of violence in the 1990s. Economists both within and outside the FRY assert that the government never took the radical economic measures that might have helped ease economic problems, such as adjusting public expenditure to the country's real economic potential, adhering to the principle of budget constraint, and making gradual structural adjustments. Instead, the government responded to the rising public expenditure deficit by printing money, which resulted in hyperinflation. The crisis culminated in January 1994, when Yugoslavia experienced a collapse of its monetary and fiscal systems and was "nearly left without a currency."[22]

In an effort to prevent total collapse, the government implemented an emergency economic package in January 1994. The Amramovic reforms, created by a seventy-four-year-old economist and former senior UN official, phased out the old FRY currency and replaced it with one introduced at parity with the deutsche mark. Although far from resolving the underlying crises, this program gave the country a relatively stable currency again, achieved relative price stability, helped raise industrial output at least temporarily, and increased real wages.[23] It also removed hyperinflation and, perhaps just as important, provided some psychological relief. In particular, citizens seem to have moved away from hoarding at this time, as goods previously held back by retailers were now back on the shelves and being replenished by producers. There was more traffic on the street than at any time in the previous two years because there was more money with which to buy the expensive sanctions-busting gasoline. In February 1994, industrial production was up 12 percent compared to the same period one year earlier; by March it was up 22 percent.

Although this growth in output appears impressive, it started from an extremely low point. Moreover, as early as midautumn of 1994, signs of instability and recession had reappeared. In 1994, UNICEF estimated that industrial production would have to increase 5 percent continuously over the next twenty-five years to return to the 1989 level, assuming, first, that the sanctions were lifted. At the same time that the government introduced these economic reforms, it also reduced subsidies to Bosnian and Krajina Serbs. This reduction in war-related expenditures, too, helped stabilize the FRY economy.

Finally, as noted above, the sanctions added greatly to both the economic and the social chaos in the FRY as well as to growing humanitarian needs. Ironically, UN organizations were supposed to compensate for UN-approved sanctions. According to UNICEF, the most important effects of sanctions included a dramatic drop in industrial output and the loss of export markets that created an uncompetitive economy that is years behind others and that is less and less market oriented. These macroeconomic trends had practical repercussions for individual households and families, not the least of which was limiting their ability to meet basic daily human needs. Although humanitarian exemptions were incorporated into UN resolutions, critical economic supplies and materials used for humanitarian purposes were often either delayed or prohibited altogether.

The Economic and Sociohumanitarian Impact of Sanctions

This and the following sections attempt to provide a picture of the humanitarian conditions in the FRY under sanctions. The information is drawn from secondary sources and existing data. Much more intensive and firsthand field research into conditions and processes is necessary to determine both the cost and the effectiveness of economic sanctions. Household surveys, in particular, could shed light on what, in their absence, are necessarily generalizations.

It is clear from existing data that sanctions in the FRY hurt the most vulnerable members of society and had less effect on those with greater resources. The data also show that sanctions had a wide reach, negatively affecting almost every sector of society (albeit to varying degrees), including industrial production, unemployment, trade, food and agriculture, water and sanitation, social and health services, and education, as well as the civil and political processes in the country. To understand better the humanitarian impact of sanctions, it is helpful to look at each of these sectors.

In Yugoslavia, the real social product (a measurement used in former socialist countries to denote the final value of goods and services produced) dropped rapidly between 1989 and 1994, falling at an average annual rate of 17.5 percent; and in 1994, it was 51.3 percent lower than in 1989 ($1,250 in 1994 compared to $3,300 in 1989).[24] In the public sector it dropped 66 percent.[25] Gross national product (GNP) also fell dramatically. In the first three months after the imposition of sanctions, industrial output dropped by 30 percent.[26] In 1994, industrial production was 36 percent lower than it was in 1989.[27] All industries were affected, and some almost ground to a halt. In 1995, out of a total of thirty-five branches of industry, the level of activity in twenty-eight industries was reportedly less than 50 percent of their 1989 levels; in sixteen branches, it was less than 20 percent.[28] Formerly the cream of the industry, the production of investment goods declined to 13 percent of its previous level; other sectors dropped to as low as 10 percent.[29] Industries particularly affected included construction, transport, catering, and tourism.[30]

As of August 1993, industrial output had fallen by 40 percent in the year following the imposition of sanctions. Retail sales were down by 70 percent. Companies that fared least badly included those that could make spare parts for imported machinery or were involved in agriculture or food processing. A few service firms such as advertising agencies also survived by shifting their efforts to their overseas offices. During the sanctions, the market favored the most flexible industries, including those that could produce a larger range of items than they had previously. For such companies it was possible to capture some of the markets vacated by foreign competitors, mostly from the Slovene and Croat firms that used to dominate industry in the former Yugoslavia.[31]

The DHA estimates that by 1994 overall industrial output dropped to one-third of its 1989 levels, with specific production activities hit particularly hard. Steel production dropped to 14 percent; automobile production dropped to 8 percent. The shortage of energy resulting from the embargo on oil and gas resulted in major reductions and even stoppages in the chemical, glass, and paper industries. The DHA report also indicated that much of the industrial infrastructure was neglected and desperately in need of repair.[32] From February to October 1994, industrial output reportedly improved owing to the government's economic stabilization policy and the elimination of hyperinflation. However, by November 1994, industrial output had started declining again, and Yugoslavia's economy went into a recession.[33]

Support of the war contributed to FRY's economic difficulties. However, the Milosevic regime had good reason to downplay these other factors in order to capitalize on public sentiment among Serbs that they were being treated unjustly. Sanctions clearly exacerbated already difficult conditions.

At the beginning of 1995, European Union observers estimated that 38 percent of the population in the FRY was unemployed. Official government figures at the end of 1994 calculated 750,000 unemployed (15.6 percent of all economically active); 900,000 redundant workers, defined as persons employed but without any work to do (i.e., 45–50 percent of all economically active); and 1.4 million pensioners.[34] In May 1995, the demand for labor was twenty-seven times lower than the labor supply. First-time job seekers made up 65 percent of all unemployed, and 55.6

percent of the unemployed were women. In all, only about 10 percent of the 10.5 million people living in the FRY were employed at the end of 1994; 60 percent of the total labor force was out of work.[35]

Moreover, many people transferred from the public to the private sector. From 1989 to May 1995, the number of employees in the state sector had dropped steadily, while the number of workers in the private sector had risen fourfold (from 60,000 to 240,000).[36] This transfer significantly affected the provision of social and humanitarian services, particularly in the health sector, and resulted in unequal access to critical services.

The breakup of the former Yugoslavia and the war destroyed interrepublic trade and reduced foreign commerce. Sanctions, too, helped render large parts of the FRY's industry idle and soon useless. The volume of consumer goods sold in 1993 was only 15 percent of the volume sold in 1990; imports were about 30 percent of those in 1989; exports were about 30 percent of their 1989 amounts. The FRY is estimated to have lost $20 billion in trade as a result of sanctions.[37] Surrounding countries with trade links to the FRY—including Romania, Bulgaria, Hungary, and Macedonia—as well as countries relying on the Danube River for trade, also reported substantial losses as a result of the sanctions.

Although self-sufficient in hydroelectricity, the FRY depends on oil and gas imports for heat and energy. By blocking these critical markets, sanctions exacerbated the recession in the FRY. Even more important, they increased the needs of the population while at the same time limiting the provision of health and human services that relied on imported products. For example, hospitals reported having insufficient heat and a limited capacity to perform necessary medical services. One of the most serious consequences of the sanctions for the health sector was the UN sanctions committee's decision, after several rounds of deliberations, to block pharmaceutical supplies and materials despite existing humanitarian exemptions. The impact of this action was even greater because of the FRY's heavy reliance on medicaments. Export-oriented industries, such as textiles, were also immediately affected and could rarely find a way of circumventing the sanctions.

The National Institute of Statistics calculated the inflation rate at its height in late 1994 at 1 percent an hour. Inflation was recorded daily, not monthly or yearly. Some stores reportedly closed down in the middle of the day for inventory and posted prices in foreign exchange (particularly deutsche marks).[38]

From December 1992 to October 1993, living costs rose 166-fold, but wages only rose 56-fold, making the situation even for working families not only extremely difficult but often precarious.[39] In 1994, UNICEF reported that pensions and minimum salaries had fallen below $10 a month, barely enough to pay utility bills. By August 1993, the inflation rate was among the highest in the world at 1,881 percent. Prices during this month were reportedly on average 19 times higher than one month earlier, with the costs of individual items increasing even more. For example, heating oil cost 114 times more; gasoline was 72 times as expensive; and beans and milk rose 38-fold above their previous month's cost. After the economic reforms in January 1994, the FRY experienced a period of relative stability from February to October. However, prices began to rise again, and by July 1995 they were 49.2 percent higher than in December 1994.[40]

The humanitarian consequences of sanctions in Serbia and Montenegro touched almost everyone within their borders. By helping to lower the standard of living, sanctions affected both household earning capacity and purchasing power. With this downward shift, population groups were more or less affected depending in large measure on their access to resources, savings, or other sources of support outside of the FRY.

The sanctions also stimulated corruption, contraband operations, and outright criminality within an economy that already was a strange combination of nationalist, mafia-like entrepreneurship, authoritarianism held in place from the days of socialist rule, and profiteers who had emerged from gun-running and other "patriotic" enterprises encouraged by the war. In the words of Sonja Licht, "Life under sanctions forced a significant proportion of society to live on the fringes of legality. The black market became a way of life."[41]

The wealthy, including the political elite, military officers, and others with access to relatives, investments abroad, or other secure sources of income in foreign exchange were least affected. Many middle-class households, however, were forced below the poverty level either because they did not have external resources or because they had exhausted their savings. Nonetheless, while sanctions made life extremely difficult for a large number of people in the middle class, the sanctions in general did not threaten their survival. Unfortunately, this was not the case for the most vulnerable members of society—the poor, sick, elderly, and, often, women and children. Without outside resources and often in need of special care, people in these population groups were forced further into poverty, sickness, and life-threatening situations. Moreover, the state, which had previously taken care of many social and health needs by providing free, high-quality health care, social services, and education, was now unable to maintain these services.

Although the country's economy had begun to decline in the early

1980s, available evidence suggests that it dropped even more sharply with the imposition of sanctions. This drop had very practical implications for both households and individuals. For example, at the beginning of 1990, the value of the minimum consumer food basket for a family of four was 80 percent of their average monthly income. By March 1993, the cost of this same basket was 3.5 times more than the average monthly salary.[42]

Employers and employees often could not keep pace with such astronomical rates of inflation. Often incomes fell below the poverty line simply because of delays in getting paid or even in cashing checks. People changed money into hard currency or bought things as soon as possible to avoid holding money that became worthless merely with the passage of time. In 1994, total household incomes in real terms dropped to only 55 to 60 percent of their 1989 value.[43] Average Serbs saw their incomes drop from $500 to $15 per month.[44] In 1993, one observer commented, "Real incomes are only a tenth of what they were three years ago and the value of the local currency has the longevity of a snowball on a summer's day."[45]

Over time, economic duress and hyperinflation exhausted the savings and economic reserves of middle-class and urban populations. At the end of 1993, 85 percent of workers and 92 percent of pensioners reportedly were below the poverty line.[46] Sources of household income also changed significantly, with more people relying on their savings, remittances from relatives and friends abroad, and in some cases the private sector or contraband.[47]

Household consumption patterns became similar to those in poor countries of the so-called Third World, where expenditures on food and basic necessities leave families with no resources even for other needs.[48] As a result of sanctions and the ongoing economic crisis, families were forced to spend an ever larger share of their incomes on food. For example, in 1990, on average 35.5 percent of a family's income was devoted to food, whereas in the first half of 1994, this figure rose to 49.5 percent. In lower-income groups, expenditures on food rose from 43 percent to 60 percent. In contrast, the share of income spent for clothes and footwear declined. Housing expenditures remained low, and outlays for furniture, education, culture, and entertainment became negligible.

In addition, except for the richest 10 percent who had substantial savings, the structure of expenditures became more or less similar across, and within, income groups; as UNICEF noted: "Citizens were rapidly becoming equal in poverty and the economic differences between the lower and middle classes, as well as between urban and rural populations, were becoming blurred."[49] Thus, sanctions helped to lower considerably the standard of living of almost everyone in the FRY, largely destroying the middle class, reinforcing a small upper class, and dramatically increasing the number of destitute. UNICEF reported that in 1994 almost 4 million people, or 38 percent of the population, had fallen below the poverty line and were unable to meet their minimum food requirements; this represented a sixfold increase over the number of poor in 1990.[50] On the other hand, about 4 percent of the population had become enormously rich through illicit trade and profiteering.[51]

A household survey conducted by the nongovernmental organization Community Information and Epidemiological Technologies International (CIET international) provides helpful and suggestive data. The households most affected included women, families with children, the elderly, the unemployed, refugees, and internally displaced persons (IDPs).[52] Families of industrial workers and miners reportedly made up 43.6 percent of the total population of the poor, while families of managers and political leaders represented only 1.4 percent.[53] Women endured perhaps the heaviest burden of the drastically reduced living standards and the challenge of meeting everyday needs. Shrinking household budgets meant more work for them, including having to use cheaper, but outdated and more time-consuming, methods of housekeeping, cooking, mending, and budgeting. Many women began growing their own vegetables or took on extra jobs in the informal sector to help make ends meet.[54]

According to CIET international, during the sanctions period, women were more likely to be unemployed than men.[55] Although the FRY constitution and labor laws protect women and guarantee absolute equality in the workplace, in practice women were concentrated in lower-paid jobs than men and were also more likely to be laid off.[56] Moreover, the types of jobs and industries in which women were employed were also the ones most affected by the sanctions and the economic crisis, including trade, catering, and tourism.[57] Conversely, CIET international found that few women held top jobs in the sectors least affected by sanctions, including factories, firms, banks, political parties, and diplomatic offices.[58]

Women also suffered from health conditions whose treatment was seriously influenced by sanctions. For example, UNICEF reported that the most frequent causes of death among women were reported to be cardiovascular diseases (61.1 percent), malignant neoplasms (14.6 percent), and respiratory diseases (4.2 percent).[59] Medical supplies and equipment needed to treat each of these illnesses were reportedly some of the most difficult to obtain during the imposition of sanctions.[60] Women and families with children also appeared to be materially worse off than others. UNICEF reported that during the second quarter of 1994, the income for families with children under eighteen was 13 percent lower than that of the average Yugoslav family and 16.4 percent lower than the income of pensioners.[61]

Existing information also suggests that the humanitarian crisis during the sanctioned period disproportionately affected children and the elderly, who along with women constitute the categories most vulnerable in all crises. By limiting the stock of many medicaments, as well as the ability of the government to provide quality health care, sanctions affected them. Dialysis and treatment for cancer or chronic illnesses were often totally unavailable.[62] Penicillin was in short supply, as were many other common medicines. Physicians were left to find creative and sometimes risky alternatives to traditional medical practices. Moreover, both children and the elderly often have greater social and health needs that were harder to meet during sanctions and often made them more vulnerable to serious health conditions.[63]

The psychological consequences of the war and crisis were often overwhelming for the elderly, in particular. During the sanctions period, the incidence of elderly suicide apparently dramatically increased. Reportedly, many elderly people lost all hope and felt that they were too great a burden on society and their families. International media reported that the humanitarian conditions in psychiatric wards were dire. With medications in short supply, heating capabilities reduced, and state services at an all-time low, patients reportedly had to be restrained more often than previously, food was ill prepared, facilities were cold, and many people had no clothes or blankets.[64]

The influx of more than 700,000 refugees from Bosnia and Croatia, including 150,000–200,000 Serbs who fled the Krajina in August 1995 when it was recaptured by Croats, not only strained the social service network and an already weak economy but also stretched household budgets still further—for many, well beyond their capacity. More than 215,000 refugees were under the age of eighteen.[65] Not only had they suffered the devastating consequences of war and being uprooted from their homes and, in many instances, families, but also their mental and psychosocial development was threatened by the indirect effects of the war and exposure to the uncertainty and stresses caused by the economic sanctions and the social crisis in the FRY.

The government in Belgrade provided for the basic necessities of the refugees, including accommodation, food, health care, education, and social services. However, over 90 percent of the refugees lived with host families, who bore the heaviest economic burden.[66] While refugees received food, social services, and other assistance, particularly from international humanitarian aid organizations and the UN High Commissioner for Refugees (UNHCR), the resources of the host families were often stretched to the breaking point.

To help them, as well as the growing number of "other" poor, the UN created a special category of beneficiary. In 1994, UNICEF estimated that 45 percent of the population living below the poverty line qualified as "social cases" dependent on humanitarian aid.[67] In many ways, the humanitarian effects of sanctions on refugees and IDPs was perhaps somewhat lessened because of the external resources received through international humanitarian aid and social services that were not available to the general public. Although host families were generous, they usually did not receive the same type of support and assistance as the IDPs and refugees. At times, this discrepancy increased tensions and contributed to additional difficulties between the local populations, on the one hand, and the refugees and IDPs, on the other. Discrepancies also influenced relations between aid organizations and local authorities.

The Decline in Public Health under Sanctions

Before the war, the health care system was well developed and accessible. Under the individual constitutions of Serbia and Montenegro as well as that of the FRY, all citizens were entitled to free and comprehensive health care. Known for its well-developed public heath system and scientific institutions, the FRY had devoted about 4 percent of its gross national product to health care.[68] A state health insurance fund was supported by contributions from employees' salaries, while the health care of uninsured persons was financed from the budgets of individual republics.[69]

With the onset of economic and social crises in the 1980s, there were substantial cuts in public expenditures for health while the needs increased. Moreover, although in 1990 the percent of the GNP allocated to health care had increased to between 10 and 15 percent, the actual value was only half that invested before the war; at the official average annual exchange rate, this amounted to $216 per capita in 1990 and $110 per capita in 1994.[70] This continuing decline and the impact of sanctions resulted in the deterioration of the health infrastructure, including the inability of the FRY to maintain facilities and equipment; frequent shortages of drugs, medical materials, diagnostic equipment, hygiene supplies, and heating fuel; and poor quality in hospital food and nutrition.[71]

Moreover, before the war, the health care system in the FRY was highly specialized, offering more doctors per person than Sweden and more medications per person than Switzerland.[72] Ironically, this level of sophistication resulted in a heavy reliance on specialized medical treatment and drugs that made the acute shortages of medicines and other medical supplies following the imposition of sanctions even more acute. Responding to the crisis in the health sector in 1993, Dr. Vuk Stambolovic, medical coordinator for the Soros Foundation, which supports reform and development projects in Eastern Europe, pointed out that "health services are surviving on humanitarian aid and the responsibility for health care is increasingly being put on the international community."[73] However, humanitarian aid could not compensate for the lack of domestic resources. Moreover, no new investments were made in the health sector; salaries were low to nonexistent; and the long-term damage was severe.[74]

These conditions dramatically highlight how economic sanctions accelerated the decline of the FRY's health care system and created a dependence on international humanitarian assistance. Much of the ultimate cost of aid was borne by outside donors—governmental, intergovernmental, nongovernmental—and the long-term investment necessary to restore the health system to self-sufficient levels will require enormous additional outside resources as well as time. An examination of key health indicators sheds some more light on the actual health conditions and problems faced during the sanctions period.

Owing to the drop in living standards, nutrition deteriorated significantly, especially among the poor.[75] Those at high risk included infants, preschool- and schoolchildren, pregnant women, and lactating mothers. The quality of food in the FRY also worsened. Almost every second sample tested in 1994 failed to meet prewar quality standards. Every second hospitalized child was reported to be anemic, while regular school checkups also indicated that children were routinely undernourished—they were not getting enough milk, meat, vegetables, and fruit, and their diets had energy deficits of 20 to 40 percent.

In spite of the humanitarian exemptions to sanctions, physicians in the FRY faced a critical shortage of certain vaccines, including those for measles, mumps, and rubella.[76] Immunizations are generally carried out through the outdated mode of vaccination drives, which lend themselves to additional sanctions-related problems, including shortages of vehicles, spare parts, and fuel.[77] These conditions resulted in a drop in the number of children vaccinated and an increase in epidemics of several diseases that formerly were almost eradicated.[78] In 1992 and 1993, the number of patients suffering from polio in Kosovo rose significantly, with the risk of a more widespread epidemic.[79]

The infant mortality rate (IMR) in the FRY is much higher than in most countries with similar levels of economic development. After dropping continuously from 1971 to 1991 (from 51.4 to 20.9 per 1,000 live births), the IMR increased in 1992 and 1993, (from 21.7 to 21.9 per 1,000 live births).[80] This represents an increase from 1991 to 1993 of 1 additional infant death in every 1,000 births.[81] Regional differences were pronounced, with the largest increase in Montenegro (11.2 per 1,000 live births in 1991 to 15 per 1,000 live births in 1993).[82] The IMR reported in Kosovo (33.6 and 33.3 per 1,000 live births, respectively, for 1991 and 1993) is the highest rate in Europe, including Macedonia and Albania (both 28 per 1,000 live births in 1991); however, these figures may reflect errors due to nonreporting or inaccurate classification, particularly given the parallel health care system of Kosovo Albanians.[83]

Perinatal and early neonatal mortality also increased, while post-neonatal mortality remained almost the same. These trends indicate deteriorating conditions and quality of services in hospitals, where most deliveries take place. Maternal mortality increased from 9 to 16 maternal deaths per 100,000 live births between 1992 and 1993.[84] The under-five mortality rate (per 1,000 live births) is a good indicator of the broader health status of a population. In the FRY, under-five mortality increased from 24.1 per 1,000 live births in 1991 to 24.9 per 1,000 live births in 1993. It rose the most in Montenegro, by 4 deaths per 1,000 live births; in Vojvodina it rose by 3 deaths; in Central Serbia it rose by 2 deaths; and in Kosovo it remained nearly the same, but, again, this may be indicative of underregistration. Children under five mostly died of respiratory diseases (20 percent); unknown causes or insufficiently defined conditions (16.1 percent); intestinal infections (15.6 percent); and fractures and other injuries (7.8 percent). These deaths undoubtedly would not have occurred with the presanctions health care services.

As a consequence of the sanctions and the ongoing economic crisis, access to health care services became increasingly unequal, and health care became accessible only for the wealthy. Many physicians transferred from the public health system to the private sector because of a lack of resources and finances. Others, often the most qualified, left the country. In the state system, the use of both out- and in-patient services dropped drastically between 1989 and 1993; the decline in the use of preventive services was even more alarming.[85] For example, the number of visits to family planning units dropped by 47 percent; pregnancy counseling dropped by 25 percent; regular checkups in health centers aimed at early detection of diseases in children and youth dropped by 28 percent; and, although compulsory for infants, preschool and school-age children, immunizations also dropped significantly during this same period.

In response to these conditions and sanctions, in 1993 and 1994 the government passed legislation to try to ease some of the strains on the health system. In 1994, the Republic of Serbia ensured the right to health care by passing the Health Care Programme During the Implementation of International Sanctions, adopted in keeping with the Strategy and Measures for Ensuring Health Care During the Implementation of Sanctions by International Organizations, passed by the Serbian government on 7 April 1993.[86] At the end of August 1994 the federal government announced a priority list of diseases and patient categories. Children under eighteen years old, pregnant women, mothers of infants, mentally handicapped persons, diabetics, and kidney and cancer patients were to be given priority. However, there were subsequent reports about the discontinuation of treatment of elderly patients with cancer.[87] After the economic reforms in January 1994, the provision of state health care services improved somewhat.[88] Pharmacies were better supplied with drugs, primarily the most frequently prescribed drugs from the list of essential drugs covered by health insurance. Hospitals were also better supplied with materials required for treating patients.

Authorized in 1990, over 3,000 private health care institutions sprang up to service the growing number of persons who could not receive care from the 309 state-operated facilities.[89] This expansion in private care was helpful to those patients who could pay for services but of limited utility to the vast majority of those unable to pay or uninsured. In addition, private sector services were often those that the state could no longer provide because of broken equipment or shortages of medical supplies, even though these services are normally part of the insurance package. Some private centers reportedly exploited the fact that their patients were insured, having some lab analyses done in state health centers, even though they were private organizations. These factors increased access and availability of critical health care services to those who could pay while limiting both for the bulk of the population as resources and physicians were removed from the state-funded health care system.

In a July 1994 rapid health assessment of a sample of 840 households in two districts of Serbia,[90] UNICEF found that 81 percent of the households surveyed believed that it was more difficult for them to get health care. Twenty-nine percent said that they had difficulties getting medical assistance for sick children, and 39 percent had trouble obtaining urgent services for adults. The primary reasons given (in descending order) were shortages of medicines, lack of money to pay for checkups or prescribed drugs, and impossibly long waiting times. Seventeen percent said that they were in need of urgent medical assistance, while one-third said that they had difficulty getting medical care because of a lack of gasoline or money.

The study also found that although in-patient admissions to hospitals were down, households generally did not have problems that necessitated in-patient treatment.[91] For example, only 3 percent of the households surveyed had members who were not admitted when necessary because they were told that their condition was not an emergency or because they were unable to cover costs in advance or buy drugs and other medical supplies. The worst period was during 1993, when patients had to bring with them to hospitals required drugs and supplies, including food. By 1994, this practice reportedly was no longer necessary. Of the households surveyed, UNICEF reported the following results: 13 percent were in need of surgical intervention and three-fourths of these received it; 14 percent were required to provide surgical material on their own; 4 percent had to pay in advance; 23 percent of hospitalization requests were turned down; 50 percent of hospitalization requests were postponed because they were not an emergency; and one-third decided not to have an operation because they had to pay in advance or provide supplies.

In September 1994, UNICEF sponsored another study that polled some 500 Serbian citizens over eighteen years of age. It examined, among other things, the use of health care services in the private health care sector and the health care costs incurred by the respondents over the previous three months. Among those surveyed, 57 percent had contact with the private health care sector. Over half of them used the services of private pharmacies; 16 percent used dental surgeries; 5 percent used private doctor's offices; and 5 percent saw private opticians. The most frequently used special medical services were ultrasound diagnostics (0.1 percent) and gynecological services (0.4 percent). Forty-five percent paid in full for the drugs prescribed; 5 percent paid for their visit to the doctor's office; 1 percent paid for hospital treatment; 1 percent paid for therapy; and 2 percent paid for diagnostic services.

Water and Sanitation

Yugoslavia has sufficient quantities of fresh water. Only 2 percent of the water supplied is used for domestic consumption; the rest goes to industry and agriculture.[91] Three-fourths of all drinking water comes from underground springs. Sixty-nine percent of Serbia's population and 68 percent of Montenegro's had access to piped water in 1989. Access was about 10 percent higher in Vojvodina and 35 percent lower in Kosovo.

There were also striking differences between urban and rural access; in 1989, for example, 91 percent of the urban population reportedly had access to piped water, while only 53 percent of the rural population had such access.

Access to sanitation in the FRY is defined as a connection to a central-ized sewerage system. According to this definition, 57.5 percent of the population had access in 1989: 79 percent of those living in urban areas, and 36 percent of those living in rural areas.

In both 1994 and 1995, UNICEF reported that the most noticeable effect of the crises on water and sanitation was the deterioration in water qual-ity due to the scarcity of chemicals that were blocked by sanctions.[92] In some areas near Bosnia, water was also frequently cut off because of the war. In addition to a lack of chemicals for water treatment, public health institutes charged with quality control faced numerous difficulties in monitoring and testing. Sanctions prohibited the import of equipment for lab analysis, spare parts, and fuel for the vehicles used to collect samples.

In 1988, about 3 percent and 23 percent of water samples tested by the Serbian Institute for Public Health (and 15.3 percent and 13.7 percent of samples tested by the federal institute for the whole country) failed tests for bacteriological and chemical contamination, respectively. By 1992, the figures for Serbia had increased to 40 percent and 62 percent, respective-ly. Among the chemical pollutants listed were nitrates and compounds of iron, manganese, and ammonia.

As a result, water-borne and water-related diseases increased during the sanctions period. For example, an outbreak of shigella with about 1,500 cases, 70.4 percent of which were children, was reported in Mace-donia in October 1993; a few instances were also reported in central Ser-bia. A study at the end of 1992 by the health institute in Novi Sad showed that the number of water-borne diseases had increased tenfold in Vojvod-ina since 1991.

Reflective of Serbia's ability to produce most of its own food with a large surplus for export, there was, by February 1994, no apparent starva-tion reported in spite of increasing impoverishment of the population.[93] As in the health sector, however, the collapse of the economy combined with economic sanctions to result in unequal access to food. Urban poor were particularly at risk, because they had little access to land to grow their own food and because sanctions prohibited the import of fuel, spare parts, equipment, and other items necessary for harvesting, transporting, and distributing food and other agricultural products to the city and beyond. Farmers often were not able to keep their trucks in good working order. At other times they could not find any fuel, or they had to purchase what little was available at astronomical prices on the black market. For these reasons, sanctions seemed to have a stronger negative humanitarian impact in urban areas than in the countryside, where food was more readily available. There were also reports of trucks being held for days at the FRY's border until necessary authorizations were obtained from the UN sanctions committee. The trucks' cargoes often spoiled during these delays.

Over time, these problems affected virtually everyone in the FRY, including the middle class. In December 1993, a bread line in the center of Belgrade reportedly formed as early as 1:00 A.M. and eventually stretched for three miles. A local charity had been giving out twenty thousand packages of food (including bread, vegetable oil, and salt) every Saturday for the previous two months. As one reporter noted, many of the people waiting in line were well-dressed, middle-class people in suits and fur coats. Sanctions had destroyed their livelihoods, even if their wardrobes were intact.[94]

The Impact of Sanctions on Education

The combined sanctions and economic crisis also greatly affected social conditions and the provision of social services throughout the FRY. Before the crisis, the FRY had a well-developed network of public institutions that provided almost complete coverage not only for health care and good access to safe water and sanitation but also to other social services, particularly education. In 1994, public expenditures for social care (including children, adult, and elderly) accounted for 0.7 percent of the country's social product.[95] The social welfare system in the FRY provided a much needed safety net for many of the country's poor.[96] With the collapse of the economy, the government became increasingly unable to meet the social needs of the population. Dwindling resources threatened the quality of social services as well as the possibility of implementing an effective social welfare policy. At the same time, the needs of the population increased dramatically owing to the sharp decline in living standards and increasing poverty brought on by the war, the economic crisis, and international sanctions. The social-psychological consequences of the war and an influx of refugees strained an already thin social support network. As Yugoslavia's social product dropped, the resources allocated to social services decreased by more than half, in real terms, which meant a continual deterioration of infrastructure, shortages of essential materials, and no new investments.[97]

Sanctions and the overall economic crisis created serious problems in the education system at all levels.[98] In some ways, this sector is easier to quantify, and its in-depth discussion here serves by analogy to suggest deterioration in all social services during this period. Access to education, previously free and available to all, became increasingly unequal.[99] By 1994, municipalities could fund only 25 to 40 percent of schools' operational costs, and other enterprises could no longer make up the shortfall; although secondary and high school education formerly had been free for all but part-time students, 20 percent of the students in this age group had to pay a fee by this time.[100] The decreased availability of public schools and the decline in their quality due to cutbacks meant that increasingly only children from wealthy families would have access to a decent education. Although school attendance in the FRY was generally high (95.5 percent), tuition and other associated costs proved to be one of the major reasons why children no longer could attend even poor schools.[101] In household surveys conducted throughout the FRY by CIET international in March 1994, over 40 percent of the children not attending school said that their nonattendance was for financial reasons; out of the children who should have been in secondary school, every second child said that finances prevented them from attending (48 percent).[102]

Financial constraints were even more common in Kosovo than in other regions in the FRY. Sixty-seven percent of the children not in school in Kosovo said their nonattendance was due to finances, compared with 35 percent in other regions. In rural areas, 56 percent cited financial constraints, compared with 6 percent in urban areas.[103] Moreover, while available funds had been cut more than half, the influx of refugees caused schools to increase their capacity by up to 10 percent.[104]

The economic crisis helped to create alarming conditions in school buildings and classrooms. In 1994, only 39 percent of all school buildings were in good condition; 37 percent were in need of repair or partial replacement; 16 percent were in need of reconstruction or total replacement; 7 percent were dilapidated; and 1.6 percent were not completed.[105] About 7,000 pupils attended classes in schools without a power supply, while 30,000 attended schools without toilets. Heating was a serious problem in the long and bitter winters in the region because of the shortage of fuel resulting from the sanctions as well as a lack of money to buy what fuel might be available. Temperatures in classrooms often reached far below the minimum required temperature of 18 degrees Celsius (about 65 degrees Fahrenheit) so that children often had to study in their winter coats. In 1994, schools were forced to take a longer Christmas break than usual.

The abysmal economic conditions also caused a scarcity of supplies, equipment, and teaching materials. Most schools were unable to provide even basic supplies such as chalk and erasers, spare light bulbs, window panes, or hygiene supplies, not to mention books and modern teaching aids.[106] Only one-third of all schools had any sort of library. Because of the restrictions on imports, the commodities necessary for producing text-books, school materials, and teaching aids were also banned. In 1994, UNICEF reported that one set of school supplies was worth three average annual salaries. Owing to the restrictions sanctions placed on education-al and cultural exchanges, regional and bilateral cooperation in education almost completely ceased. Exclusion from international cooperation and information exchange made it difficult to provide the quality of education necessary for economic growth and development.[107]

Yugoslavia traditionally has had a high literacy rate. In 1981, only 10.8 percent of the total population was illiterate.[108] In 1995, UNICEF reported that 5 to 10 percent of children were not enrolled in primary school, even though enrollment was compulsory; 10 to 15 percent in the last primary grade failed to graduate; and 30 percent of the relevant age did not con-tinue after elementary school.[109] In 1994, CIET international found that rural children were twice as likely as urban children not to be in school. Children of the unemployed, those who were living from savings or humanitarian aid, were several times more likely not to be in school than the children of office workers (22 percent compared to 6 percent).[110] The long-term consequences of nonattendance, including a drop in literacy, will make themselves felt for the foreseeable future. As elsewhere, the most pronounced impact will be on the poor and disadvantaged.

The impacts of the crisis were also felt at the university level and recorded by CIET international. In 1993, the University of Belgrade scaled down its operations, halting production and purchase of all scientific pub-lications. Departments were given only 3 to 4 percent of the funds required for normal operations. The monthly salary of full professors with thirty years of experience was the equivalent of $62; staff technicians received about $25 per month. Requests for heating oil had already been turned down by authorities, who said that even hospital requests were not being approved. In June 1993, deans of several colleges at the Univer-sity of Belgrade warned that the colleges would not be able to open in the fall because of the sanctions. Faculty from archaeology, engineering, and technology claimed to be facing almost complete collapse; veterinary medicine faculty said that they had no funds for fieldwork that was an essential part of their core curriculum; and mining professors warned that they had nothing in the labs to work with because they hadn't been able to buy a single chemical substance for a year.[111]

Other universities also closed or, for the first time, began charging tuition. For example, the medical school in Novi Sad decided to charge $7,000 per year and teach in English in the hope of attracting foreign students. Sanctions also contributed to the flight of some of the best and brightest from the FRY. Vlastimir Matejic, who served as minister for science and technology in the short-lived cabinet of Prime Minister Milan Panic, estimated that 20 percent of the researchers working in the natural sciences and technology had left the country in 1992 alone.[112]

The Political Context and Civil Society under Sanctions

A significant if normally ignored consequence of sanctions stemmed from the ban on educational, scientific, and cultural exchanges. Although not necessary under Resolution 757, sanctions were extended to educational cooperation among scholars. France and Germany suspended their support to language and cultural instruction for pupils from Serbia and Montenegro. Isolating the intellectual and academic elite had disastrous, even if unintended, consequences. In particular, it cut off the very people most likely to oppose the war in Bosnia and denied them the critical support from the international community that might have facilitated internal change and fostered opposition to Milosevic's policies.

On the humanitarian front, physicians and others felt extremely frustrated, and later demoralized, by their inability to communicate and exchange scientific and professional information with the outside world. More important, as the sanctions regime continued and negative humanitarian effects increased, the need to consult with other professionals grew. The Serbian Medical Association and other scientists went to great lengths to document reliably the humanitarian crisis and the range of negative impacts in order to support their requests for critical medicines and humanitarian supplies. For example, although it was one of the founding and most active members, the Serbian Medical Association's membership was suspended during the Forty-sixth General Assembly of the WHO in 1993. Serbian doctors registered their complaints and noted the special duty of physicians to be neutral and provide medical care to all, regardless of politics and factors other than medical considerations.[113]

The ban on cultural, scientific, and educational exchange was counterproductive in that it isolated the few independent media still left in Serbia and Montenegro. Over the years, Milosevic had consolidated much of his power by implementing tight controls and limiting both the flow and the content of public information. Although one radio and television station and two independent papers existed, they had few resources and were greatly limited in what they could report. Isolating them even further helped consolidate Milosevic's power and increased public support for the war in Bosnia. Most Serbs saw themselves as victims of the world's aggression. Denying them independent reports of alternate perspectives contributed to the misinformation provided in the mainstream media.

The relatively small antiwar movement in Serbia—including the Belgrade Circle, the Center for Antiwar Action, and others—tirelessly fought the government's policies in Bosnia and Croatia. Occasional antiwar demonstrations as well as theater and other cultural events were complements to the opposition parties in parliament that had, to varying degrees, antiwar platforms. At the same time, some people in the antiwar movement supported—or at least understood—the imposition of sanctions. Many also recognized that lifting sanctions, once imposed, was a sensitive question of timing because doing so could "reward" Milosevic and send the wrong message in support of the war. Sanctions thus hurt the antiwar movement and civil society as a whole because they dealt a crushing blow to the independent media. With critical material embargoed and independent agencies and philanthropic groups constrained from providing grants and travel resources, the few existing oppositional voices were even more easily silenced.[114]

Conclusion

Like many other half-articulated and partially implemented policies used by outsiders to influence the behavior of participants in Yugoslavia's wars, sanctions were much less effective politically than they might have been, and they certainly provided too little and too late, especially for the Bosnian Muslims. Yet the delay is attributable not to sanctions per se but to decisions by the West and the United Nations to pursue sanctions as a preferred instrument of policy throughout much of the four years of violent conflict without more vigorous diplomacy and military action as part of a cohesive strategy.

The analysis of the economic situation in Serbia and Montenegro demonstrates that sanctions were one of several factors contributing to disastrous economic circumstances facing citizens and political authorities. As the decade commenced, the various economic (and soon to be distinctly political) regions of what had been the Yugoslav federated state faced a debt crisis brought on by a decade of borrowing that had not resulted in economic growth. This crisis was amplified by the structural shocks of attempting to reorient the economy throughout the early 1990s to an unabashed open market. With the breakup of the former state into a number of new entities and the emergence of intranational violence, earlier trading patterns disappeared. This dissolution and the economic impact of the war itself soon combined to wreak economic havoc. As a final layer of hardship, sanctions effectively removed foreign commerce as a way of compensating for the loss of internal trade. In many ways, the greatest negative impact of sanctions was to delay the resolution of some of the economic and social conditions underlying the war, including the FRY's transition to a democracy and market economy, as well as its effective integration into Europe.[115]

The dramatic declines in per capita income and overall economic growth resulting from sanctions and the general political crisis had negative, but not disastrous, humanitarian effects for citizens of Serbia and Montenegro. Humanitarian crises, in the form of the dire need for lifesaving emergency supplies to besieged populations, appeared throughout the war. But they occurred most acutely and frequently in Bosnia, where Serbs holding towns hostage refused to permit relief supplies to reach the suffering, as opposed to the sanctioned parts of the FRY. There is no small irony, however, in the fact that many of the humanitarian needs in Serbia and Montenegro were brought about by UN decisions to impose sanctions, which the UN system and NGOs were then called upon to help mitigate.

Were sanctions *necessary* to compel action by Slobodan Milosevic? Or would he have finally complied because of the ongoing economic and social disintegration already under way? If these factors still would not have led him to the negotiating table, would not the changed circumstances and the facts on the ground in Bosnia (Croatian retaking of the Krajina; the strengthening of the Croatian and Bosnian Federation, including military capabilities; and the "map" emerging in Bosnia itself) themselves have done so by the summer of 1995?

On balance, it seems difficult to argue with the view that sanctions alone failed to force the warring parties in the former Yugoslavia to negotiate. Certainly the sanctions and their effects provided Milosevic with a face-saving tool with which to fight the internal political forces in the FRY who still supported the war. Yet in the longer term, mounting international pressures of varying sorts and internal war weariness, especially significant economic dislocations of which sanctions were surely a part, also played a role in stimulating peace talks. In the shorter term, the successful Croatian military blitzkrieg of August-September 1995 brought the benefits of a cease-fire into clearer focus for some of the parties. The more assertive military stance by the North Atlantic Treaty Organization also seems to have played a particularly persuasive role in moving the

Bosnian Serbs to negotiate.[116]

In light of the military and other factors that contributed to the final settlement in Dayton, the assertion of the 1996 UN report that sanctions were "the single most important reason"[117] for Serbian acceptance of a negotiated peace settlement is open to challenge. Nonetheless, even if sanctions were not the decisive factor, they seem to have been at least a contributing factor in pressuring the government in Belgrade to moderate its policies. The fact that the Milosevic regime severed its ties with the Bosnian Serbs in 1994, prior to the shift in battlefield fortunes in 1995, is particularly significant in suggesting that the coercive pressure of sanctions influenced policymaking in Belgrade. The UN report's conclusion that the sanctions "modified the behavior of the Serbian Party"[118] seems legitimate. Sanctions were effective, at least partially, in convincing Belgrade to shift its policies toward support of a negotiated solution. As one of many political, military, and economic factors, sanctions contributed to the deteriorating gains and increasing costs that Milosevic associated with his support of the Bosnian Serbs.

Notes

The authors are especially grateful to George A. Lopez for his guidance and efforts in improving the argument and presentation of this chapter.

1. For a discussion of these phases and trends, see Richard Ullman, "Introduction: The World and Yugoslavia's Wars" and "The Wars in Yugoslavia and the International System after the Cold War," in *The World and Yugoslavia's Wars*, ed. Richard Ullman (New York: Council on Foreign Relations Press, 1996), 1–41; and Susan L. Woodward, "The Use of Sanctions in the Former Yugoslavia: Misunderstanding Political Realities," in *Economic Sanctions: Panacea or Peacebuilding in a Post–Cold War World?* ed. David Cortright and George A. Lopez (Boulder, Colo.: Westview, 1995), 141–52.

2. For a discussion of the UN incapacity in this regard, see Thomas G. Weiss, "Collective Spinelessness: U.N. Actions in Former Yugoslavia," in *The World and Yugoslavia's Wars*, ed. Ullman, 59–96.

3. *Report of the Copenhagen Roundtable on United Nations Sanctions in the Case of the Former Yugoslavia, held at Copenhagen on 24 and 25 June 1996*, Annex prepared by the Security Council Committee established pursuant to resolution 724 (1991) concerning Yugoslavia, S/1996/776, 24 September 1996, 3.

4. Edward M. Luttwak, "Toward Post-Heroic Warfare," *Foreign Affairs* 74, no. 3 (May/June 1995):118.

5. A full and nuanced account of the complex set of factors that led to the breakup of Yugoslavia is beyond the scope of this chapter. This section highlights the major factors that relate to sanctions and humanitarianism. This context

derives from the better sources in the field, notably Susan L. Woodward, *Balkan Tragedy: Chaos and Dissolution after the Cold War* (Washington, D.C.: Brookings Institution, 1995); Warren Zimmermann, "Origins of a Catastrophe: Memoirs of the Last American Ambassador to Yugoslavia," *Foreign Affairs* 74, no. 2 (March/April 1995): 2–21; Steven Burg and Paul Shoup, *Ethnic Conflict and International Intervention: The Crisis in Bosnia-Herzegovina, 1990–1993* (New York: M. E. Sharpe, 1994); and Misha Glenny, *The Fall of Yugoslavia: The Third Balkan War*, rev. ed. (New York: Penguin Books, 1994).

6. Data from the 1991 census, discussed in Steven L. Berg, "Why Yugoslavia Fell Apart," *Current History* 92, no. 577 (November 1993): 358.

7. Albanian pronunciation is *Kosova*, but for purposes of this article the traditional spelling and pronunciation are used.

8. For discussion of this strategy and action at varying times during the wars, see Ian Lupis, *War Crimes in Bosnia-Herzegovina* (New York: Human Rights Watch/Helsinki, 1994); and Human Rights Watch/Helsinki, *Bosnia and Herzegovina: The Unindicted, Reaping the Rewards of "Ethnic Cleansing"* (New York: Human Rights Watch, 1997).

9. Woodward, *Balkan Tragedy*. The following section draws upon her chap. 3, 47–81.

10. The observations conform to the classic appeal of sanctions in many situations; see George A. Lopez and David Cortright, "The Sanctions Era: An Alternative to Military Intervention," *Fletcher Forum of World Affairs* 19, no. 2 (Summer/Fall 1995): 78–81. As regards these approaches in this case, see Woodward, *Balkan Tragedy*, 144–45. See also her "Use of Sanctions in Former Yugoslavia: Misunderstanding Political Realities," in *Economic Sanctions*, 141–51. The authors draw heavily upon her framework in this chapter.

11. In fact, the situation on the U.S. side was even more confused and counterproductive. The suspension of U.S. aid took the form of the Nickles amendment, which actually had been passed at the end of 1990 to come into effect automatically on 5 May 1991 if Serbian human rights violations against ethnic Albanians in Kosovo did not end. When Congress was not satisfied with Serb behavior in May, it let the amendment stand. But then Secretary of State James Baker exercised the executive right to grant a waiver and claimed that the Yugoslav government had met its pledges to the human rights framework of the Helsinki accords.

12. See the interpretation by Claudia von Braunmühl and Manfred Kulessa, *The Impact of UN Sanctions on Humanitarian Assistance Activities, A Report on a Study Commissioned by the United Nations Department of Humanitarian Affairs* (Berlin, December 1995), 12.

13. For an analysis of the general trends in these arms supplies to Bosnia and other conflicts, see Aaron Karp, "Small Arms: The New Major Weapons," and Michael T. Klare, "The Global Trade in Light Weapons and the International System in the Post–Cold War Era," both in *Lethal Commerce: The Global Trade in Small Arms and Light Weapons*, ed. Jeffrey Boutwell, Michael T. Klare, and Laura W. Reed (Cambridge: American Academy of Arts and Sciences, 1995), 17–30, 31–43, respectively.

14. von Braunmühl and Kulessa, *Impact of UN Sanctions*, 113.

15. For an assessment of the various European concerns and actions, see Stanley Hoffman, "Yugoslavia: Implications for Europe and European Institutions," in *The World and Yugoslavia's Wars*, ed. Ullman, 97–121.

16. Tom Hundley, "Embargo Softens Serb Hard-liners," *Chicago Tribune*, 21 October 1994, 6.

17. See von Braunmuhl and Kulessa, *Impact of UN Sanctions*, 113.

18. Tom Hundley, "Lessened Sanctions Still Crimp Yugoslavs: UN Extends Easing of Bans, Won't Go Further," *Chicago Tribune*, 14 January 1995, 1.

19. In light of the paucity of data on the economic and social impacts of sanctions in the FRY, statistics in the next two sections of this chapter rely extensively on two unpublished internal documents from UNICEF's Belgrade office, "A Situation Analysis of Women and Children in the Federal Republic of Yugoslavia 1994" and "A Situation Analysis of Women and Children in the Federal Republic of Yugoslavia 1995." These documents are cited with UNICEF's permission and hereafter are cited as "UNICEF 1994" and "UNICEF 1995."

20. "UNICEF 1994," 7; and "UNICEF 1995," 11.

21. "UNICEF 1995," 8.

22. The citation and preceding figures are from "UNICEF 1995," 12.

23. The economic statistics in the next three paragraphs are from "UNICEF 1995," 12.

24. "UNICEF 1995," 3, 8.

25. "UNICEF 1995," 8.

26. "UNICEF 1995," 3, 12.

27. "UNICEF 1995," 9.

28. "UNICEF 1995," 9.

29. "UNICEF 1995," 8.

30. "UNICEF 1995," 3, 9.

31. "Business in Serbia Crumbling," *Economist*, 14 August 1993, 65.

32. von Braunmühl and Kulessa, *Impact of UN Sanctions*, 120–23.

33. "UNICEF 1995," 9.

34. Data in this paragraph are from "UNICEF 1995," 8–10.

35. von Braunmühl and Kulessa, *Impact of UN Sanctions*, 65.

36. "UNICEF 1995," 9.

37. Data in the next three paragraphs are from "UNICEF 1994," 7–8.

38. Kifner, "For Belgrade's Broken Middle Class," A20.

39. Data in this paragraph are from "UNICEF 1994," 8.

40. "UNICEF 1995," 10.

41. Sonja Licht, "The Use of Sanctions in the Former Yugoslavia: Can They Assist in Conflict Resolution?" in *Economic Sanctions*, ed. Ullman, 158.

42. "UNICEF 1994," 8.

43. "UNICEF 1995," 10.

44. "A Price No One Can Justify," *Newsweek*, 6 December 1994, 31.

45. "Business in Serbia Crumbling," 65.

46. "UNICEF 1994," 9.

47. "UNICEF 1994," 13.

48. Data in this paragraph are from "UNICEF 1994," 14.

49. "UNICEF 1995," 14.

50. "UNICEF 1995," 13.

51. "UNICEF 1994," 9.

52. Community Information and Epidemiological Technologies International, *Social Conditions for Health in Serbia and Montenegro* (New York: CIET international, May 1994). Data in the following paragraphs are extracted from this report, in which one of the authors, Julia Devin, participated.

53. "UNICEF 1995," 13.

54. See "UNICEF 1995," 4, 23.

55. CIET, *Social Conditions;* see also "UNICEF 1994," 9.

56. "UNICEF 1995," 4, 23.

57. See CIET, *Social Conditions;* and "UNICEF 1995," 3, 24.

58. "UNICEF 1995," 24.

59. "UNICEF 1995," 38.

60. See for example, "UNICEF 1994," 18.

61. "UNICEF 1995," 25.

62. See "UNICEF 1994," 18; and "Humanitarian Aid for ex-Yugoslavia," WHO Area Office-Briefing for Interagency Mission in September 1993, prepared 27 August 1993, which cites 4,000 dialysis patients and difficulty maintaining equipment due to the sanctions as well as a shortage of drugs for chronic illnesses.

63. Personal interviews with physicians from the Serbian Medical Association conducted by Julia Devin in 1993–1994.

64. "A Price No One Can Justify," *Newsweek,* 6 December 1994.

65. "UNICEF 1995," 15.

66. "UNICEF 1994," 10; and "UNICEF 1995," 15.

67. "UNICEF 1994," 9.

68. "UNICEF 1995," 31; and "UNICEF 1994," 17.

69. "UNICEF 1995," 31.

70. See "UNICEF 1995," 31; and "UNICEF 1994," 17. The following discussion of health draws upon Mary Black, "Report," *British Medical Journal,* 30 October 1993, 1135–37.

71. "UNICEF 1995," 31.

72. Black, "Report," 1135.

73. Quoted in Black, "Report," 1135.

74. "UNICEF 1995," 31.

75. Data in this paragraph are from "UNICEF 1995," 39.

76. "UNICEF 1995," 5.

77. "UNICEF 1995," 35.

78. "UNICEF 1994," 13; and "UNICEF 1995," 34.

79. "UNICEF 1995," 5.

80. "UNICEF 1995," 19.

81. "UNICEF 1995," 38.

82. "UNICEF 1995," 19; and "UNICEF 1994," 12.

83. "UNICEF 1994," 12.

84. Data in this paragraph are from "UNICEF 1995," 38.

85. Data in this paragraph are from "UNICEF 1995," 38.

86. "UNICEF 1995," 33.

87. "UNICEF 1994," 13.

88. "UNICEF 1995," 34.

89. "UNICEF 1995," 32–33.

90. Data in the next three paragraphs are from "UNICEF 1995," 35–36.

91. Data in this paragraph are from "UNICEF 1995," 22.

92. Data in the next three paragraphs are from "UNICEF 1994," 22–23.

93. "The Sanctions Alternative," *Economist*, 12 February 1994.

94. Kifner, "For Belgrade's Broken Middle Class," A20.

95. "UNICEF 1995," 28.

96. "UNICEF 1995," 3–4.

97. "UNICEF 1995," 3–4, 13–14.

98. "UNICEF 1994," 21.

99. "UNICEF 1995," 40.

100. "UNICEF 1994," 22.

101. "UNICEF 1994," 19–22.

102. This section draws upon CIET, *Social Conditions*, and Julia Devin's direct observations.

103. CIET, *Social Conditions*, 21.

104. "UNICEF 1994," 22.

105. School data are from "UNICEF 1995," 42.

106. "UNICEF 1994," 21.

107. "UNICEF 1995," 41.

108. "UNICEF 1994," 21; and "UNICEF 1995," 44.

109. "UNICEF 1995," 43.

110. CIET, *Social Conditions*, 20.

111. Dusko Doder, "UN Sanctions on Serbia Devastate Its Colleagues," *Chronicle of Higher Education* 39 (9 June 1993): A33.

112. "Economic Sanctions, Fighting in Bosnia Prompt Scholars to Flee Yugoslavia: 20 Percent of Scientists Leave Country; U. of Belgrade Loses Hundreds of Staff Members," *Chronicle of Higher Education* 39 (5 May 1993): A41–A43.

113. See Milan Popovic, president, Ethics Committee of the Serbian Medical Association, "Letter to the Attention of the President of 46th General Assembly of WHO and Related Associates," published in *The Impact of UN Security Council Sanctions on the Health of the Population of FR Yugoslavia*, a collection from the Federal Ministry of Labour, Health and Social Policy, The Federal Institute for Public Health, the Ministry for Health of the Republic of Serbia, Belgrade, 7 April 1994.

114. Licht, "Use of Sanctions," 158.

115. See Woodward, "Misunderstanding Political Realities."

116. See Dick A. Leurdijk, *The United Nations and NATO in Former Yugoslavia, 1991–1996: Limits to Diplomacy and Force* (The Hague: Netherlands Atlantic Commission, 1996).

117. *Report of the Copenhagen Roundtable*, 3.

118. *Report of the Copenhagen Roundtable*, 13.

6

Humanitarian Effects of the Coup and Sanctions in Haiti

Sarah Zaidi

On 8 October 1991, the Organization of American States (OAS) imposed trade sanctions, allowing exemptions for humanitarian assistance, against Haiti's de facto government and its military rulers. They were prescribed in response to the military coup, organized by General Raoul Cédras and police chief Michel François, that had ousted the seven-month-old government of democratically elected President Jean-Bertrand Aristide. The coup unleashed a campaign of terror and repression against the civilian population, including extrajudicial executions, disappearances, torture, rape, limitations on freedom of association and assembly, and disruption in personal and professional activities.[1]

From the beginning, the political will to enforce sanctions was lacking because the sanctions were not in response to an internationally perceived threat to peace and security. The OAS, in June 1991, had ratified the Santiago accord mandating the nonrecognition of a regime that seized power from a popularly elected government and restoring the constitutional government. Haiti was the first test. Perhaps most important, the United

Figure 6.1 Haiti

189

States did not take action to ensure that sanctions were internationally respected. Sanctions were porous, were only halfheartedly maintained by many OAS members, and were not binding on states outside the OAS. As a result, illegal and legal trade flourished, and the military junta and those close to it profited. Over the course of the next three years, sanctions were progressively tightened, as the United States and the United Nations Security Council supported these measures; but questions about sanctions compliance persisted.

Assessing the humanitarian effects of these sanctions is a complex challenge. The effects of sanctions cannot be separated from the human rights abuses perpetrated by the coup and Haiti's deep-rooted and widespread poverty. Prior to sanctions, the majority of Haitians were already living on the margins of society and suffered many hardships. Sanctions resulted in inflation, as the value of the Haitian gourde declined against the U.S. dollar, and everything became more expensive. But the coup was responsible for much of the suffering, since the political violence prevented Haitians from earning a living wage or using services. Wage earners were afraid to go to work; and as the price of transport increased, many found it unprofitable to show up at their jobs. Peasants, representing 70 percent of the population, were unable to engage in agricultural activities and were actively targeted by the military junta as part of the ongoing political repression. As a result, local production declined. Although deeply affected by sanctions, the poor supported the economic embargo and wanted tighter enforcement. By contrast, the well-off elites were far less hurt by sanctions but lamented that the sanctions were hurting the poor and should be lifted.

International agencies reacted to the effects of sanctions but failed to acknowledge the underlying political context of the coup. As individuals, staff recognized the severity of repression. But as representatives of their agencies, they ignored political realities and focused strictly on the humanitarian effects of sanctions. The impression given by international agencies, operating both inside and outside Haiti, was one of deteriorating health and environmental conditions. However, during the three years (1991–1994), no new research was conducted either by the UN agencies or by nongovernmental organizations (NGOs). Hence no reliable statistics exist for this period. Although it is impossible to quantify the humanitarian impact, several trends can be discerned by directly examining the flows of humanitarian assistance and by extracting from the experience of community-based groups and projects.

UN agencies and NGOs responded by providing such traditional humanitarian assistance as food; but water and sanitation projects, considered part of the development agenda, were halted. Moreover, food assistance, often in the form of cooked meals, was targeted for certain areas and was politically motivated. Despite the circumscribed focus of humanitarian assistance, these agencies played a part in the broader politicization of sanctions—a nonforcible, international coercive instrument frequently used to address political problems rather than forcible military intervention.

The experience of community-based and international nongovernmental organizations interviewed for this study is summarized below. First, activities of all programs such as agricultural development, water and sanitation, women's issues, education, and good governance were halted. Community-based health programs were temporarily interrupted and faced greater operational constraints than in earlier years. Second, the health care providers reported a drop in the number of patients seen but noted an increase in the rate of certain illnesses, such as tuberculosis, typhoid, and other water-borne diseases. Third, most service providers (health or clerics) interviewed felt a marked demoralization, indifference, and helplessness amongst the staff, including themselves, and those Haitians coming to seek assistance.

This paper focuses on the humanitarian effects of sanctions vis-à-vis the coup and evaluates the international responses. It seeks to determine whether sanctions effectively targeted the military junta. Were the three years of sanctions an important factor in bringing about the exit of the military rulers? The first section briefly presents the economic, social, and political background of Haiti that is essential to situate a judgment about sanctions. There follows an examination of the period of the coup, the sanctions, and diplomatic responses. Next, humanitarian effects and subsequent responses are analyzed. Finally, there is a discussion of the extent of the success (or failure) of sanctions in achieving the political goal of forcing Cédras from power and restoring the popularly elected Aristide government and of whether the humanitarian consequences justified this result.

Background to the Crisis

Haiti, the first black republic in the New World, has often been in a state of crisis.[2] In 1804 the enslaved people of Haiti declared independence, only to find themselves in a world hostile to self-governing blacks. Economic divisions within Haitian society led to political polarization between those wanting to engage in world trade and those interested in subsistence agriculture. The peasantry lost out to new masters from the commercial class, who were backed by the military. The clash over economic priorities resulted in political instability and provided the United States a pretext for invading Haiti. After nineteen years of occupation that ended in 1934, the United States left behind the Garde d'Haiti, later known as the Forces Armées d'Haiti (FADH), to protect American interests and investments.

In 1957, Dr. François Duvalier, favorite of the army and Washington, came to power. Under "Papa Doc" state repression, exercised through paramilitary forces responsible only to him, was aimed at eliminating political opposition, in particular those trying to change social and economic conditions. After the death of his father in 1971, Jean-Claude Duvalier took over as president for life. He attempted to diversify the economy by giving foreign investors favorable terms to encourage manufacturing industries. However, for the most part, the lack of infrastructure such as electricity, roads, and running water did not attract investment beyond the boundary of Port-au-Prince, the Haitian capital. The vast majority of Haitians, particularly in rural areas, remained poor and saw little or no improvement in their lives (see table 6.1). Large flows of international aid produced few tangible results among the poor.

In recent decades, the peasants began to organize at the grassroots level and in church communities to address the structural causes of their poverty.[3] Inspired by liberation theology, the poor struggled to improve their situation both economically and socially and to protect their interests against external forces.[4] In the urban streets, *ti legliz* (little churches) served as agents of change. In early 1987, Duvalier and his family were forced to leave Haiti in the face of popular uprisings, work stoppages, and school strikes, as the Haitian grassroots movement surged forward to mobilize openly and participate in the political process.

The Constitutional Referendum of 1987 served as a catalyst for democratic change, only to be crushed by the military in the public murders of two presidential candidates and a gruesome massacre of voters at a polling place on 29 November 1987. Since the massacre had been witnessed by foreign and local journalists, Washington suspended aid, although secretly the security forces continued to receive $10 million a year from the Central Intelligence Agency (CIA).[5] The military remained in power until the government of Supreme Court judge Ertha Pascal Trouillot managed (with help from the international community) to organize the first free and fair elections in Haitian history on 16 December 1990. Jean-Bertrand Aristide, a parish priest in Cité Soleil and leader of the popular political movement Lavalas, was swept into office with 67 percent of the vote.

Table 6.1
Trends in Indicators of Development

Real Gross Domestic Product (purchasing power parity, dollars)	
1960	921
1987	925
1993	1,050
Life Expectancy (years)	
1960	42.2
1975	50.0
1987	55.0
1993	56.2
Under-Five Mortality Rate (per 1,000 births)	
1960	294
1988	171
1995	127
Population with Access to Potable Water (percent)	
1975	12
1985	35
1990–95	28

Source: Information in this table is adapted from the United Nations Development Programme, *Human Development Report 1990, 1994, and 1996* (New York: Oxford University Press, 1990, 1994, and 1996).

From the start, amidst the hopes of the majority and the fears of the minority, the conflict between pro- and anti-Aristide forces politicized all aspects of Haitian society. For the vast majority of Haitians, especially the peasants, the political and social movement that brought Aristide to power was a symbol of "real" change. This represented an emphatic no to the military, paramilitary forces, extortion, repression, and lack of state accountability, and a long-awaited yes to economic and social justice. For the Haitian elite and the military, the new government meant unwelcome fiscal accountability and participation in building state structures. According to Claudette Werleigh, who afterwards served as foreign minister:

> While the elections of 1990 inspired hope for Haiti's impoverished majority, fear of losing their privileges and power struck the nation's economic elite. For the first time they found that it was not they who influenced the choice of the new government, nor the new president who had long advocated on behalf of the poor.[6]

The Life Cycle of the Coup

On 29 September 1991, Lt. Gen. Raoul Cédras halted the democratic process and forcibly seized the government. The familiar reign of military and paramilitary terror began again for the majority of Haitians, targeting the urban and rural supporters of Aristide and Lavalas. It is estimated that at least one thousand persons were killed in the first few weeks following the coup. Thousands more were arrested, beaten, and tortured.[7] These and other events in this section are found in summary form in table 6.2.

Despite diplomatic outcries from the OAS, little action was taken to restore Aristide. The OAS officially condemned the crisis and imposed trade sanctions against the military government, but the regional organization lacked the resources and political will to enforce these measures. When the first oil tanker, a Colombian ship flying the Liberian flag, delivered fuel after the coup to the military government and suffered no retaliatory measures, it became readily apparent that sanctions had little support (particularly from the United States). Few states cared about the restoration of the democratically elected government.

For the majority of Haitians, who had been exploited for more than two centuries and who were finally mobilized against what has become known as the "predatory" state, sanctions became a primary, perhaps the only outside, political symbol. Many hoped for stronger international intervention, such as military involvement or tightened enforcement. As diplomatic mission after diplomatic mission failed to affect the de facto government, Haitians began to believe that the OAS's efforts to restore Aristide had little chance of success, while the military was consolidating its power by adopting a Duvalierist form of governance.[8] OAS members were inconsistent in their responses, in particular the Republican administration of George Bush. Nonetheless, ongoing sanctions became a token of Haitian popular resistance, at whatever personal cost, and remained central to the struggle for democracy and the return of Aristide.[9]

The lack of response from Washington convinced the coup leaders that as time elapsed, they could be recognized as legitimate leaders of Haiti. There were several reasons for making such an assumption. First, as the violence and terror continued hand-in-hand with the failing diplomatic negotiations and ineffective sanctions, Haitian refugees began to flee on rickety boats for Miami. The Bush administration forcibly repatriated thousands, labeling them economic refugees and dismissing their claims of political asylum. President Bill Clinton continued with the policy of his predecessor, even though during his campaign he had promised to reverse it. Second, several months after the coup the Bush administration made special exemptions to the sanctions that allowed American businesses to maintain their export-assembly factory operations in Haiti.[10] Third, the CIA continued to support the military. There were numerous nocturnal flights. The purpose and contents of these flights were never publicly discussed, but several Haitians reported that these planes carried materials to refurbish the army. Later, other reports surfaced regarding CIA payments to Haitian officers, including Cédras, involved in drug trafficking.[11] Fourth, the CIA also initiated a smear campaign against Aristide, portraying him as psychologically unstable.

The UN Security Council began to take an active role in Haiti in early 1993, responding to a request by President Aristide for a human rights mission. In February, the UN and OAS sent a joint human rights mission to monitor abuses and political progress. Despite repeated human rights violations reported by the observers and concerns expressed over civilian safety, policymakers in Washington and New York downplayed the mission's efforts.[12] The Security Council, led by the U.S. administration, continued to follow inconsistent Cold War policies. UN and U.S. negotiators meanwhile tried to work out a diplomatic arrangement for the reinstatement of civilian government and amnesty for those who had orchestrated and participated in the coup. General Cédras, recognizing the inconsistencies and confusion within the international community, clung to his defiant position.

Frustrated with Cédras's refusal of an acceptable solution, the UN Security Council passed Resolution 841, which imposed more comprehensive sanctions in mid-June 1993, cutting off all fuel and arms. The United States imposed its own unilateral sanctions, freezing the assets of the members of the military junta. These more forceful measures seemed to have an immediate effect. A few days later, the military leaders came to the bargaining table, and in July the two sides negotiated a resolution of the crisis, the Governors Island agreement.

The ten-point accord, signed first by Cédras and then later, reluctantly, by Aristide, was fatally flawed. It allowed lifting sanctions once an interim government was named but before the actual transfer of power. It contained provisions to resume economic assistance to Haiti before Aristide's reinstatement. The agreement lacked an enforcement mechanism in the event of noncompliance, beyond the likelihood of renewed sanctions. International forces were to land before Aristide's return, but they were under strict orders not to intervene if they encountered human rights abuses.[13]

Mixed policy signals concerning the role of the military and its

Table 6.2

Time Line of Selected Events Related to the Imposition of Sanctions on Haiti

1991	
7 February	Jean-Bertrand Aristide is inaugurated as president.
29 September	Military coup led by Lt. Gen. Raul Cédras ousts Aristide. The coup unleashes violence and political repression.
6 October	OAS imposes regional sanctions that lack serious enforcement. Sanctions are porous and soon violated by vessels carrying fuel originating in an OAS member state.

1992	
January	Negotiations continue between the OAS and the military with a focus on installing an interim government. The military wants sanctions lifted. Talks fail. Meanwhile, repression prevails as thousands of Haitians flee.
August	Aristide requests that OAS sponsor a multinational mission to monitor human rights abuses and political progress. Instead of the 3,000 observers requested, only 18 are permitted by the military government.

1993	
January	Bill Clinton is inaugurated as U.S. president. During his electoral campaign, he had proposed a swift solution to the Haitian situation. But he alters position, in particular asylum for Haitian refugees.
February	A joint UN-OAS–sponsored civilian mission, with an additional 400 observers, is deployed to promote and protect human rights as guaranteed in the constitution. Despite repeated recommendations from the members of the mission to tighten sanctions, there is no international action. Observers note that even in their presence, violence continues. Meanwhile, the UN special envoy attempts to bring the military to the negotiating table.
16 June	UN Security Council imposes a fuel and arms embargo. The U.S. freezes bank accounts and revokes visas of supporters of the coup and its leaders.
3 July	Cédras and Aristide sign the Governors Island agreement. The 10-point acord provides for Aristide's return on 30 October, a lifting of the sanctions as soon as an interim government is installed, and the presence of 1,100 UN police and military personnel.
27 August	Robert Malval is ratified as interim prime minister. Sanctions are lifted. UN observers report an increase in the number of deaths as violence escalates. The U.S. insists that the process remains on track.

Table 6.2—*continued*

1993 *(continued)*

| 11 October | USS *Harlan County*, with the first major contingent of UN forces (U.S. and Canadian troops), is unilaterally withdrawn by the Clinton administration when it confronts a staged demonstration. The UN reimposes sanctions and evacuates all personnel, including human rights observers. Political repression worsens. |

1994

January	U.S. domestic pressure builds, as U.S. demands reinstatement of the exiled government. U.S. Congressmen chain themselves to the White House fences. Randall Robinson, an internationally respected figure of the U.S. African American community, goes on a hunger strike.
May	U.S. government refugee policy allows for screening of asylum seekers and settlement in safe havens established outside the U.S. Other governments refuse to participate in the safe haven programs, and refugees are settled in Guantanamo Bay.
21 May	UN Security Council institutes comprehensive sanctions, yet some fuel and other goods are delivered through the Dominican Republic and Haitian ports.
31 July	UN observers are expelled by the military rulers. UN Security Council passes Resolution 940 authorizing the creation of a multilateral force.
15 September	Preparations made for military invasion of Haiti are delayed. President Clinton sends former president Jimmy Carter to work out a peaceful departure by the coup leaders. Carter announces an agreement with Cédras. UN-authorized and U.S.-led forces land on Haitian soil and are welcomed by Haitians. Sanctions are lifted.

takeover of the government continued to emanate from Washington and then New York. Soon after the signing of the agreement, human rights abuses escalated. Close associates of Aristide were killed in broad daylight. The UN and the United States largely turned a blind eye to these actions, however, and continued with the process agreed upon at Governors Island. Sanctions were lifted on 27 August, as planned, and trade resumed. In October, the first set of UN forces, composed of U.S. and Canadian soldiers, approached aboard the USS *Harlan County*. When the troops were confronted by a demonstration organized by armed thugs, the right-wing Front for the Advancement and Progress of Haiti

(FRAPH), the United States unilaterally recalled the ship, thereby giving the Haitian military time for a longer siege.

In response to the defiance of the coup leaders, the UN reimposed sanctions, but again without the political will to enforce them. The sanctions continued to be transgressed by ships carrying fuel and other items. The border between Haiti and the Dominican Republic was traversed thousands of times with illicit goods. The United States and the UN continued their ambivalent policies, including the failure to enforce and strengthen sanctions.

The refugee issue was pivotal in changing Washington's policy. In 1994, thousands of boat people continued to leave Haiti. Because of the influx of refugees, the United States proposed a policy to screen asylum seekers and settle them in safe havens before allowing them onto U.S. soil. This proposal was not enthusiastically received by other members of the Western Hemisphere, and in the end a safe haven was established on Guantanamo Bay, Cuba.[14] Thousands of refugees, some with the human immunodeficiency virus, were contained in a small camp, and reports of human rights abuses began to filter out into the media. Political pressure for a resolution of the refugee crisis and the return of Aristide began to build from the Congressional Black Caucus, an important partner in Clinton's domestic coalition; from Randall Robinson, a prominent African American and leader of the antiapartheid movement; and from the Haitian diaspora. These and other groups called for tightening sanctions and using military force, if necessary.

Comprehensive trade sanctions were imposed in May 1994 by Security Council Resolution 917, which banned commercial flights, financial transactions, and trade. The military rulers, however, continued their defiance. In retaliation for the tightened sanctions, they expelled UN/OAS human rights observers. Meanwhile, the increased pressure from lobbying groups in the United States attracted growing media attention to the human rights abuses perpetrated by the junta rulers.

As the Haitian reality began to take hold in the public consciousness, the Clinton administration pledged to address the situation immediately.[15] UN policy was tightened at the end of July; UN Security Council Resolution 940 authorized the creation of a multinational force to remove the dictatorship.

In a last-minute effort to avoid American casualties, former U.S. president Jimmy Carter, Senator Sam Nunn, and retired chairman of the Joint Chiefs of Staff Colin Powell were sent to negotiate the departure of General Cédras and his retinue of military officers. The Carter mission succeeded and offered a graceful exit and safe haven in Panama for coup leaders. The violent regime was dutifully removed, but without its having to answer to any charges of human rights violations. The multinational forces, led by the United States, descended on Haitian soil without incident to restore democracy.

The Humanitarian Effects and Response

As noted earlier, many ordinary Haitians supported sanctions. "Better to live in an empty house where you eat dry bread in peace than a full house eating meat in violence," commented a peasant during an interview after the restoration of democracy.[16] The political repression violated not only civil and political rights but also economic and social rights. Nonetheless, the sanctions exacted a further toll on peasants, town dwellers, and urban residents.

From the beginning, the sievelike sanctions merely inconvenienced the well-to-do. They paid higher prices for luxury goods and gasoline, but in some cases they also benefited from the thriving contraband trade. The poor, however, were hit hard by rampant inflation. Food became extremely expensive. Transport costs rose. Public hospitals had no medicine or medical supplies. In the countryside, the already deforested land was cleared of the remaining trees, which were used for fuel or sold as charcoal.

The violence and political repression resulting from the coup completely disrupted the lives of Aristide's supporters. Thousands fled for their lives. The residents of slums in Port-au-Prince escaped to the countryside. Military soldiers pillaged homes and offices of Aristide's backers. People were systematically uprooted and killed. Haitian human rights organizations estimate that close to three thousand persons were killed during the first few months of the coup.

In the absence of an overt conflict, the humanitarian effects of sanctions assumed critical importance for those involved in relief operations. However, at the heart of the international relief debate was the difficulty of quantifying humanitarian effects. How much suffering should have been attributed to sanctions, to effects of the coup, and to historical poverty? The community of humanitarians, by name impartial and neutral, were reluctant to examine the historical and political context. Yet for the many Haitians who lived through the coup and sanctions, the debate about their suffering was unimportant, even irrelevant. They had been economically exploited and politically repressed for centuries. Although the sanctions caused suffering and were largely ineffective, Haitians considered them an important political commitment, however symbolic.

The lack of available data is the critical problem in assessing the impact of sanctions. Haiti has few sources of information; routinely registered data are incomplete and unreliable, and there is no vital registration system. Cross-sectional surveys undertaken by research institutes are the most reliable source of information, along with information from several nongovernmental organizations. Save the Children/U.S. in Maissade and the Child Health Institute, a local NGO, routinely collect data from health facilities in several locations. However, during the coup, reporting even from these sources diminished. Although written records, such as total number of patients seen and the types of diagnoses, were kept by the community-based health projects, much of this information has not yet entered the public domain.

Health reports published during the sanctions period largely regurgitated what was already known about the situation prior to sanctions. The Pan American Health Organization (PAHO) published annual reports, and the United States Agency for International Development (USAID) published monthly reports throughout the three years of economic coercion. These reports document the constant devaluation of the gourde vis-à-vis the dollar and the rising price of basic commodities. Otherwise, each report contains similar information from year to year or month to month.

Sanctions severely affected both urban and rural populations. In the cities, already limited government services were suspended. Drinking water output dropped by 50 percent owing to the lack of electricity, fuel, and spare parts.[17] Garbage collection ceased, and sewage treatment plants were not maintained. The lack of proper refuse removal and sanitation resulted in pronounced fecal contamination of the water supply in the capital. In the rural areas, aid programs for agricultural development, health, water, and sanitation plants were halted. The already deforested countryside deteriorated further as rural Haitians cut trees to be made into charcoal. Although the effects of sanctions were evident to the observer, there is little data that would stand up to scientific scrutiny.

The health situation was not clearly documented, but it appears to have worsened during sanctions for several reasons. First, most regular health care programs were cut back or suspended. Many NGOs completely closed operations; others cut back on services because of the lack of goods and cash. Additional humanitarian relief was not enough to meet the needs. There were reported shortages in drugs and other supplies. The violence and political repression made it difficult for people to move around and seek services. According to those interviewed, patients were often unable to gather at a clinic since groups of civilians were viewed suspiciously by the military and subject to harassment. As health services and infrastructure deteriorated during the three years, particularly in the public sector and in rural areas, the health situation almost certainly deteriorated as well.[18]

Dr. Paul Farmer, a figure familiar with Haitian affairs and a physician at the Clinique Bon Sauveur, an ambulatory clinic that provides services to the poor in the Central Plateau region in Haiti, has published a study summarizing the clinic's experience. He reports on four types of effects witnessed at the clinic that are generalizable to other organizations operating during these years. He notes: (1) interruption of all outreach activities such as AIDS prevention, distribution of contraception, the women's literacy project, and community organizing; (2) demoralization among all health care workers, including several resignations; (3) a decrease in the number of patients seen but an increase in the severity of illness of, and the distances traveled by, patients seeking treatment; and (4) treatment of their first reported cases of politically motivated rape and an increase in the number of assaults.[19]

An important health issue, not classified under the umbrella of humanitarian effects or response, was the increase in the rate of homicide and injuries as a result of political violence. It is likely (although not documented) that the rate of mortality increased for young men and women, given the well-documented repressive nature of the military regime. Such human rights groups as Amnesty International, Human Rights Watch, and the National Coalition for Haitian Refugees reported on the killings and the violations of human rights.

The inherently violent nature of the regime was minimized, as humanitarian agencies focused on more traditional humanitarian outcomes and responses. Deaths among Aristide supporters could not become part of the humanitarian dialogue because they were the result of the coup and not caused by sanctions. Similarly, the underlying reasons why agricultural output declined or the health situation deteriorated were not part of humanitarian discourse.

Haitians who had voted for Aristide paradoxically saw sanctions as a means of guaranteeing his return and that of democracy. In several interviews about the effects of sanctions and their significance, community leaders, peasants, and workers all commented that life had become very expensive but that they supported sanctions as a way to help resolve the political crisis. It was a period of solidarity; everyone shared in one another's suffering. This was their sacrifice for the return of Aristide. "Haitians, poor and oppressed but proud, could work and struggle for justice and a better world." A group of women interviewed in a small hamlet said that what they wanted was "diplomacy without hypocrisy."

The Economy

The economy deteriorated significantly because of the coup and the subsequent sanctions. Although there was never any apparent shortage of goods and fuel during the crisis, prices rose out of the reach of the majority of Haitians. The Haitian gourde depreciated rapidly against the U.S. dollar during the crisis, dropping about 11.4 percent on average per quarter. Two years into the crisis, the Haitian gourde had dropped 200 percent, a landmark in the currency's continuing devaluation. On 30 September 1991, one dollar was worth 7.5 gourdes; on 15 August 1994, it was worth 18.53 gourdes. The economy of the poorest country in the region was being destroyed, and the purchasing power of the poor's income was even more inadequate.

Prices for basic foods and charcoal continued to increase. Prices of rice, corn, and beans, the three staples found in all Haitian markets, rose at a steady rate of about 15 percent per quarter. The price of sweet potatoes (a staple food source of the poor) rose 100 percent between December 1993 and April 1994. There was never any shortage of foodstuffs in the market, but prices were beyond the reach of most Haitians. For example, the cost of preparing food at home to feed a family of five could be as much as 25 gourdes a day.[20]

The provision of emergency food relief, including two cooked meals a day, by donor agencies was one of the primary means of support for the Haitian poor. In the northwest region of Haiti, CARE's beneficiaries increased to 625,000 from the presanctions workload of 15,000 persons. Similar programs were managed by Catholic Relief Services (CRS) and Adventist Development and Relief Agency (ADRA) in the southern and central parts of Haiti. Most of the food aid provided to NGOs was through USAID's PL480 program. According to a program officer involved in food distribution, programs in Haiti were massive and aimed at keeping the rural population in place and pacified. Another viewpoint suggested that food was a bandaid that was not applied strategically. It was not a targeted nutritional intervention for women and children but blanket feeding by Washington.

The coup leaders were not interested in minimizing the economic effects of sanctions. As legitimate businesses were hurt, many were forced into buying contraband. A new class of wealthy merchants in parallel markets emerged who had a strong interest in supporting the military state that in fact sustained their well-being. The de facto government could have imposed price controls to bring down skyrocketing inflation; but the military leaders themselves were profiting from the sanctions. Those who shipped humanitarian products and were engaged in trade with the expatriate communities of relief workers, journalists, and diplomats also profited from the shortages induced by sanctions. For most Haitians the effects of sanctions meant *la vie chère* (the expensive life). Food aid cushioned somewhat the humanitarian impact, but this aid reached only a limited number of people.

Nutritional Status of Children

From a review of the available data, it appears that sanctions had little impact on the nutritional status of Haitian children, the most vulnerable of vulnerable groups. Children already suffered from unprecedented high levels of malnutrition compared with other children of the Western Hemisphere. One-third of all children, measured by the Waterlow classification in which weight for height is normal but height for age is low, were chronically malnourished. In the 1980s, the Child Health Institute identified several geographical areas of Haiti that were susceptible to fluctuations in food availability because of drought conditions. In the 1990s, the northern and northwest regions reported a high prevalence (6.3 percent) of severe malnutrition (low weight-for-height and height-for-age indicators).

During the coup and sanctions, the Child Health Institute maintained its routine collection of information on nutritional status from several of its health facilities. The nutritional situation varied in different parts of the country, but malnutrition levels remained more or less constant through the crisis period (see table 6.3).[21] In 1994, the nutritional situation deteriorated slightly for children at health centers in Port-au-Prince and in the north. Earlier, in March 1993, Action Internationale Contre la Faim (International Action Against Hunger) conducted an anthropometric survey among children aged six months to five years in Gonaïves (in the Artibonite valley, considered to be part of the north). The prevalence of acute malnutrition, measured by a weight-for-height ratio of less than -2 standard deviation, was 10.4 percent, and the prevalence of severe malnutrition, at -3 standard deviation, was 7.1 percent.

In addition, an insignificant increase was reported in the ratio of low birthweight (less than 2.5 kilograms) births. The overall birth rate in centers remained low, possibly because women interviewed reported not having seen their husbands frequently over this three-year period.

Excess Child Mortality and Measles

A humanitarian assessment of the sanctions published by researchers at Harvard University sent mixed signals regarding the effects of sanctions.[22]

Table 6.3

Malnutrition among Preschool Children, 1992–1995

| Year | Region (no. health facilities reporting) | Total Sample | % Malnourished* | | |
			Mild (M1)	Moderate (M2)	Severe (M3)
1992	Haiti (38)	23,572	33.25	13.56	3.51
	Port-au-Prince (6)	5,455	42.33	16.96	2.37
	North (15)	12,447	31.57	13.02	2.58
	Northwest (3)	955	32.82	12.21	11.04
	South (14)	4,825	23.64	11.07	4.71
1993	Haiti (36)	20,830	32.04	13.71	3.55
	Port-au-Prince (4)	4,628	42.11	17.80	3.24
	North (17)	10,764	32.82	13.35	2.58
	Northwest (3)	986	30.54	15.11	12.32
	South (12)	4,452	20.01	10.31	4.59
1994	Haiti (42)	30,260	34.03	17.01	4.70
	Port-au-Prince	7,600	36.44	19.66	4.85
	North (17)	15,017	35.44	17.44	4.01
	Northwest (3)	1,062	30.54	12.43	12.62
	South (13)	6,529	29.19	13.91	4.81
1995 (Jan.–Aug.)	Haiti (42)	34,853	33.54	15.43	4.19
	Port-au-Prince (9)	9,879	35.41	16.71	4.32
	North (17)	15,690	34.76	15.50	3.46
	Northwest (3)	1,251	27.92	12.40	13.29
	South (13)	8,033	30.02	14.22	4.37

Source: USAID, *USAID Monitoring Report: Haiti.* Pre-School Children Nutritional Status in Selected Institutions. (June and November 1993; May, June, and August 1994; and August–October 1995).

*Categorization according to percentage in Gomez classification (mild, moderate, and severe malnutition) using the weight-for-age index.

Although the report acknowledged that the coup was the triggering event of the crisis and contained several good recommendations on alleviating civilian suffering, it attributed to sanctions one thousand excess deaths per month among children under five years of age. This increase in mortality paralleled the rise in the severity of the measles epidemic, which was exacerbated by the low levels of vaccination coverage and the marginal nutritional status of children.[23] This report of the excess mortality attributed to sanctions was widely covered by the media.[24] Those opposing sanctions argued that they should be lifted because they were killing the most vulnerable. Those supporting sanctions believed that the policy should continue as a matter of international solidarity.

The Harvard team's claim of excess deaths was based on data collected by Save the Children/U.S. from Maissade in the Central Plateau. The findings showed that mortality for children between one and four years of age and those under five increased 64 and 32 percent respectively from calendar year 1991 to 1992. The mountainous region, one of the poorest in Haiti, had experienced a severe measles epidemic, largely attributable to historically low levels of vaccination. The epidemic began in June 1991, peaked in 1992, and continued until 1993. According to the Save the Children/U.S. representative in Maissade, the epidemic had nothing to do with the political situation or the sanctions; the vaccine supply was full. The difficulty was in reaching the people because of the absence of passable roads. Therefore, this estimate of excess mortality should not have served as the basis for national debate on whether sanctions should be lifted or maintained. Nonetheless, these deaths became one of the most controversial issues for humanitarian relief efforts within UN circles.

Late in 1993, the implementation of a measles vaccination campaign also became embroiled in controversy. Some humanitarian agencies that wanted to press ahead felt that the interim constitutional government approved under the Governors Island agreement was impeding the campaign, wanting to delay it until Aristide's return, since the benefits of such an effort could otherwise be credited to the military government.[25] The constitutional authorities replied that they did not discourage the UN from pressing ahead, and even provided a check to carry out the campaign.[26] The decision to delay, taken by the Comité National pour l'Éradication de la Rougeole (National Committee for the Eradication of Measles), was based on other reasons: the difficulty of gathering people under the military government; thefts of propane gas, which made it difficult to sustain refrigeration; and the fact that the children who were to be vaccinated in schools were going to be on vacation. Moreover, there was no perceived urgency to vaccinate children, since the epidemic was over.

These two incidents concerning measles are suggestive of the tensions within any sanctions regime when it comes to assessing humanitarian effects and delivering humanitarian assistance. They also highlight the tensions faced by UN personnel in field operations between the need to demonstrate a deterioration in health in order to justify assistance, on the one hand, and the issue of who receives credit for providing that aid, on the other. In a country that has been placed under sanctions to punish the leadership, UN agencies providing humanitarian assistance have less room to maneuver than their NGO counterparts. UN humanitarians could not attribute suffering to sanctions, but at the same time they had to portray the increased suffering as humanitarian to receive additional funds for assistance. In the absence of any established criteria of what constituted humanitarian assistance, including the items allowed under exemption procedures, these agencies became victims of the larger political issues surrounding sanctions.

The Experience of the Clinique Bon Sauveur

During the three years, the Clinique Bon Sauveur continued to serve the population of the lower Central Plateau region, regarded as pro-Aristide by the local authorities.[27] In 1990, 448 new cases of tuberculosis were diagnosed among the 33,000 patients seen at the clinic. While in 1993 the number of new diagnoses of tuberculosis cases remained high at 409, the number of patients seen was almost halved, to 17,428. Although the number of patients visiting the clinic in 1993 decreased substantially compared to 1990, the number of cases diagnosed for typhoid, measles, and HIV infection remained high and even increased when compared with statistics from 1990. The clinic documented its first four cases of politically motivated rape, not seen prior to 1991, and noted an increase in the number of injuries—in particular, a doubling of injuries inflicted during torture and assaults, types of injuries rarely seen previously by the staff.

Humanitarian Assistance

During the sanctions period, international assistance shifted from development to humanitarian activities, especially the provision of food. In the past, Haiti received large amounts of assistance for most of its development activities—in fact, it ranked in per capita terms as the most aid-dependent country in the Western Hemisphere. Once sanctions were imposed, virtually all development projects and programs ceased. Available humanitarian assistance was prioritized into food and health, with very limited support provided for agriculture, education, job creation, the private sector, and democracy. The United States had the most generous program, totaling $74 million in the last year of sanctions, from October 1993 to September 1994. Over 50 percent of U.S. bilateral assistance was in the area of food. In addition, 55 percent of total humanitarian assistance provided by the UN was food aid. The United States, with Canada, was also one of the largest contributors to UN-administered programs.[28]

Large amounts of food aid, channeled primarily through international NGOs, was aimed at regions historically vulnerable to poverty and famine. Food aid was not distributed in the form of dry goods but as cooked meals served through feeding programs functioning from schools and canteens. As one CARE staff member noted, the availability of meals was designed to keep poor Haitians in place so that they would not take boats or migrate to the cities. Food was a stopgap measure to stem the tide of suffering and to prevent still more Haitians from looking to escape. Yet it was never adequate to meet the needs of the people.

Ironically, one result of sanctions was an increase in the budgets of humanitarian agencies and more targeted assistance than through the development projects of the past. Budgets for most UN organizations increased dramatically. For example, prior to sanctions, the in-country budget of the UN Children's Fund (UNICEF) was approximately $2 million, but by the end of sanctions, its budget was closer to $12 million. Similarly, the budget of the UN Fund for Population Activities increased from $200,000 to $3.5 million. PAHO's budget at one point during sanctions was estimated at $32 million. Budgets of international private relief organizations, such as CARE and Catholic Relief Service, also increased substantially. A large proportion of this assistance went to programs and projects designed to cushion the effects of sanctions and was unlike the development aid programs during the Duvaliers' time, which observers generally agree were wasted or corrupted.

Local organizations working with community and grassroots groups were negatively affected by sanctions and received almost no assistance for their projects. International agencies were unable to provide substantial funds to these groups because their activities were not usually considered to be part of humanitarian requirements. Moreover, they had difficulty receiving funds from abroad because the regime actively prevented them from receiving any donations. For example, a check given by the Catholic Church to a church-based group engaged in grassroots activities was never cleared by the military government. It was eventually returned to the Vatican. Even when they were able to procure funds, these local groups were unable to engage effectively in projects because their members were persecuted and because both transport and available materials were expensive. Haitian civil society and democratic movements were severely affected during these years.

Overall, humanitarian assistance cushioned some of the effects of sanctions. Although this assistance was limited, it reached its targeted population and most likely prevented an already precarious nutritional and health situation from deteriorating even further. But the lack of assistance in other sectors, such as agriculture or community organizing, had unfortunate and immediate consequences for Haitian society. The amount of assistance given was insufficient to meet even the basic needs of over 6.5 million Haitians.

An Effective Response?

From the beginning, the international political response to the overthrow of the democratically elected government of President Aristide was mixed. The coup had unleashed a tremendous amount of violence and terror, but the sanctions imposed in response to the coup were unenforced and proved to be politically ineffective. The OAS and the UN, following Washington's leadership, lacked the political will to enforce sanctions. Aristide and his supporters had hoped for a comprehensive embargo that would lead to quick restoration. But the sanctions were repeatedly violated as goods flowed into Haiti.

The three years of sanctions affected the various sectors of Haitian society in different ways. The wealthiest members paid a little more for their necessities and increased their wealth by renting out property or owning profitable businesses, such as gasoline stations. The small entrepreneurs and middle class, not associated with the military, were decapitalized. Many went out of business or saw production decline. The urban poor and peasants could not afford to purchase basic goods, given the high prices. They lost their jobs and other means of livelihood. They were in large part Aristide supporters and paid a dear price for their allegiance, often in blood. The military rulers and their associates profited from illegal trade because they were in a position to consolidate economic and political power.

The ensuing negotiations between the OAS, the United States, and the military ended in repeated failures. The Governors Island agreement was defied by the military rulers. It collapsed when UN forces confronted by a rabble were recalled. Meanwhile, sanctions remained porous, and thousands of Haitians fled on rickety boats hoping to reach the shores of Miami. The military took advantage of the confusion and inconsistencies.

Although porous, sanctions helped damage an already weak Haitian economy. The gourde depreciated against the dollar, and prices increased dramatically for most staple items. The reduced purchasing power adversely affected an already destitute population. Basic food items, such as cassava, rice, and beans, became very expensive, as did fuel for cooking. The increased need for charcoal contributed to an increased rate of deforestation and devastation of the local environment. Other goods, such as transport, also grew dear in price because of the high price of gasoline. There were severe shortages in the health sector. Agricultural output was reduced because peasants were politically targeted by the regime, and there were shortages of supplies.

Despite the observable effects of sanctions, there is enormous difficulty in quantifying their actual impact. Limited available data made humanitarian claims to justify assistance or understand the effects of sanctions more a political than a targeted response. The data, collected either through population-based studies or vital registration systems, necessary to understand the effects of sanctions were unavailable. In addition, the baseline information needed to observe the changes resulting from sanctions was of poor quality. Information on utilization of health services was kept at the community level. Although this may be the most reliable source of information, there are problems of generalization to the larger situation. On the basis of other sanctions experience, such as Iraq and the Federal Republic of Yugoslavia, the humanitarian community generally believed that sanctions affected the poor and vulnerable sectors of the population. However, it was difficult to determine the proportion of suffering attributable to sanctions and the portion attributable to the coup. The fact was that they were intertwined.

While the international response was essentially humanitarian, it was within a political framework of traditional U.S. foreign policy towards Haiti. For example, the international assistance provided, mostly in the area of food, was seen by many as a rural pacification policy, keeping the poor and vulnerable in their homes and on their land and out of boats headed toward the Florida coast. Yet humanitarian assistance reached many of the people who required help. This was an improvement compared with the millions of dollars that disappeared during the Duvalier and post-Duvalier periods, and the assistance may have averted a larger crisis. But was this the most effective use of humanitarian assistance?

There was visible tension within humanitarian operations, particularly in UN-administered efforts, as to the politicizing effects of sanctions. On one hand, by criticizing sanctions and highlighting the humanitarian effects, international agencies were viewed as legitimizing the de facto authorities. On the other hand, by remaining silent on the humanitarian effects of sanctions, international agencies also were viewed as accepting civilian suffering for larger political gains. In the absence of political gains, these agencies appeared to condone suffering despite their humanitarian programs.

In addition, most humanitarian agencies—governmental, intergovernmental, nongovernmental—work with a narrow definition of what constitutes suffering. For example, nutritional effects on women and children are seen as humanitarian needs. However, excess deaths of young men and the increase in violence due to repression do not fall under the humanitarian rubric. Although these deaths may not be directly sanctions related, they are part of the broader framework of the reason sanctions were imposed. Such a narrow definition of the humanitarian agenda has created confusion in setting priorities and in assisting beneficiaries.

Since every sanctions regime has been unique and the targeted countries are at different stages of development, it is difficult to assess the political effectiveness and the humanitarian impacts of sanctions. In particular, the sanctions on Haiti were not the comprehensive type seen in Iraq or the former Yugoslavia, but they did affect the poor and most vulnerable. Despite the sanctions' ineffectiveness and inconsistency, the Haitian people supported sanctions because for three years this was the only feasible option presented by the member states of the OAS and the UN. In the absence of tighter enforcement or military intervention, sanctions were seen as the only means to political freedom and the return of democracy. Ultimately, sanctions were politically ineffective, and U.S. soldiers eventually brought the return of the democratically elected regime. The question in the minds of many Haitians was, "Why three years of suffering? Why not earlier military intervention?"

Notes

1. The author was part of a seven-person team that investigated the international responses to Haiti's crises of the last decade. The interested reader is referred to Robert Maguire et al., *Haiti Held Hostage: International Responses to the Quest for Nationhood, 1986–1996*, occasional paper no. 23 (Providence, R.I.: Watson Institute, 1996).

2. For a more detailed historical review, see Paul Farmer, *The Uses of Haiti* (Monroe, Maine: Common Courage Press, 1994); Michel-Rolph Trouillot, *Haiti: State against Nation: Origins and Legacy of Duvalierism* (New York: Monthly Review Press, 1990); and James Ridgeway, ed., *The Haiti Files* (Washington, D.C.: Essential Books, 1994).

3. See Robert Maguire, "Haiti's Emerging Peasant Movement," *Cimmarón* 2, no. 3 (Winter 1990): 28–44; and Robert Maguire, "The Peasantry and Political Change," *Caribbean Affairs* 4, no. 2 (April–June, 1991): 1–15.

4. Gustavo Gutierrez, *A Theology of Liberation: History, Politics, and Salvation* (Maryknoll, N.Y.: Orbis, 1988).

5. Farmer, *Uses of Haiti*, 141–42.

6. Claudette Antoine Werleigh, "The Use of Sanctions in Haiti: Assessing the Economic Realities," in *Economic Sanctions: Panacea or Peacebuilding in a Post–Cold*

War World? ed. David Cortright and George A. Lopez (Boulder, Colo.: Westview, 1995), 161–71.

7. National Coalition for Haitian Refugees (NCHR), Americas Watch, and Physicians for Human Rights, *Return to the Darkest Days: Human Rights in Haiti since the Coup* (New York: NCHR, 1992).

8. See Pamela Constable, "Dateline Haiti: Caribbean Stalemate," *Foreign Policy* no. 89 (Winter 1992): 175–90.

9. In several interviews that took place in January 1996, people said that supporting sanctions was the only form of resistance left to them. They were unable to hold public demonstrations. There was no free press or freedom of expression. Although they suffered and would have preferred military intervention right after the coup, they said that they would have supported sanctions for another ten years.

10. The National Labor Committee estimated that $67,629 million worth of clothing was imported from Haiti in 1992. National Labor Committee, *Haiti after the Coup: Sweatshops or Real Development?* (New York: NLC, 1993). A recent study by the committee reports that Haitian assembly workers had less buying power in 1995 than they did in 1990. A minimum-wage ($2.40) job provides less than 60 percent of the bare minimum needs for a family of five.

11. Tim Weiner, "CIA Formed Haitian Unit Later Tied to Narcotics," *New York Times,* 14 November 1993, A1.

12. For more details, see Ian Martin, "Haiti: Mangled Multilateralism," *Foreign Policy,* no. 95 (Summer 1994): 72–89. William O'Neill, "Recent Development: Human Rights Monitoring vs. Political Expediency: The Experience of the OAS/UN Mission in Haiti," *Harvard Human Rights Journal* 8, no. 101 (1995): 1–29.

13. William O'Neill, "Reconciling the Irreconcilable: The Troubled Outlook for U.S. Policy toward Haiti," *Haiti Study Group Info Circular,* no. 2 (October 1995): 1–57.

14. Farmer, *Uses of Haiti.*

15. See B. Gellman and R. Marcus, "US Boosts Pressure on Haitians: Use of Force to Oust Junta Not Ruled Out," *Washington Post,* 4 May 1994, on Lexis/Nexis; and James O. Goldsborough, "Who Will Blink First as the Haitians Die?" *San Diego Union-Tribune,* 2 May 1994 on Lexis/Nexis.

16. Mr. Luc, Syndicate Travaller Agriculture de Savanete, interview by author, Mirebalais, January 1996.

17. Pan American Health Organization, *Health Situation Analysis 1993.* (Port-au-Prince, Haiti: PAHO, 1993).

18. Cesar Chelala, "Fighting for Survival," *British Medical Journal,* 20–27 August 1994, 525–26.

19. Paul Farmer, "Haiti's Lost Years: Lessons for the Americas," *Current Issues in Public Health* (1996): 143–51.

20. Sarah Castle, "Women and the Household in Haiti," a subreport submitted to the Harvard Center for Population and Development Studies, August 1993.

21. USAID, *USAID Monitoring Report: Haiti.* Pre-School Children Nutritional Status in Selected Institutions. (June and November 1993; May, June, and August 1994; and August-October 1995).

22. Harvard Center for Population Studies, "Sanctions in Haiti: Crisis in Humanitarian Action" (Cambridge: Program on Humanitarian Security Working Paper Series, November 1993).

23. The estimates of malnutrition suffered from sampling limitation; few children reported for measurements. Maissade, the community where the sampling took place, was the home of the Mouveman Peyizan Papaye (MPP), supporters of Aristide and leaders in the peasant grassroots movement. Many families were targets of repression and violence by the coup leaders.

24. Howard French, "Haiti's Sanctions Toll on Kids Told," *New York Times*, 9 November 1993, A1. Christopher Wilson, "Doctors Say Harvard Study Wrong on Haiti Sanctions," *Reuters*, 24 November 1993, for Lexis/Nexis.

25. Director of country office for UNICEF, interview by author, Port-au-Prince, 1996.

26. Minister of health for the interim constitutional government, interview by author, Port-au-Prince: 1996.

27. For more information, see Farmer, "Haiti's Last Years."

28. USAID, *USAID Monitoring Report*, August 1994, 12.

Part III

Conclusions

7

Political Gain and Civilian Pain

Thomas G. Weiss, David Cortright, George A. Lopez, and Larry Minear

This volume has presented a framework for analyzing the humanitarian impacts and political effectiveness of multilateral economic sanctions, drawing from the experiences of South Africa, Iraq, the former Yugoslavia, and Haiti. This chapter addresses recurrent themes in the country experiences, suggests points at which the original analytical framework may itself need revision, and examines issues emerging from the use of sanctions as a policy tool, particularly the limitations of the current sanctions "regime." It assesses humanitarian aspects and the complex and troublesome dynamics of weighing civilian pain against political gain. Moreover, this chapter addresses policy concerns and further research.

An Overview of Recent Experience

Of the four country situations examined in this volume, multilateral economic sanctions appear to have been a major success only in the case of South Africa. Sanctions helped to dismantle South Africa's entrenched apartheid system, opening the way to a representative black-majority government for the first time in that nation's history. Through the gradual escalation of economic pressure, sanctions curtailed South African access to international finance, forced the apartheid regime to pay a surcharge of some 50 percent for oil purchases on world markets, and contributed to declining growth rates. By depriving the military of spare parts, sanctions also compromised South Africa's air superiority (a factor especially relevant in the Angolan war). Political authorities sought to deflect the full force of sanctions through import substitution, resulting in greater self-sufficiency in the energy and arms sectors. These changes also had unintended and positive side-effects, including the relaxation of apartheid strictures and, through broadened education and job opportunities for black workers, the reinforcement of organized efforts against apartheid.

The experience in Iraq has been generally negative. Imposed in August 1990 in the immediate aftermath of Iraq's invasion of Kuwait, multilateral economic sanctions did not force the exit of Iraqi troops. That was accomplished instead by the forty-three-day war by the United States and its allies in January-February 1991. Following the war, sanctions remained in place for more than six years, without any noticeable effect in diminishing Saddam Hussein's power.[1] Yet sanctions had some limited impact in achieving secondary goals. According to Rolf Ekeus, head of the United Nations special commission charged with eliminating Iraq's weapons of mass destruction, sanctions were "very important" in pressuring Saddam Hussein to accept UN demands.[2]

Iraq took steps to comply with some of the conditions specified in Security Council Resolution 687 for lifting sanctions, including acceptance of the UN Boundary Commission's redrawn borders with Kuwait, the destruction of certain weapons of mass destruction, and the creation of the UN Compensation Fund. However, the United States and the United Kingdom insist that Iraq must also comply with the requirement of Resolution 688 to cease repression of the civilian population, which further delays the lifting of sanctions. Efforts since mid-August 1991 to use the sale of Iraqi oil to underwrite the costs of humanitarian relief and other international activities in Iraq finally bore fruit when Resolution 986 went into effect in December 1996. As of late 1996, Eric Hoskins judged that the regime appeared "well-entrenched and in firm control" while the condition of the civilian population was "dismal."

The experience with sanctions in the former Yugoslavia also has received mixed reviews. Imposed in May 1992 against the Federal Republic of Yugoslavia (FRY; that is, Serbia and Montenegro), the economic blockade was tightened later in 1992 and again in 1993 in an effort to force Slobodan Milosevic to suspend his support for the Bosnian Serbs and to accept the various peace agreements being negotiated by UN and European Community diplomats. That the Bosnian Serbs signed the Dayton agreement in November 1995 gives the impression that sanctions achieved their purpose. Indeed, soon after sanctions were imposed, the Milosevic regime seemed to adjust its policies, urging (although without success) the Bosnian Serbs to accept the Vance-Owen plan in 1993 and lending support to subsequent negotiations and the Dayton accords. Edward Luttwak argues that sanctions "moderated the conduct of Belgrade's most immoderate leadership" and "induced whatever slight propensity has been shown to negotiate."[3] A report to the UN from a roundtable discussion held in Copenhagen in June 1996 expressed the view that UN sanctions were "the single most important reason for the government in Belgrade changing its policies and accepting a negotiated peace agreement."[4]

Yet questions remain about the precise role of sanctions in persuading Milosevic to join the peace process and about the actual impact of such pressure on the Bosnian Serbs themselves. Available evidence at this writing in early 1997 suggests that sanctions bear an indirect relation to the process of negotiating an end to the war. In a broader sense, the link between the Dayton accords themselves and a durable peace in the former Yugoslavia also remains uncertain. There is no doubt, however, about the significant levels of pain inflicted on the FRY economy.

The experience of sanctions in Haiti was even more ambiguous. Responding to the military coup that ousted democratically elected president Jean-Bertrand Aristide in September 1991, the Organization of American States (OAS) levied sanctions that proved highly porous. In June 1993 the UN Security Council imposed more comprehensive sanctions. These seemed to have an immediate positive effect, as Haiti's military rulers accepted negotiations and signed the Governors Island accord supposedly restoring Aristide to office. When sanctions were lifted before Aristide's actual return, however, the military regime reneged on its promises. The sanctions were then reimposed in October 1993 and tightened in May 1994, but with little or no impact on the junta's intransigence. When the regime finally stepped aside in September 1994, the decisive factor was not sanctions but the show of U.S. military force authorized by the United Nations. This outcome and the suffering caused by sanctions raised the question of why so much civilian pain had been meted out for so little political gain. Ironically, sanctions were encouraged and supported by many of the poor who suffered from them and resisted by junta leaders and Haitian elites, many of whom were enriched by the measures.

In analyzing these four experiences, it may be useful to establish a continuum with respect to the correlation between economic sanctions and political change. On the positive end would be South Africa, on the negative end Haiti and Iraq, with the former Yugoslavia somewhere in the middle. Additional research—not to say future developments—might shift the locations somewhat, with the Yugoslav experience perhaps most susceptible to repositioning. In each instance, however, the observed political changes, or the lack thereof, had multiple causes and points of resistance. Each situation was characterized by a complex interaction of diplomatic, military, and economic influences. In no case were sanctions the definitive factor in bringing about political change; but in each instance economic coercion played at least some role in generating pressures for negotiation or compromise.

A second continuum might usefully correlate economic sanctions with civilian pain. For reasons indicated in the early chapters by the editors and made concrete in the four country studies, there are serious analytical and methodological difficulties in establishing precise correlations. Perhaps the most daunting challenge is disaggregating the effects of sanctions from other causes of social distress. In South Africa, economic sanctions exacerbated problems ranging from drought to militarization, from economic restructuring to urbanization and global recession. Similarly, war and government oppression in Iraq, war and the transition to a market economy in the former Yugoslavia, and military repression in Haiti contributed to civilian distress. Despite the complexities of multiple causality, the country cases demonstrate the possibility of disaggregating the various factors at work and establishing a rough correlation between sanctions and suffering.

The connections between sanctions and political change and those between sanctions and civilian pain point toward a third set of relationships: between political change and human suffering. Civilian pain is justified by the imposition of sanctions on the grounds that it makes an indispensable contribution toward agreed changes in policy by a targeted government. Suffering associated with a failed political strategy is more difficult to justify than similar suffering accompanying a successful political strategy. In either instance, however, political options involve major humanitarian risks that should be explicitly recognized. As a major study by the Carnegie Commission on Preventing Deadly Conflict concludes, it is no longer possible to ignore "the plight of innocent civilians, especially children and the elderly, in countries that are the targets of comprehensive sanctions."[5]

Sanctions as a Policy Tool: Regime Issues

The country cases illustrate the variety of sanctions experiences in the early post–Cold War period. The cases are of sufficient unevenness and particularity, however, to suggest that what exists is less what social scientists refer to as a "regime" than a set of ad hoc arrangements, managed by improvisation, with little consistency from one setting to the next. Moreover, there exist little accountability and no agreed process for routine postsanctions evaluation. A regime, by contrast, involves "principles, norms, rules, and decision-making procedures around which actor expectations converge in a given issue-area."[6] Critics of sanctions, among them some humanitarian organizations, have identified the absence of consistent application of exemptions by the United Nations and member states as an element undermining what arguably is a nascent sanctions regime. Delays in processing requests for approval of waivers for humanitarian matériel weaken the system further.

Economic sanctions are authorized under Article 41 of Chapter VII of the UN Charter, which also contains provisions for the use of military force. Given the charter's commitment to the pacific settlement of disputes, forcible coercion is to be utilized only after nonforcible options have been tried and exhausted. The case studies, however, suggest two seemingly contradictory sets of complications.

On the one hand, economic sanctions are sometimes used as a prelude to military force rather than as an alternative to it. In Iraq, Hoskins notes, "there was evidence, prior to January 1991," when the UN Security Council authorized the use of force, that sanctions were having a powerful economic impact and "were indeed causing hardship among the Iraqi population." Early suggestions that options be prepared for an assessment of humanitarian and other impacts were dismissed out of hand: such an assessment would be irrelevant for the Security Council, which was clearly predisposed to authorize military force.[7] Indeed, the Iraq experience led humanitarian, religious, and other groups that actively supported sanctions as an alternative to war to conclude that such an approach was not given a serious chance to succeed in the circumstances. "Economic sanctions and the UN Charter," wrote one of those who monitored the situation closely, "rather than serving as the 'threshold for peace,' became a 'trap door to war.'"[8]

On the other hand, sanctions are also faulted for preventing the prompt use of military force. To the extent that economic sanctions are politically ineffective, the issue is particularly excruciating. Sarah Zaidi recalls that many Haitians understandably asked, "Why three years of suffering? Why not earlier intervention?" Even when sanctions have ostensibly been more politically effective, as in the former Yugoslavia, serious questions arise. The Implementation Force's (IFOR) more robust terms of engagement, had they accompanied the deployment of the UN Protection Force (UNPROFOR) troops three years earlier, might have mooted the need to impose economic sanctions, with their attendant pain. From both humanitarian and political standpoints emerges the need to review the charter's assumption that a graduated application of first economic and then military coercion is necessarily the best approach for all situations. Three observers summarized the irony: "It seems that risk-averse policymakers and pacifistic humanitarians have formed a common discourse on the merits of sanctions based on their value as a *symbolic* rather than as a *strategic* instrument of international concern."[9]

The complications from the four-country experiences suggest the need for greater clarity in the objectives of sanctions. In the words of former UN Secretary-General Boutros-Ghali, "While recognizing that the Council is a political body rather than a judicial organ, it is of great importance that when it decides to impose sanctions it should at the same time define objective criteria for determining that their purpose has been achieved."[10] The evidence suggests that sanctions work better when objectives are clearly specified and carefully targeted. Clear objectives permit analysts and governmental decisionmakers to assess success or failure more precisely.

Yet as the earlier discussion in this chapter illustrates, even clearly specified objectives are difficult to evaluate, all the more so when attaining them is not readily achieved by external pressure. Finding durable solutions to ethnic tensions in the former Yugoslavia, for instance, may be facilitated by sanctions but will not be accomplished solely by them. Sanctions can pressure parties to come to the negotiating table, as may have been the case in the former Yugoslavia, but they are not a tool for creating lasting solutions to ethnic violence. Sanctions and other political initiatives can help lay the groundwork for reconciliation, but reknitting torn societies will require more than externally imposed measures.

One complicating factor is that sanctions, discussed in the Security Council by representatives of UN member states with diverse political perspectives and agendas, are born of compromise. In the case of Iraq, the lead was taken by the United States and the United Kingdom, which brought to bear great pressure on recalcitrant Security Council members with divergent views. For example, when Yemen announced its intention to vote against Resolution 678, authorizing the use of "all necessary means" (that is, military force) to expel Iraq from Kuwait, U.S. officials warned that this would be costly and threatened to deny economic aid. After the Yemeni ambassador cast his country's no vote, Secretary of State James Baker observed that this had been "the most expensive vote he had ever taken."[11] The United States moved quickly to cut off bilateral economic assistance. In the case of the former Yugoslavia, the ambivalent and conflicting strategies of the European Union (EU) and the United States played themselves out in the Security Council and other forums, and the language of the resulting resolutions often reflected the lack of agreement on objectives and means.

Like other measures taken by politicians, the formulation and imposition of sanctions involves a cosmetic or public relations element. In the case of South Africa, there is a question whether sanctions represented a bona fide attempt to dismantle apartheid or, as in Crawford's view, were undertaken "simply to placate domestic constituencies or as symbolic expressions and punishment for apartheid." What makes the application of sanctions attractive to politicians is not necessarily what makes them effective in the country on which they are imposed. In fact, there may be little correlation. A highly touted mechanism for sending political messages, sanctions are sometimes less clear devices for communication than expected and sometimes convey messages other than those intended. As mentioned at the outset of this volume, it was not so much a humanitarian preference for nonforcible sanctions that mattered; rather, they were attractive because of the low domestic political costs in Western countries, combined with virtually no loss in credibility in failing, which would not have been the case with forcible sanctions.

If sanctions are to be a means of sending messages, the conditions of their imposition and of their lifting might logically be occasions for discussions with the targeted authorities. In the South African case, lengthy discussion preceded the imposition of sanctions, clarifying their intent while also giving the government and elites time to react. In the other cases, sanctions initially were imposed more quickly, allowing little opportunity for discussion. If sanctions are to serve as an instrument of diplomacy and persuasion, debate about their terms of application may provide an occasion for dialogue, reducing the likelihood of their eventual imposition.

Closely related to the question of the objectives of sanctions is the issue of their coverage. In several cases, specifically targeted measures seem to have succeeded in catching the attention of the authorities. In South Africa, divestment campaigns seem to have been particularly effective in doing so. In the former Yugoslavia, air travel, telecommunications, and sports boycotts seem to have been the most telling. In Haiti, it was not until bank transfers by the elites were interdicted that sanctions began to be taken seriously by the de facto authorities, although even then the measure did not produce an immediate policy change.

There is also evidence to suggest, however, that sanctions gained in effectiveness as they became more inclusive. Only in the case of Iraq were sanctions comprehensive from the outset; in other instances they became more so over time, as demonstrated by the charts in each chapter. Those imposed against South Africa eventually touched nearly every aspect of society, with the slow but steady strengthening of cumulative pressure taking its toll on the apartheid regime. In the former Yugoslavia, UN efforts to broaden the sanctions and tighten their enforcement seemed to enhance their impact. In Haiti, the substitution of comprehensive UN sanctions for partial OAS measures sent a strong message of broad international condemnation and packed a stronger economic wallop. Many in Haiti believed that had the embargo been as comprehensive from the outset in September 1991 as it became three years later, its early effectiveness would have been enhanced.

Whether sanctions are broad or narrow, leakage as a result of loose implementation or control weakens their impact. Effectiveness is also circumscribed when some commercial items are intentionally excluded. The revision of the embargo against Haiti to allow export to the United States of manufactured items from U.S.-owned companies, for example, sent a message that commercial benefits were more important than political change. The U.S. government's import into Haiti of oil for its own uses from the Dominican Republic in violation of the embargo was also less than helpful.[12] If sanctions are to be effective in sending a coherent political message, that message must be consistently and unequivocally reinforced on the ground.

The four cases examined here reflect wide variations in how sanctions mechanisms are prepared, implemented, monitored, adjusted, and removed. With respect to Iraq, sanctions followed within less than a week the events that triggered them. In Haiti as well initial OAS sanctions came swiftly and were promptly endorsed by the UN, although more comprehensive UN sanctions followed a year and a half later. In the cases of South Africa and the former Yugoslavia, sanctions came only after extensive reflection and soul-wrenching debates and then were implemented incrementally.

Whether sufficient time exists, or is taken, to review policy options before deciding on the nature and breadth of a set of sanctions, one essential element is the anticipation of efforts by the targeted authorities to subvert or blunt the sanctions' effects. As Crawford argues from the South Africa experience, "understanding target resistance is essential." Contingency planning for resistance and subversion needs to be incorporated into the initial discussions. Resistance should be expected from private as well as government quarters. The closing of normal commercial channels can be expected to generate efforts by businessmen, sometimes with government blessing, to establish illegal operations or parallel markets. Once such markets are established, as the Yugoslav experience indicates, the creation of vested interests in the continuation of sanctions can work against the achievement of their political objectives.

With respect to implementation, a key question concerns the correlation between multilateralism and effectiveness. Although the four sets of sanctions sooner or later received the UN's imprimatur, specific variations are potentially instructive. In the case of South Africa, individual countries took the lead. In Haiti and the former Yugoslavia, the initiative came from regional organizations—the OAS and the EU. The correlation between multilateralism and effectiveness is not clear, however. Although the broadest possible international political consensus is helpful, there is no substitute for tough enforcement measures, which may or may not be UN related.

Moreover, individual governments play a key role in shaping the contours of multilateral action. Thus in the case of Haiti, pressure from Washington in the summer of 1994 led to a tightening of the UN embargo, while unilateral U.S. actions such as the suspension of air traffic and the freezing of Haitian assets reinforced the bite of UN measures.[13] This would suggest that a combination of regional initiative, multilateral endorsement, and major-power support may prove formidable. The UN General Assembly's approval of sanctions against South Africa made them legitimate, whereas the imposition by the Security Council in the other three instances conveyed a less wide endorsement, in the view of some, because of the less representative nature of the council.

There are important lessons to be learned from the implementation of sanctions in Yugoslavia. The work of sanctions assistance missions (SAMs) organized by the Organization for Security and Cooperation in Europe and other European institutions is widely held to have injected overdue rigor into the monitoring process. Those involved have concluded that the SAM system provided "valuable assistance" in the implementation of sanctions and that the unprecedented cooperation and support provided by European agencies was the "main reason for the effectiveness of sanctions" against the former Yugoslavia.[14] The fact that monitors worked only during daylight hours initially opened the doors to considerable embargo-running during their off-hours. Subsequently, military personnel at checkpoints received explicit instructions to be implemented round the clock while the monitors were "on call," an arrangement that proved more effective. Nonetheless, the SAM system may not be easily repeatable in settings that lack the legal and institutional resources available to monitors along the Yugoslav borders.

Regarding the removal of sanctions, only one of the four sets of sanctions remains in place: those against Iraq. Sanctions against South Africa were relaxed gradually: some were removed after the release of Nelson Mandela in February 1990, but others remained in place until all-race multiparty elections were held. In the case of the former Yugoslavia, they were also relaxed in stages, with an initial lifting of some travel restrictions and the ban on participation in cultural and sports activities waived in September 1994 following Belgrade's sealing of its border with Bosnia, and a complete lifting of UN sanctions in November 1995, after the signing of the Dayton accord. The sequenced removal of sanctions has not been without controversy. As indicated by Devin and Dashti-Gibson, medical professionals in the former Yugoslavia were critical of terminating the bans on sports and cultural exchanges before ending those on critical medical supplies. There was also discussion by U.S. officials in December 1996 of possible reimposition of sanctions if President Milosevic failed to respect the results of November 1996 municipal elections in Serbia or if he used force against those demonstrating in the streets. In the case of Haiti, sanctions were removed in late 1994 after the change of governments, following a false start in the previous year. Chastened by the failure after the initial Governors Island agreement in 1993, the UN did not lift sanctions again until the regime had truly stepped aside and Aristide had been restored.

The continuation of sanctions against Iraq has been justified on the basis of Iraq's refusal to comply fully with Security Council Resolutions 687 and 688. Without discussing here whether Iraq's partial compliance with Resolution 687 merits some easing of sanctions (a subject addressed below), or whether the prohibition against internal repression in Resolution 688 is unenforceable, it is hard to avoid the impression that sanctions have been maintained primarily because of the American and British desire to punish and contain Iraq and remove Saddam Hussein from power. These are not the purposes for which sanctions were initially imposed. Moreover, the terrible human suffering that continued sanctions have caused is unjustifiable in the absence of any significant political gain.[15]

From recent experience, then, it is clear that sanctions can take on a life of their own. They are easier to impose than to implement, easier to levy than to lift. Given sanctions' highly political nature, interpretations of their success may change over time. Faulted for "moving the goalposts" as the game is being played, backers of sanctions defend their evolution in a given setting as a necessary response to changing political circumstances. As a political device in a highly politicized setting, however, sanctions as they exist today are highly vulnerable to politicization. Changes in both policy and operation are needed if sanctions are to become more principled and consistent, more effective and accountable—in short, to function as an international regime rather than an ad hoc and arbitrary set of mechanisms.

Humanitarian Aspects

In the four cases studied here, economic sanctions had four major and largely negative implications for humanitarian action. First, they were generally associated with increased humanitarian requirements and stepped-up pressure on human rights. Second, the need occasioned by sanctions often outran the capacity of humanitarian organizations to respond. Third, sanctions impaired international responses because relief supplies, while exempted from sanctions, still had to pass through a sanctions framework and review process. Fourth, the independence and effectiveness of humanitarian activities were often compromised by association with the political agenda of sanctions.

Sanctions often worsened the suffering of those already affected by war or other serious difficulties. They often broadened the ranks of sufferers to an even larger portion of the population, and their effects fell disproportionately on the most vulnerable. The result in some cases was to transform a situation of major humanitarian needs into one of genuine humanitarian crisis. In Iraq, according to Hoskins, "annual per capita income was estimated at $335 in 1988 . . . and fell to $65 in 1991 and $44 in 1992. These levels are far below the international poverty line of $100 established by the World Bank. Based on personal income and calorie-purchasing power, the prevalence of poverty has now become greater in Iraq than in India." In addition, human rights violations became "increasingly common" as the government confronted the increasing desperation of Iraqi citizens.

Impacts were also serious, if less dramatic and well documented, in the former Yugoslavia. Devin and Dashti-Gibson argue that sanctions "added to a vicious cycle of increasing needs and decreasing resources." They "increased the needs of the population while at the same time limiting the provision of health and human services that relied on imported products." In Haiti as well, sanctions added to the suffering caused by military repression and compounded the problems of impoverishment and underdevelopment. In South Africa, the health of the black majority population was appalling, although Crawford's data do not demonstrate that conditions were "severely degraded by sanctions."

The scale of the increased suffering often outdistanced the ability of international organizations to respond. Iraq's dependence on imports for 70 percent of its food and 75 percent of its medicines before sanctions meant disaster when these supplies were cut off. Items in short supply in the health sector—medicines, vaccines, syringes, anesthetics, and materials used for surgery, radiology, laboratory, and diagnostic tests—were officially exempted from sanctions. Obviously, the exemption curtailed the flow of items that were avowedly intended to be unaffected.

In the former Yugoslavia as well, "United Nations sanctions spread the suffering experienced by refugees to local populations," according to Devin and Dashti-Gibson. In late 1993, the population in Serbia for which UN programs were intended numbered 565,000, not all of whom were being reached. However, the UN estimated that between 50 and 90 percent of the remaining 10 million Serbians experienced serious sanctions-related hardships.[16] In the health sector, Devin and Dashti-Gibson note that "humanitarian aid could not compensate for the lack of domestic resources."

The magnitude of the distress alarmed UN humanitarian officials on the ground in Belgrade. A memo sent to New York in mid-1993 cast what UN staff were observing in broader terms. "The imposition of economic sanctions will inevitably affect the humanitarian situation in the area concerned. Declining local resources will always result in declining standards of health care, education, housing, social services, and so forth. The contradiction lies in imposing sanctions while at the same time asking agencies of the UN system to provide humanitarian aid."[17]

The impacts of sanctions were not uniformly negative. In South Africa, for example, Crawford writes that "most indicators of health continued to show some improvement . . . even after the imposition of the most biting economic sanctions of the mid-1980s." In Haiti during the time of sanctions, the budgets of some humanitarian organizations such as UNICEF, the Panamerican Health Organization, Catholic Relief Service, and CARE received significant increases, which benefited particularly, in Zaidi's view, "programs and projects designed to cushion the effects of sanctions." Nonetheless, "additional humanitarian relief was not enough to meet the needs."

Impacts varied from country to country, but nowhere were humanitarian activities able fully to compensate for the additional hardship caused by sanctions. Many assume that humanitarian pass-through arrangements offset or at least moderated such hardship. However, a study carried out in 1995–1996 for the UN Department of Humanitarian Affairs noted that "extensive experience in recent sanctions cases has shown [that] humanitarian assistance cannot be expected to meet all the basic needs of vulnerable groups and of the population at large." The authors, Claudia von Braunmühl and Manfred Kulessa, conclude that "the amount of information available today on the devastating economic, social and humanitarian impacts of sanctions no longer permits [the international community] to entertain the notion of 'unintended effects.'"[18] In other words, sanctions should be expected to create hardship beyond the capacities of agencies to cushion.

An example cited by a senior UN humanitarian official suggests a cavalier attitude on the part of sanctions proponents toward civilian pain. Returning from a UN fact-finding mission to Iraq in 1991, Prince Saddrudin Aga Khan detailed for the U.S. and UK ambassadors the plight of Iraqi civilians. He was reportedly told brusquely to concentrate on mopping up the damage rather than criticizing sanctions for their alleged impacts. "That's what you're paid to do." At an off-the-record discussion organized by the Humanitarianism and War Project in early 1994 on improvements needed in the international response to the situation in the former Yugoslavia, an ambassador who served on the UN Security Council dismissed all suggestions of changes in the practice of sanctions as inimical to their basic purpose: to cause civilian suffering. To reform sanctions, he said, would be to weaken them.

Despite the exemptions allowed, sanctions impaired the ability of humanitarian actors to import the requisite relief supplies, equipment, and personnel. The hardships that resulted in Iraq, the former Yugoslavia, and Haiti were serious. In the case of South Africa, the magnitude of the problem is not documented. Resources were channeled into South Africa through an array of multilateral, bilateral, nongovernmental organization (NGO), and corporate programs and trust funds, although UN agencies themselves were not present.

Perhaps the best-documented difficulties are those in Iraq. The original Security Council resolution of August 1990 did not include an exemption for foodstuffs for civilian consumption, although Hoskins notes that this omission was corrected in April 1991 and may have been by default rather than by design. Once the monitoring mechanism was in place, however, "shipments of humanitarian supplies to Iraq" were delayed by an extensive search procedure; "legitimate shipments destined for local consumption in Jordan" were also held up. "The absence of any published lists of allowable items meant that states, NGOs, private firms, and even United Nations agencies themselves were forced to submit requests for nearly every item being considered for import into Iraq."

In the former Yugoslavia, the first two years of the sanctions caused enormous hardship for humanitarian groups. Interviewed in Belgrade in 1993, WHO officials noted that "sanctions make the life of humanitarian organizations almost impossible." Not only did they experience difficulty in importing essential items; requests by local authorities also encountered difficulties. "In addition to its time-consuming, case-by-case review of requests for commercial drug imports, the Sanctions Committee refused to authorize imports of raw materials from which a relatively advanced Serbian pharmaceutical industry could manufacture drugs itself."[19] The fact that UN peacekeeping personnel experienced none of the difficulties encountered by the UN's humanitarian organizations made the situation particularly irritating. As time passed, the Sanctions Committee instituted improvements in its procedures for reviewing humanitarian exemption requests. The overall experience is chronicled in the committee's final report to the Security Council, S/1996/946 of 15 November 1996.

Management of exemptions also had hidden costs, not only for humanitarian organizations but also for a wider circle of institutions. Hoskins observes that in Iraq "sanctions demand extraordinary amounts of time from all those concerned—agencies, suppliers, shippers, as well as Sanctions Committee members. . . . The international community—almost without exception—has felt constrained and incapacitated by the sanctions regime." Such was also the early experience in the former Yugoslavia. Members of the committee spent their time in the detailed review of exemption requests, with little consideration of broad policy matters. More efficient and transparent pass-through arrangements would have allowed greater attention by the Sanctions Committee, not to say the Security Council itself, to the effects of sanctions—positive and negative, political and humanitarian.

In a 1995 letter, the five permanent members of the Security Council addressed the humanitarian impact of sanctions. "While recognizing the need to maintain the effectiveness of sanctions imposed in accordance with the Charter," the ambassadors of China, France, the Russian Federation, the United Kingdom, and the United States wrote, "further collective actions in the Security Council within the context of any future sanctions regime should be directed to minimize unintended adverse side-effects of sanctions on the most vulnerable segments of targeted countries."[20] The statement from "Perm Five" is noteworthy not only for its expressed humanitarian concerns but also for the view that existing sanctions are effective and constitute a "regime." In interviews, senior UN humanitarian officials have characterized such expressions of concern for humanitarian impacts as "crocodile tears." They serve as "balms to the consciences of people who know perfectly well the impacts of sanctions on civilians," commented one who requested anonymity.

The sanctions committees themselves have taken steps to streamline the review process. It is no longer true, as Hoskins wrote of Iraq, that "Every spare part required by a UN agency or NGO [must] go before the Sanctions Committee for approval." "No-objection" procedures allow agencies to proceed with shipments within a time certain unless a member of a sanctions committee raises questions. Major agencies such as the United Nations High Commission for Refugees (UNHCR) and the International Committee of the Red Cross confirm that significant improvements have been made, in part as a result of their own initiatives in New York. But smaller agencies, particularly those without close ties to the UN system, still experience difficulties. Moreover, agencies that pride themselves on their nonpolitical nature must have individual governments plead their case in the UN review process.

The theory and practice of sanctions has been the subject of recent intergovernmental debate in the Subgroup on the Question of United Nations Sanctions of the Informal Open Ended Working Group, created by the UN General Assembly to review proposals in the secretary-general's *Agenda for Peace*. The subgroup's recommendations begin with the observation that "an effectively implemented regime of collective Security Council sanctions can operate as a useful international policy tool in the graduated response to threats to international peace and security." Approaching sanctions as "a matter of utmost seriousness and concern," the subgroup urges that "sanctions should only be resorted to with utmost caution, when other peaceful options provided by the Charter are inadequate" and with "as thorough consideration as possible to the short and long term effects." A number of recommendations are made to facilitate the work of aid organizations, including "Further improvements in the working methods of sanctions committees that promote transparency, fairness and effectiveness." The subgroup urges that "the concept of 'humanitarian limits of sanctions' deserves further attention and standard approaches should be elaborated by relevant U.N. bodies."[21]

Humanitarian organizations differ in their assessments of how effective actual reforms have been and how much can be expected of additional ones now under discussion. Larger agencies seem to be experiencing fewer difficulties in 1996 than earlier; some smaller agencies, especially those that are reluctant to seek the political support of member states, may still experience problems. Some analysts have dismissed the reforms as "minor procedural changes to defuse the dissatisfaction" of Security Council members.[22] Whatever the current situation, it is apparent that further changes are needed. Fully cognizant of recent developments, the DHA study made a sweeping but constructive recommendation: that "established international institutions, when acting within their recognized humanitarian assistance mandate, should not be subjected to sanctions regimes."[23]

Sanctions also situate humanitarian efforts on highly politicized terrain, creating discomfort for humanitarian agencies that often prefer to think of themselves as apolitical. Sanctions also associate humanitarian actors with highly unpopular political measures. Humanitarian activities carried out within the framework of economic sanctions are inevitably caught in serious contradictions. Since "imposing sanctions is by definition a political act, [it] is therefore inevitable that the delivery of humanitarian services is a component of that political act, and that entails politicization of humanitarian efforts."[24] The negative impacts of sanctions place aid officials in what many believe are untenable and contradictory positions. Employed by governmental, intergovernmental, and nongovernmental organizations, they are part of a system that is pressing to bring about political change. At the same time, they witness firsthand the damage to civilian life and infrastructure that may undermine the prospects for such change. "Humanitarian agencies, particularly those within the UN system, have felt uneasy being so closely associated with both the implementation and the enforcement of sanctions," Hoskins observes. "Many of the system's humanitarian personnel have misgivings about the role of the world organization as both sanctioner and caregiver."

Exercising what they considered their ethical obligation as professionals, ranking officials of the World Health Organization (WHO), the UN High Commission for Refugees, and the International Federation of Red Cross and Red Crescent Societies (IFRC) in Belgrade noted "the detrimental effect of the sanctions on the health of the people and on the health care system." UNHCR's chief of mission in Belgrade reached the conclusion in late 1993 that "trying to implement a humanitarian program in a sanctions environment represents a fundamental contradiction."[25] Functioning in Haiti also raised similar ethical dilemmas. Zaidi notes that publicly voiced criticisms of sanctions played into the hands of the de facto authorities, while silence appeared to be acquiescence to the suffering of civilians. Humanitarian officials were hard-pressed to maintain international solidarity while remaining fully integrated into a political strategy aimed at international isolation.

Sanctions may undercut the effectiveness as well as the credibility of humanitarian activities. In the case of the former Yugoslavia, the unpopularity of economic sanctions, associated by the Milosevic government, and indeed by the people of Serbia and Montenegro, with the United Nations, was transferred to aid activities carried out by the UN and affiliated groups. The absence of an embargo against Croatia and the management of aid efforts in Serbia from Zagreb confirmed suspicions about a nefarious and one-sided political agenda. The padding of beneficiary lists and other actions by local Serb officials to undermine relief activities became acts of defiance making programs hard to administer. In Haiti, sanctions also illuminated a kind of schizophrenia within the United Nations system. In this case, however, the schism tended to be among humanitarian agencies rather than between them and the political and peacekeeping sides of the world organization.[26]

In sum, humanitarian action within the framework provided by economic sanctions has often produced the worst of all possible worlds. By their mission, emergency relief and human rights agencies are thrust into situations of exacerbated and acute human needs and physical peril. At the same time, they are expected to cushion the additional impacts of sanctions among civilians, a task well beyond their means. Their responsiveness is impaired by the strictures of sanctions, even though improvements have been made in the exemption process. Their integrity is called into question by recipient populations, who associate humanitarian organizations with the purveyors of sanctions, and by sanctioners, who perceive relief efforts as softening the bite of sanctions.

The Pain-and-Gain Calculus

The four case studies and accompanying analytical material in this volume have explored the necessary and inevitable tensions between the pain of economic sanctions for civilian populations and the resulting political gains. In both practice and theory, the separation of pain from gain and the analysis of either in isolation from the other has proved impossible. In the real world of opprobrious political leaders and vulnerable populations, decisionmakers understand the pain caused by economic coercion. For their part, humanitarian actors and vulnerable peoples have a stake in changing the behavior of repressive authorities by political means.

The challenge of framing the pain-and-gain calculation and of managing sanctions initiatives was well stated by the International Federation of Red Cross and Red Crescent Societies. An article in its *World Disaster Report 1995* provided a careful review of the risks associated with sanctions experienced in Iraq, the former Yugoslavia, and Haiti. Drawing on its experience in these three countries as well as on discussions in Geneva and New York of the policy issues at stake, the federation framed the issue as follows:

> With its Fundamental Principles and the Geneva Conventions, the International Red Cross and Red Crescent Movement has a duty to assist those suffering, including those who live under sanctions. When it finds that those

sanctions are designed and implemented to systematically affect vulnerable groups, that their impact is so severe that ever-wider sections of the population sink into poverty, that humanitarian aid is totally inadequate and humanitarian agencies are denied the means to operate, then there is a need to ask of the Security Council: Where is the balance between politics and humanitarianism?[27]

In assessing that balance, analysts confront serious methodological difficulties in both the political and the humanitarian realms. The complexities of measuring political gain were explored earlier—how can analysts explain the motivations of a targeted regime or disaggregate the influence of sanctions from other factors? Sanctions played at least some role in exerting pressure on targeted leaders in each of the four cases; but their effectiveness varied from case to case, and their overall impact was ambiguous.

On the humanitarian side, the challenge is also to disaggregate sanctions effects from other factors. The complexity of the methodological task, discussed in chapter 2, has been more than amply demonstrated by the cases. In each instance, sanctions exacerbated already existing hardships. In South Africa, Crawford notes that the impacts of sanctions were hard to "disentangle" from the consequences of "apartheid, drought, militarization, economic restructuring, urbanization, and global recession." In the case of Iraq, the decade-long war with Iran had taken its toll, as did the 1991 Gulf War, before sanctions added to the causes of suffering.

Devin and Dashti-Gibson point out that in the former Yugoslavia, the combination of war and its dislocations, huge refugee flows, and the austerity measures associated with the post–Cold War transition to a market economy were already causing hardship among civilians before sanctions were imposed. The consequences of the loss of trade with markets in what was once Yugoslavia wreaked greater hardship among civilians in Serbia and Montenegro than did the loss of foreign trade due to sanctions. In Haiti, Claudette Werleigh has argued that the coup d'état "and not the embargo was the root cause of any suffering."[28] Zaidi agrees that the impacts of the sanctions there "cannot be separated from the human rights abuses perpetrated by the coup and Haiti's deep-rooted and widespread poverty."

Notwithstanding how much the problems predating and complicating sanctions caused major suffering among civilians, each of the chapters found demonstrable, if not always quantifiable, links between sanctions and civilian pain. Crawford's analysis shows that sanctions in South Africa had direct effects that caused hardships, although she also identifies indirect effects that in some ways benefited black workers. The case of Iraq is less ambiguous. Hoskins presents evidence that "the number of deaths that have occurred as a result of war-related damage and the continued application of sanctions . . . has greatly surpassed the number of civilian casualties during the war itself." His review of the impacts in the water, health, agriculture, and education sectors documents that "it has been the impact of sanctions, not war-related damage, that has been most responsible for the continued hardship and suffering of the Iraqi population."

In the Federal Republic of Yugoslavia, according to Devin and Dashti-Gibson, sanctions "increased the needs of the population while at the same time limiting the provision of health and human services that relied on imported products." Their careful formulation is noteworthy because sanctions did not cause but rather "accelerated the decline of the FRY's health care system and created a dependence on international humanitarian assistance." Zaidi's analysis shows that conditions in Haiti violated minimum humanitarian standards and that the imposition of sanctions in this situation caused inevitable hardships.

In sum, the cases in this volume confirm that economic sanctions are, in the words of former UN Secretary-General Boutros Boutros-Ghali, a "blunt instrument."[29] Uneven in political utility, they are nevertheless capable of causing serious humanitarian consequences. When political gain is evident, civilian pain seems tolerable and justifiable. Such was the case in Haiti and South Africa, where, in addition, the vast majority of the population embraced the pain of sanctions as a possible stepping-stone to meaningful political change. However, when political gain is less apparent, as in Iraq and the former Yugoslavia, civilian pain is less tolerable and justifiable.

Whether sanctions are successful or otherwise, the present state of calibrating pain and gain has left much to be desired. If sanctions are to continue to enjoy a prominent place in the international tool kit—and there is every indication that they will—there is no substitute for making calculations more systematic and nuanced. The tension between political and humanitarian values necessitates closer attention. The humanitarian limits of sanctions require fuller articulation and protection.

Associated Policy Concerns

Sanctions in the four cases raise three especially pertinent policy concerns: the effects of sanctions on domestic political dynamics within targeted countries, on the costs of reconstruction and development, and on the perceived levels of international engagement and responsibility. Taken together, they highlight the overarching issue of accountability for sanctions.

The first policy concern emanates from the conventional assumption that civilian pain will produce political gain in the form of altered behavior by political authorities or even their overthrow. Yet, sanctions assume "a societal transmission belt from economic damage to political change"[30] that often does not exist, or at least does not function very effectively in particular circumstances. Sanctions can have precisely the opposite effect. As demonstrated by Saddam Hussein, political leaders of a sanctioned country can solidify their position by mobilizing civilians to "rally round the flag" in patriotic response to external coercion. As suggested by the experience in Haiti and South Africa, sanctions can also spark the opposite effect. Domestic opponents of a targeted regime may gain legitimacy and increased political support from their compatriots as a result of the solidarity that sanctions provoke.

The contribution to an "internal opposition" effect depends on the existence of a legitimate democratic opposition movement and its expressed support for sanctions. "[I]f the targeted country has a domestic opposition to the policies of the government in power," the U.S. General Accounting Office has observed, "sanctions can strengthen this opposition and improve the likelihood of a positive political response to the sanctions."[31] In its 1993 study *Dollars or Bombs*, the American Friends Service Committee argued that sanctions are morally justified when there is "significant support for sanctions within the target country among people with a record of support for human rights and democracy, or by the victims of injustice."[32] Lori Fisler Damrosch makes a similar point in highlighting the significance of internal opposition in both the South African and the Rhodesian cases. She attaches "great significance to the fact that the authentic leadership of the majority populations called for the imposition, strengthening, and perpetuation of sanctions." When legitimate opposition voices plead for sanctions as a strategy of transformation, she believes, "that voice should carry great weight."[33] One of the elements in the greater success of sanctions imposed on South Africa was the support that they enjoyed from the African National Congress. Conversely, in Iraq and the former Yugoslavia, targeted authorities sought to manipulate public opinion, making sanctions a scapegoat for their own shortcomings. International strategies should reflect these realities and be formulated accordingly.

By contrast, a sizable (though not majority) democratic opposition movement existed when sanctions were imposed in the Balkans, but leaders were uncertain about the wisdom of sanctions and found themselves largely disempowered and further isolated by the sanctions process.[34] In the former Yugoslavia, internal pressures against Slobodan Milosevic intensified after the war ended and sanctions had been lifted. The flowering of opposition political activity was triggered by the annulment of elections by the Milosevic regime in late 1996, although the widespread disenchantment with the economic circumstances of the country may have played a contributing role.

Sanctions may even undercut the ability of domestic actors to organize against opprobrious regimes. Sanctions often sever essential contact with the outside world, especially when they prevent access to communications equipment and supplies. The experience during the siege of Sarajevo was a case in point. The priority given by the United Nations to emergency food and medicine was logical on its face, although its wider political impacts were untoward. "You cannot refuse to allow spare parts for Sarajevo's radio transmitter through the blockade on the grounds that they are not 'humanitarian,'" observed one Bosnian journalist in an interview with the editors, "and then, based on CNN and Sky News, think that you are getting accurate information about people's priorities. The world has kept some of us alive through its humanitarian relief programs, but it has done nothing to enable Bosnians to speak for themselves."

Similarly, in Haiti one of the results of the international oil embargo was the closing of several independent radio stations that lacked the means to power their generators. While the pressure applied against the authorities by the embargo was important, the international strategy of building up domestic pressure on the illegitimate regime was undercut when sanctions forced alternative voices off the air. In view of the thrust of sanctions—to isolate a country—it should come as no surprise that the local availability of information diminishes and that domestic opposition groups may suffer accordingly.

The logic of the sanctions instrument suggests that as targeted states comply, external pressure should be eased, rewarding compliance with a partial or complete lifting of coercive measures. As noted earlier, this approach was applied in the former Yugoslavia when travel restrictions and the ban on participation in international cultural and sports activities were lifted in response to Belgrade's closing of the border with Bosnia and its increased cooperation with the peace process. The Security Council's decision sent a message of encouragement to the Milosevic regime that further compliance would result in further relaxing. In Iraq, by contrast, Baghdad received no encouragement or relief from partial compliance, instead facing unrelenting pressure. However grudging and halfhearted its responses, Iraq in November 1994 formally recognized the redrawn borders established by the UN Iraq-Kuwait Boundary Demarcation Commission. A year earlier, Baghdad had accepted the provisions of Security Council Resolution 715 and agreed to station a permanent UN weapons inspection team on its territory. Had these concessions been met with an easing of pressure, it is conceivable that Baghdad might have responded with still further gestures toward compliance and the Iraqi people might have received some relief from the pain of sanctions.

A sanctions policy becomes dysfunctional when it leans disproportionately toward the punitive "stick" at the expense of a positive "carrot." Effective sanctions policy must be responsive to political changes, even while maintaining the threat of continued punishment. As Alexander George has emphasized, coercive diplomacy requires a mix of carrots and sticks. What the latter cannot accomplish in isolation may often be achieved with the aid of incentives. Too little attention has been paid to the use of inducement strategies to influence targeted regimes. A new study by the Carnegie Commission on Preventing Deadly Conflict examines recent cases where inducement strategies have defused international crises, highlighting the importance of combining diplomatic tools.[35]

A second policy concern associated with sanctions involves the heightened costs of reconstruction and development in a postsanctions environment. Although the data for South Africa are unclear, the cases of Iraq and the former Yugoslavia provide substantial evidence of dramatic and far-reaching damage. The cost of rebuilding Iraq's economy from the ravages of sanctions and war is placed at nearly $300 billion. As chapter 4 indicates, Iraq faces the cost not only of replacing destroyed infrastructure (an estimated $232 billion) but also of rebuilding the destruction from the war with Iran ($67 billion), paying war reparations to Iran ($97 billion) and Kuwait ($100 billion), and settling its foreign debt ($86 billion). Having required decades to construct but less than a decade to destroy, the Iraqi economy surely faces a lengthy uphill struggle to reconstruct.

In the Federal Republic of Yugoslavia, the domestic social product during the early years of sanctions plummeted from $26.6 billion in 1990 to an estimated $10 billion in 1994. Devin and Dashti-Gibson estimate the cost of sanctions at some $20 billion in lost trade alone. These sizable economic costs were borne not only by the targeted country but also by its neighbors. The ripple effects of sanctions raise difficult political and financial issues for the United Nations, whose charter Article 50 contains a specific provision to bring to the Security Council's attention the need to address possible compensation to affected third parties.

In contrast to Iraq and the former Yugoslavia, where presanctions economies functioned reasonably well, sanctions in Haiti were overlaid upon "an already fractured economy. The longer the crisis, the heavier was the toll on the economy, on the already vulnerable ecology, and on the country's infrastructure." Workers in business and industry as well as farmers were particularly hard hit by the resulting "distortion of the Haitian economy."[36] Haiti also experienced a serious "brain drain." In Iraq and South Africa as well, the flight of skilled professionals undoubtedly complicates reconstruction. A 1996 overview by the Yugoslav authorities of the impacts of sanctions on society highlighted the reconstruction challenge. They identify

> "immeasurable losses . . . due to the impossibility of our representatives to take part in the work of a series of international organizations, the absence of scientific, cultural and sports interchange in an international framework, the extensive brain-drain, the markedly deteriorated health condition and lower education and cultural activity levels of the population, the increased mortality and decreased population birth rates."[37]

Reconstruction requires not only financial investment but also measures to address dysfunctional patterns that have developed under sanctions. War economies create expanded opportunities for black marketeering and smuggling, a situation exacerbated by sanctions. A pattern of illicit trade and other forms of criminality emerged in Iraq, the former Yugoslavia, and Haiti. When these economic activities are dominated by paramilitary forces and military groups, as in Haiti and the former Yugoslavia, the result is the enrichment and strengthening of the very perpetrators of wrongdoing against whom sanctions were targeted. The power of these criminal elements may persist in the postsanctions environment and impede political reform and economic reconstruction efforts. After sanctions are lifted, incentives for black marketeering must be eliminated in order to restore normal patterns of production and trade.

A third policy concern relates to subsequent levels of international engagement. Faced with reconstruction and development challenges of the magnitude just described, formerly targeted countries are in dire need of outside assistance. The burden of rebuilding falls heavily on the recovering nation itself. South Africa and the former Yugoslavia received significant pledges of postsanctions aid from the international community, although more was promised than delivered. Iraq has had no promises of assistance.

UN officials in Serbia and Montenegro observed a net decrease in humanitarian assistance, which they attributed to the imposition of economic sanctions. It is difficult for the outside world, on the one hand, to stigmatize and isolate a reprobate regime and, on the other, to maintain a commitment to helping its people after sanctions are lifted. Parliaments and publics have difficulty understanding how aid ministries can provide assistance while foreign ministries are promoting isolation. Repeated assertions that the outside world's quarrel is with a given regime but not with its citizens are not adequate to prevent erosion in the levels of outside assistance.

If sustaining reasonable levels of emergency relief for sanctioned countries is difficult, reconstruction and development are even more problematic. Emergency responses are typically more generous than responses to appeals for resources to meet postconflict needs. Ironically, the responses to such appeals are most undependable at precisely the time when the country's needs are greatest and outside resources most essential. The effort to resituate a pariah country on the international donor agenda faces competition for aid among various countries, loss of donor interest and attention, and, in the case of some sanctioned countries, a hardening of attitudes toward the leadership.[38]

The issue goes beyond charity to touch upon legal as well as moral obligations. Admittedly, the status of international rights to food and development are a matter of some dispute. However, international obligations to provide humanitarian and development assistance are arguably heightened when international economic coercion itself has contributed to the imperiled nutritional and health status of a population. "With the imposition of sanctions the international community has assumed an additional responsibility for the restoration of peace and human rights in the target country or between that country and the one that suffered from aggression."[39]

International responsibility includes an obligation to provide assistance for the repair of an economy and the restoration of social well-being. Experience also suggests that successful postwar reconstruction efforts can pay handsome dividends in shaping the economic and political behavior of former adversaries and preventing future conflict. In larger compass, the imposition of sanctions—however repugnant the act that triggers it—does not fulfill the international community's responsibilities. Instead, economic coercion implicates outsiders in the thorny and long-term tasks of finding durable solutions to deeply rooted problems.

This third policy concern raises the overarching issue of accountability. The pain-and-gain calculus involves life-and-death issues for civilian populations in sanctioned countries, which are framed, although not created, by international enforcement actions. Yet "there has been an astonishing lack of public debate over the moral and legal implications of a policy that imposes such enormous costs on a civilian population."[40] The IFRC assessment referenced earlier makes the essential point: "If the UN Charter is both about peace and security and about respect for fundamental human rights, there is the expectation that the Security Council assumes explicit responsibility for both the political and humanitarian dimension in its decisions."[41] International accountability for sanctions—their imposition, management, removal, and reconstruction—must be clarified, with an eye to defining the humanitarian limits of sanctions.

The UN Security Council and other sanctions-imposing authorities, whether regional or unilateral, are not free to pursue political options in a humanitarian vacuum. Because sanctions have in many cases proved more devastating in the humanitarian sphere than effective in the political, those imposing sanctions have an obligation to proceed with caution. Nor does the incorporation of humanitarian exemptions into sanctions programs moot responsibility by those who advocate sanctions for their impacts on vulnerable populations. In sum, there remains a need for a clearer, more transparent, and accountable framework of acceptable sanctions practice.

Issues for Further Research

The bulk of this chapter has rightly concerned itself with summarizing the lessons of the case studies and addressing their policy implications. This volume began with a concern about the relationship between theory and policy, especially as configured in the available literature. As a result of the preceding survey of broad concerns across four difficult cases, two issue clusters emerge as the agenda for future research: those dealing with sanctions generally and those relating to assessing the sanctions' humanitarian impact.

A number of high-priority areas exist in research on economic sanctions, which make up a formidable agenda for enterprising and thoughtful scholars. The first (albeit most ironic) involves undertaking more serious *economic* analyses of economic sanctions and their impacts. Specifically, the field needs serious studies, using modeling methods or statistical analyses across cases, of the economic reverberations of sanctions through a targeted economy over time. This volume's contributors have reported a variety of economic data and trends and interpreted—by combining the data with a variety of health, social, and political indicators—the economic and humanitarian impact of sanctions. The cases in this volume have focused primarily on the social and humanitarian sectors, but with only one or two exceptions there were no economic studies to replicate methodologically, or to test further empirically, the structural changes that occur in a particular economy over time.[42]

One simple example underscores the anomaly of an economic research gap on economic sanctions. In nearly every sanctions case, analysts agree that economic sanctions create favorable conditions for the development of a local black market. Whereas it is relatively easy to detect the emergence of such a market, especially in weapons, there is less clarity regarding the precise contours of such a parallel market, who emerges as winners and losers, and whether the market will endure in a postsanctions environment, to the detriment of recovery and development.

This volume's methods and cases suggest that to be effective, sanctions must be credible, and that to be credible, sanctions policies must become more grounded in a wider diplomatic policy. Imposing sanctions, in such a broader context, would establish the basic building blocks of sanctions as a legitimate international regime, not as a set of ad hoc measures highly provisional in nature and selective in application. The weakness of sanctions in the early post–Cold War era has not been their failure to convey political messages, but rather that those messages lack consistency and accountability.

The overall impacts of sanctions, and not merely their humanitarian consequences, vary widely from country to country. Researchers should emphasize the impact of the conscious links (or lack thereof) between the use of sanctions and the structure and process of wider diplomatic policies on the prospects of accomplishing certain goals. Assessments of particular schemes for accountability and transparency that can be easily implemented should be explored, along with the correlation, if any, between the breadth of sanctions and their impact. Is it politically possible to construct a global regime, with adequate operational and accountability safeguards, for applying economic coercion with the requisite finesse and precision?

Another ripe research area lies in systematic consideration of what are called "smart sanctions."[43] For practical and humanitarian reasons, there is little doubt that far greater focus and investigation into this possibility are urgently required. A smart sanctions strategy of targeted constraints on the financial assets and capital vulnerabilities of elites, rather than traditional trade sanctions imposed on vulnerable populations, has the potential for assuring both a more humane and a more effective sanctions policy. How such sanctions can be imposed swiftly and effectively and whether such action requires the same level of multilateral support to be successful are but two of the important associated research questions.

The literature generally accepts that sanctions with multilateral institutions at their core will be highly effective and marked by a willingness of sanctioners to continue to cooperate; but the four case studies appear to question these findings considerably. Future research will need to examine the correlation, if any, between multilateralism and effectiveness, employing a wider range of cases than this volume or that of Lisa Martin and Edward Mansfield discussed in chapter 1. What precisely is the value added of an endorsement of sanctions by the United Nations, and, within the world body, by the General Assembly as well as the Security Council? Does endorsement mean better chances for operational success, or merely more convoluted procedures? Does multilevel endorsement enhance the likelihood that any number of states may become free riders, or that large states more often than not will "hijack" the process to serve their own interests?

Each new crisis has the tendency to rivet attention upon the behavior of a particular reprobate country and the efforts of the international community, using sanctions, to alter the behavior of its political authorities. Often an afterthought is the extent to which international strategies respect existing international law. Policy research that distilled a set of legally based benchmarks and ground rules in such matters as proportionality and discrimination would add to the body of legal thinking relevant to sanctions. It also might help constrain future excesses of zeal.

Finally, attention should be focused on the criteria to measure the impact of sanctions on political change. A more sophisticated understanding is needed of the ways in which external pressures, including sanctions, influence the decisionmaking of leaders in targeted states. In light of the number of sanctions cases that have concluded, it would be useful to conduct a series of interviews with authorities targeted by sanctions to identify more fully the impacts on their own perceptions and decisionmaking. Rational-actor theories and unitary decisionmaking models undoubtedly have only limited utility for evaluating the real-world decisions of political leaders contending with multiple pressures, domestic and external. But what decisional dynamic applies to the perception of sanctions pressure? In a related manner, research needs to be conducted on precisely how sanctions affect the various political forces and dynamics within a targeted nation, especially the status of, or potential for, democratic opposition movements.

On the humanitarian side of the gain-and-pain link, a number of research issues flow directly from the research design and the comparative cases examined in this volume. Beyond generic issues, additional research is needed on humanitarian impacts in each of the four countries in question. As all the contributors to the case studies made clear—and this was more than modesty or excessive academic self-protection—data that permit clear judgments are not available. Even in the case of Iraq, where the most ample information is available, additional work is needed to verify existing data and trace the differing causes of humanitarian suffering; in fact, debate about this case has generated more controversy than others in spite of the data. In the case of South Africa, more information about the nature of outside assistance provided and the extent to which it softened the impacts of sanctions would be useful. In the case of the former Yugoslavia, additional work on the effects of the sanctions on the Republic of Serbia also would be helpful. The Haiti experience offers potential lessons in the challenges of providing humanitarian assistance without providing tacit political support for a regime that has overthrown elected authorities.

The relative success in applying in the case studies the indicators suggested in chapter 2 increases the desirability of what to date have been mainly political calls for further research aimed at developing a comprehensive checklist of indicators on sanctions impact to be used in a pre-assessment of the likely impacts of sanctions, in the monitoring of those impacts, and in discussions of refocusing or lifting sanctions. In formulating such a checklist, it would be important to take into account the most reliable and readily available data and to discuss widely with scholars and practitioners the best means for collecting such data.

Looking to yet-to-be sanctioned countries, more in-depth reviews of recent experience, including household surveys, should be mounted with an eye toward remedying potential problems. For example, consideration should be given to developing a protocol regarding standard and uniform humanitarian exemptions that could be incorporated wherever sanctions are imposed. The credibility of sanctions would be enhanced if standardized exemptions procedures were in place prior to the decision to impose such measures.

Research on the monitoring of humanitarian impacts is essential. Taken together, assembling better data and utilizing it in setting sanctions policies could, in the words of the 1995 DHA study, help "rescue a humanitarian assessment from the vagaries of political debate."[44]

Independent scholarly inquiry also is necessary in order to subject the activities of the Security Council to more rigorous outside analysis. "Strategic preparatory studies [prior to imposing sanctions] have not been carried out under the aegis of the Security Council," observes one former secretariat official, "nor have terminated sanctions regimes ever been subjected to a critical evaluation by the Council." [45] Although there is no substitute for having both pre- and postassessment tasks carried out by the council itself, independent policy research can promote such work and encourage its objectivity.

These suggestions raise the question of outside evaluation and review of sanctions practices. If policymakers act on what many have identified as a pressing need—namely, the development of a protocol within the UN Security Council to guide the imposition of different types of sanctions in response to identified needs within targeted states—then more consistent and multifaceted approaches are essential. The implications are wide ranging, encompassing both macro issues such as the place of economic coercion in the post–Cold War world and more micro issues such as approaches to humanitarian exemptions and possible compensation to neighboring states. Despite the increasing reliance on sanctions and a growing body of experience regarding their use, a host of critical issues remain underexplored.

There is an indispensable role for independent analysts in evaluating dispassionately the political utility of sanctions. Objectivity is otherwise difficult to achieve. The Security Council may be expected to overstate the political utility of sanctions and minimize the humanitarian consequences, while UN aid agencies may exaggerate the human costs and minimize the utility of political initiatives. In fact, given the complexity of the issues and the confusion over indicators, a strong case can be made for the creation of an independent "Sanctions Watch," which over time would develop expertise and objectivity in both political and humanitarian spheres.

Notes

1. For a discussion of the early period, see Patrick Clawson, *How Has Saddam Hussein Survived? Economic Sanctions, 1990–93,* McNair Paper 22 (Washington, D.C.: National Defense University, 1993).

2. Statement of Rolf Ekeus, Conference on Nuclear Nonproliferation and the Millennium: Prospects and Initiatives, Carnegie Endowment for International Peace, Washington, D.C., 13 February 1996.

3. Edward N. Luttwak, "Toward Post-Heroic Warfare," *Foreign Affairs* 74, no. 3 (May/June 1995): 118.

4. *Report of the Copenhagen Roundtable on United Nations Sanctions in the Case of the Former Yugoslavia,* held at Copenhagen, 24– 25 June 1996, S/1996/776, 3.

5. John Stremlau, *Sharpening International Sanctions: Toward a Stronger Role for*

the United Nations (New York: Carnegie Corp., 1996), 44.

6. Stephen D. Krasner, "Structural Causes and Regime Consequences: Regimes as Intervening Variables," in *International Regimes*, ed. Stephen D. Krasner (Ithaca, N.Y.: Cornell University Press, 1983), 1.

7. One particular incident is reported in Larry Minear et al., *United Nations Coordination of the International Humanitarian Response to the Gulf Crisis, 1990–1992*, Occasional Papers Nos. 18, 21 (Providence, R.I.: Watson Institute, 1992).

8. Jack T. Patterson, "The Political and Moral Appropriateness of Sanctions," in *Economic Sanctions: Panacea or Peacebuilding in a Post–Cold War World?* ed. David Cortright and George A. Lopez (Boulder, Colo.: Westview, 1995), 90.

9. Rodney G. Allen, Martin Cherniak, and George J. Andreopolos, "Refining War: Civil Wars and Humanitarian Controls," *Human Rights Quarterly* 18, no. 4 (November 1996): 747–81, quote on 777, emphasis in original.

10. Boutros Boutros-Ghali, *Supplement to An Agenda for Peace*, para. 68, reproduced in *An Agenda for Peace 1995* (New York: United Nations, 1995).

11. Lawrence Freedman and Efraim Karsh, *The Gulf Conflict, 1990–1991: Diplomacy and War in the New World Order* (Princeton, N.J.: Princeton University Press, 1993), 233–34.

12. For a brief discussion of the U.S. action, see Robert Maguire et al., *Haiti Held Hostage: The Quest for Nationhood, 1986–1996*, Occasional Papers Nos. 23, 49 (Providence, R.I.: Watson Institute, 1996),.

13. Maguire et al., *Haiti Held Hostage*, 39.

14. *Report of the Copenhagen Roundtable*, 14.

15. This makes Iraq the classic case noted by Lisa Martin, and by Edward Mansfield in his comparative book review that includes her work—namely, that powerful states may choose to "hijack" the coalition of actors in a sanctions case in order to advance their own interests. See Lisa Martin, *Coercive Cooperation: Explaining Multilateral Economic Sanctions* (Princeton, N.J.: Princeton University Press, 1992); and Edward Mansfield, "International Institutions and Economic Sanctions," *World Politics* 47 (July 1995): 575–605.

16. Minear et al., *Humanitarian Action in the Former Yugoslavia*, 94.

17. Confidential communication to the authors.

18. Claudia von Braunmühl and Manfred Kulessa, *The Impact of UN Sanctions on Humanitarian Assistance Activities: Report on a Study Commissioned by the United Nations Department of Humanitarian Affairs* (Berlin: Gesellschaft für Communication Management Interkultur Training mbH—COMIT, 1995), 66.

19. Minear et al., *Humanitarian Action in the Former Yugoslavia*, 94–95.

20. Letter dated 13 April 1995 addressed to the president of the Security Council, document S/1995/200, Annex, 1.

21. Subgroup on the Question of United Nations Imposed Sanctions of the Informal Open Ended Working Group of the General Assembly on An Agenda for Peace, "Provisionally Agreed Text," 10 July 1996, paras. 1, 20, 33.

22. Paul Conlon, "The UN's Questionable Sanctions Practices," in *Aussen Politik* 46, no. 4 (1995): 336.

23. von Braunmühl and Kulessa, *Impact of UN Sanctions*, 18.

24. Sarah Zaidi, "Comment on DHA and the IASC Study on Sanctions and

Humanitarian Assistance," letter of 14 February 1996, 1.

25. See Minear et al., *Humanitarian Action in the Former Yugoslavia*, 92–103.

26. See Maguire et al., *Haiti Held Hostage*, 44–55.

27. International Federation of Red Cross and Red Crescent Societies, "UN Sanctions and the Humanitarian Crisis," in *World Disasters Report 1995* (Geneva: IFRC, 1995), 19–27, quotation on 19.

28. Claudette Antoine Werleigh, "The Uses of Sanctions in Haiti: Assessing the Economic Realities," in *Economic Sanctions*, ed. Cortright and Lopez, 166.

29. Boutros-Ghali, *Supplement*, para. 70.

30. von Braunmühl and Kulessa, *Impact of UN Sanctions*, 30.

31. U.S. General Accounting Office, *International Trade: Issues Regarding Imposition of an Oil Embargo against Nigeria*, November 1994, GAO/GGD-95-24, 12.

32. American Friends Service Committee, Working Group on International Economic Sanctions, *Dollars or Bombs: The Search for Justice through International Economic Sanctions* (Philadelphia: American Friends Service Committee, 1993), 9.

33. Lori Fisler Damrosch, "Civilian Impact of Economic Sanctions," in *Enforcing Restraint: Collective Intervention in Internal Conflicts*, ed. Lori Fisler Damrosch (New York: Council on Foreign Relations, 1993), 302.

34. Sonja Licht, "The Use of Sanctions in Former Yugoslavia," in *Economic Sanctions*, ed. Cortright and Lopez, 161–72.

35. See David Cortright, ed., *The Price of Peace: Inducement Strategies for International Conflict Prevention* (Lanham, Md.: Rowman & Littlefield, forthcoming).

36. Werleigh, "Uses of Sanctions in Haiti," 166–67.

37. Federal Republic of Yugoslavia, "Consequences of Sanctions for the Economy and Foreign Trade of the Federal Republic of Yugoslavia" (unpublished and undated).

38. See Judith Randel and Tony German, eds., *The Reality of Aid, 1996* (London: Earthscan, 1996).

39. von Braunmühl and Kulessa, *Impact of UN Sanctions*, 33.

40. Roger Normand, "Iraqi Sanctions, Human Rights, and International Law," *Middle East Report* 26 (July-September 1996): 40.

41. IFRC, "UN Sanctions and the Humanitarian Crisis," 21.

42. The few exceptions to this rule are the studies, cited in chaps. 1 and 2, by David Matthew Rowe, "Surviving Economic Coercion: Rhodesia's Responses to International Economic Sanctions" (Ph.D. diss., Duke University, 1993); and William LeoGrande, "Making the Economy Scream: Economic Sanctions against Sandinista Nicaragua," *Third World Quarterly* 17, no. 2 (1996): 329–48. Also relevant is some of the work of the public choice school; see William H. Kaempfer and Anton D. Lowenberg, "A Model of the Political Economy of Investment Sanctions: The Case of South Africa," *Kykos* 39, no. 3 (1986), 377–96; William H. Kaempfer and Anton D. Lowenberg, "The Theory of International Economic Sanctions: A Public Choice Approach," *American Economic Review* 78, no. 4 (September 1988): 792–93; and William H. Kaempfer and Michael H. Moffet, "The Impact of Anti-Apartheid Sanctions on South Africa: Some Trade and Financial Evidence," *Contemporary Policy Issues* 6 (October 1988): 118–29.

43. For an introduction to the idea of "smart sanctions" and their utility in the

case of Nigeria in 1996–1997, see David Cortright and George A. Lopez, *Smart Sanctions on Nigeria,* Occasional Paper No. 10 (Notre Dame, Ind.: Joan B. Kroc Institute for International Peace Studies, 1996).

44. von Braunmühl and Kulessa, *Impact of UN Sanctions,* 34.

45. Conlon, " Questionable Sanctions Practices," 330.

Selected Bibliography

Before 1980

Adler-Karlsson, Gunnar. *Western Economic Warfare, 1947–1967: A Case Study in Foreign Economic Policy.* Stockholm: Almqvist & Wiksell, 1968.

Baldwin, David A. "The Power of Positive Sanctions." *World Politics* 24 (October 1971): 19–38.

Barber, James. "Economic Sanctions as a Policy Instrument." *International Affairs* 55 (July 1979): 367–84.

Bienen, Henry, and Robert Gilpin. *Evaluation of the Use of Economic Sanctions to Promote Foreign Policy Objectives.* Seattle: Boeing Corp., 1979.

Brown-John, C. Lloyd. *Multilateral Sanctions in International Law: A Comparative Analysis.* New York: Praeger, 1975.

Davis, Jennifer. *U.S. Dollars in South Africa: Context and Consequence.* New York: Africa Fund, 1978.

Doxey, Margaret P. "International Sanctions: A Framework for Analysis with Special Reference to the UN and Southern Africa." *International Organization* 26 (1972): 532–35.

Freedman, Robert Owen. *Economic Warfare in the Communist Bloc: A Study of Soviet Economic Pressure against Yugoslavia, Albania, and Communist China.* New York: Praeger, 1970.

Galtung, Johan. "On the Effects of International Economic Sanctions with Examples from the Case of Rhodesia." *World Politics* 19 (April 1967): 378–416.

Garson, John R. "The American Trade Embargo against China." In *China Trade Prospects and US Policy*, ed. J. A. Cohen. New York: Praeger, 1971.

Guichard, Louis. *The Naval Blockade, 1914–1918.* New York: D. Appleton, 1930.

Highley, Albert E. *The First Sanctions Experiment: A Study of League Procedures.* Geneva: Geneva Research Centre (July 1938).

Hoffmann, F. "The Functions of Economic Sanctions: A Comparative Analysis." *Journal of Peace Research* 3 (1967): 140–59.

Jack, D. T. *Studies in Economic Warfare.* New York: Chemical Publishing, 1941.

Kapinger, Leonard T. *The United Nations and Economic Sanctions against Rhodesia.* Lexington, Mass.: Lexington Books, 1979.

Knorr, Klaus. "International Economic Leverage and Its Uses." In *Economic Issues and National Security*, ed. K. Knorr and F. Traeger. Lawrence, Kans.: Regents Press, 1977.

———. *The Power of Nations.* New York: Basic Books, 1975.

Lillich, Richard B. "Economic Coercion and the International Legal Order." *International Affairs* 51 (July 1975): 358–71.

Losman, Donald L. *International Economic Sanctions: The Cases of Cuba, Israel, and Rhodesia.* Albuquerque: University of New Mexico Press, 1979.

Medlicott, W. N. *The Economic Blockade.* 2 vols. London: Longman, Green, 1952.

Mersky, Roy M. *Conference on Transnational Economic Boycotts and Coercion.* Dobbs Ferry, N.Y.: Oceana Publications, 1978.

Mitrany, D. *The Problem of International Sanctions.* London: Oxford University Press, 1925.

Olson, Richard Stuart. "Economic Coercion in World Politics with a Focus on North-South Relations." *World Politics* 31, no. 4 (1979): 471–94.

———. "Economic Coercion in International Disputes: The United States and Peru in the IPC Expropriation Dispute of 1968–1971." *Journal of Developing Areas* 9 (April 1975): 395–414.

Schreiber, Anna P. "Economic Coercion as an Instrument of Foreign Policy: U.S. Economic Measures against Cuba and the Dominican Republic." *World Politics* 25 (April 1973): 387–413.

Strack, H. R. *Sanctions: The Case of Rhodesia.* Syracuse, N.Y.: Syracuse University Press, 1978.

Wallensteen, Peter. "Characteristics of Economic Sanctions." *Journal of Peace Research* 5 (1968): 248–67.

Walzer, Michael. *Just and Unjust Wars: A Moral Argument with Historical Illustrations.* New York: Basic Books, 1977.

Wu, Yuan-Li. *Economic Warfare.* New York: Prentice Hall, 1952.

1980–1989

Abbott, Kenneth W. "Coercion and Communication: Frameworks for Evaluation of Economic Sanctions." *International Law and Politics* 19, no. 78 (1987): 781–802.

———. "Linking Trade to Political Goals: Foreign Policy Export Controls in the 1970s and 1980s." *Minnesota Law Review* 65 (1981): 739–889.

Alting von Geusau, Frans A. M., and Jacques Pelmans. *National Economic Security: Perceptions, Threats, and Policies.* Tilburg, The Netherlands: John F. Kennedy Institute, 1982.

Anglin, Douglas G. "United Nations Economic Sanctions against South Africa and Rhodesia." In *The Utility of International Economic Sanctions*, ed. D. Leyton-Brown. New York: St. Martin's Press, 1987.

Askin, Steve. "The Business of Sanctions Busting." *Africa Report* (January/February, 1989): 18.

Ayubi, Shaheen, Richard E. Bissell, Nana Amu-Brafih Korsah, and Laurie A. Lerner. *Economic Sanctions in U.S. Foreign Policy*. Philadelphia: Foreign Policy Research Institute, 1982.

Baldwin, David A. *Economic Statecraft*. Princeton, N.J.: Princeton University Press, 1985.

———. "Economic Sanctions as Instruments of Foreign Policy." Paper presented at the annual meeting of the International Studies Association, Atlanta, 1984.

Bayard, Thomas O., Joseph Pelzman, and Jorge Perez-Lopez. "Stakes and Risks in Economic Sanctions." *World Economy* 6 (March 1983): 73–87.

Becker, Abraham S. "Economic Leverage on the Soviet Union in the 1980s." Office of the Under Secretary of Defense for Policy, Santa Monica, Calif.: Rand Corp., 1984.

Becker, Charles M. "The Impact of Sanctions on South Africa and Its Periphery." *African Studies Review* 31 (September 1988): 61–88.

Booth, Alan R. "South Africa's Hinterland: Swaziland's Role in Strategies for Sanctions-Breaking." *Africa Today* 36, no. 1 (1989): 41–50.

Brady, Lawrence J. "The Utility of Economic Sanctions as a Policy Instrument." In *The Utility of International Economic Sanctions*, ed. D. Leyton-Brown. New York: St. Martin's Press, 1987.

Caras, James. "Economic Sanctions: United States Sanctions against Libya." *Harvard International Law Journal* 27 (Spring 1986): 672–78.

Carswell, Robert. "Economic Sanctions and the Iran Experience." *Foreign Affairs* 60 (Winter 1981–82): 247–65.

Carter, Barry E. *International Economic Sanctions: Improving the Haphazard U.S. Legal Regime*. Cambridge: Cambridge University Press, 1988.

Clarizio, Lynda M. "United States Policy toward South Africa." *Human Rights Quarterly* 11 (May 1989): 249–94.

Coker, Christopher. *The United States and South Africa, 1968–1985: Constructive Engagement and Its Critics*. Durham, N.C.: Duke University Press, 1986.

Commonwealth Group of Eminent Persons. *Mission to South Africa: The Commonwealth Report*. London: Commonwealth Secretariat, 1986.

Cooper, J. H. "The Welfare Effects of Sanctions." *Journal for Studies in Economics and Econometrics* 0(25) (August 1986): 2–11.

Cross, E. G. "Economic Sanctions as an Instrument of Policy." *International Affairs Bulletin* 5 (1981): 19–29.

Daoudi, M. S., and M. S. Dajani. *Economic Diplomacy: Embargo Leverage and World Politics*. Boulder, Colo.: Westview, 1985.

————. *Economic Sanctions: Ideals and Experience*. London: Routledge & Kegan Paul, 1983.

DeKieffer, Donald E. "Foreign Policy Trade Controls and the GATT." *Journal of World Trade* 22 (June 1988): 73–80.

————. "Incentives: Economic and Social." *Case Western Reserve Journal of International Law* 15 (Spring 1983).

Doxey, Margaret P. "International Sanctions in Theory and Practice." *Case Western Reserve Journal of International Law* 15 (Spring 1983).

————. "International Sanctions: Trials of Strength or Texts of Weakness?" *Millennium* 12 (May 1983): 79–87.

————. *Economic Sanctions and International Enforcement*. New York: Oxford University Press, 1980.

Elagab, Omer Yousif. *The Legality of Non-forcible Counter-measures in International Law*. Oxford: Clarendon Press, 1988.

Ellings, Richard J. *Embargoes and World Power: Lessons from American Foreign Policy*. Boulder, Colo.: Westview, 1985.

Falkenheim, Peggy L. "Post Afghanistan Sanctions." In *The Utility of International Economic Sanctions*, ed. D. Leyton-Brown. London: Croom Helm, 1987.

Finney, Lynne Dratler. "Development Assistance—A Tool of Foreign Policy." *Case Western Reserve Journal of International Law* 15 (Spring 1983).

Flores, David A. "Export Controls and the US Effort to Combat International Terrorism." *Law and Policy in International Business* 13 (1981): 521–90.

Gordon, D. F. "The Politics of International Sanctions: A Case Study of South Africa." In *Dilemmas of Economic Coercion: Sanctions in World Politics*, ed. M. Nincic and P. Wallensteen. New York: Praeger, 1983.

Green, Jerrold D. "Strategies for Evading Economic Sanctions." In *Dilemmas of Economic Coercion: Sanctions in World Politics*, ed. M. Nincic and P. Wallensteen. New York: Praeger, 1983.

Hanlon, Joseph, and Roger Ormand. *The Sanctions Handbook*. Harmondsworth, England: Penguin Books, 1987.

Harrison, Glennon J. "Panama: Trade, Finance, and Proposed Economic Sanctions." Congressional Research Service Report for Congress, Report No. 88–188E, 1988.

————. "The U.S. Trade Embargo against Nicaragua after Two-and-a-Half Years." Congressional Research Service Report for Congress, Report no. 87-87E, 1987.

Hayes, J. P. *Economic Effects of Sanctions on South Africa*. London: Trade Policy Research Centre, 1987.

Hirschman, Albert O. *National Power and the Structure of Foreign Trade*. Expanded ed. Berkeley and Los Angeles: University of California Press, 1980.

Holland, Martin. "The Other Side of Sanctions: Positive Initiatives for Southern Africa." *Journal of Modern African Studies* 26, no. 2 (1988): 303–18.

Hufbauer, Gary Clyde, and J. J. Schott. *Economic Sanctions in Support of Foreign Policy Goals*. Washington, D.C.: Institute for International Economics, 1983.

Joyner, Christopher. "The Transnational Boycott as Economic Coercion in International Law: Policy, Place, and Practice." *Vanderbilt Journal of Transnational Law* 17 (1984).

Kaempfer, William H., and Anton Lowenberg. "The Theory of International Economic Sanctions: A Public Choice Approach." *American Economic Review* 78 (September 1988): 786–93.

———. "A Model of the Political Economy of International Investment Sanctions: The Case of South Africa." *Kyklos* 39, no. 3 (1986): 377–96.

Kaempfer, William H., and Michael H. Moffet. "Impact of Anti-Apartheid Sanctions on South Africa: Some Trade and Financial Evidence." *Contemporary Policy Issues* 6, no. 4 (October 1988): 118–29.

Kapstein, Jonathan. "South Africa: The Squeeze Is On." *Business Week* Industrial/Technology Edition, September 1989, 44–48.

Khan, Haider Ali. *The Political Economy of Sanctions against Apartheid*. Boulder, Colo.: Lynne Rienner, 1989.

———. "The Impact of Trade Sanctions on South Africa: A Social Accounting Matrix Approach." *Contemporary Policy Issues* (October 1988): 130–40.

Klinghoffer, Arthur Jay. *Oiling the Wheels of Apartheid: Exposing South Africa's Secret Oil Trade*. Boulder, Colo.: Lynne Rienner, 1989.

Kriesberg, Louis. "Carrots, Sticks, De-escalation: U.S.-Soviet and Arab-Israeli Relations." *Armed Forces and Society* 13, no. 3 (1987): 403–23.

Lawson, Fred H. "Using Positive Sanctions to End International Conflicts: Iran and the Arab Gulf Countries." *Journal of Peace Research* 20, no. 4 (1983): 311–28.

Lenway, Stefanie Ann. "Between War and Commerce: Economic Sanctions as a Tool of Statecraft." *International Organization* 42 (Spring 1988): 397–426.

Leyton-Brown, David, ed. *The Utility of International Economic Sanctions*. New York: St. Martin's Press, 1987.

Lindsay, James M. "Trade Sanctions as Policy Instruments: A Re-examination." *International Studies Quarterly* 30 (1986): 153–73.

Lipton, Merle. "Sanctions and South Africa: The Dynamics of Economic Isolation." Special Report no. 1119. London: Economist Intelligence Unit, 1988.

Lombard, Joseph C. "The Survival of Noriega: Lessons from the U.S. Sanctions Against Panama." *Stanford Journal of International Law* 26 (Fall 1989): 315–69.

Love, Janice. "The Potential Impact of Economic Sanctions Against South Africa." *Journal of Modern African Studies* 26, no. 1 (1988): 91–111.

Lowenberg, Anton D. "An Economic Theory of Apartheid." *Economic Inquiry* 27 (January 1989): 57–74.

Lundborg, Per. *The Economics of Export Embargoes: The Case of the US-Soviet Grain Suspension*. London and New York: Croom Helm, 1987.

Marantz, Paul. 1987. "Economic Sanctions in the Polish Crisis." In *The Utility of International Economic Sanctions*, ed. D. Leyton-Brown. London: Croom Helm, 1987.

Maren, Michael. "Fortress South Africa." *Africa Report* 34 (March/April 1989): 31–33.

Mayall, J. "The Sanctions Problem in International Economic Relations: Reflections in Light of Recent Experience." *International Affairs* 60, no. 4 (1984): 631–42.

Miller, J. "When Sanctions Worked." *Foreign Policy* 39 (1980): 118–29.

Moorsom, Richard. *The Scope for Sanctions: Economic Measures against South Africa.* London: Catholic Institute for International Relations, 1986.

Morse, Duane D., and Joan S. Powers. "U.S. Export Controls and Foreign Entities: The Unanswered Questions of Pipeline Diplomacy." *Virginia Journal of International Law* 23 (1983): 537–67.

Moyer, Homer E., Jr. *Export Controls as Instruments of Foreign Policy: The History, Legal Issues, and Policy Lessons of Three Recent Cases.* Washington, D.C.: International Law Institute, 1988.

Moyer, Homer E., Jr., and Linda A. Mabry. "Export Controls as Instruments of Foreign Policy: The History, Legal Issues, and Policy Lessons of Three Recent Cases." *Law and Policy in International Business* 15 (1983): 1–171.

Neff, Stephen C. 1988. "Boycott and the Law of Nations: Economic Warfare and Modern International Law in Historical Perspective." *British Yearbook of International Law 1988.* Oxford: Oxford University Press, 1988.

Nincic, Miroslav, and Peter Wallensteen, eds. *Dilemmas of Economic Coercion: Sanctions in World Politics.* New York: Praeger, 1983.

Nossal, Kim Richard. *Rain Dancing: Sanctions in Canadian and Australian Foreign Policy.* Toronto: University of Toronto Press, 1994.

———. "International Sanctions as International Punishment." *International Organization* 43, no. 2 (1989): 301–22.

Orkin, Mark. *Sanctions against Apartheid.* New York: St. Martin's Press, 1989.

Paarlberg, Robert L. "Lessons of the Grain Embargo." *Foreign Affairs* 59 (Fall 1980): 144–62.

Paul, Karen. "Political Consequences of Ethical Investing: The Case of South Africa." *Journal of Business Ethics* 7 (September 1988): 691–97.

Perlow, Gary H. "Taking Peacetime Trade Sanctions to the Limit." *Case Western Reserve Journal of International Law* 15 (Spring 1983).

Renwick, Robin. "Economic Sanctions." Harvard Studies in International Affairs no. 45. Cambridge: Harvard University Center for International Affairs, 1981.

Rode, Reinhard, and Hanns D. Jacobsen. *Economic Warfare or Detente: An Assessment of East-West Relations in the 1980s.* Boulder, Colo.: Westview, 1985.

Sarna, A. J. *Boycott and Blacklist: A History of Arab Economic Warfare against Israel.* Totowa, N.J.: Rowman & Littlefield, 1986.

Schott, Jeffrey J. "Trade Sanctions and US Foreign Policy." Washington, D.C.: Carnegie Endowment for International Peace, 1982.

Sikkink, Kathryn. "Codes of Conduct for Transnational Corporations: The Case of the WHO/UNICEF Code." *International Organization* 40, no. 4 (1986): 815–40.

Sullivan, Mark P. *U.S. Sanctions and the State of the Panamanian Economy.* Congressional Research Service Report for Congress, Report No. 88-578F, 1988.

United Nations Economic Commission for Africa. *South African Destabilization: The Economic Cost of Frontline Resistance to Apartheid.* New York: Africa Recovery, October 1989.

U.S. Congressional Research Service, Library of Congress. *China Sanctions: Some Possible Effects.* Washington, D.C.: Congressional Research Service, 1989.

———. *U.S. Economic Sanctions Imposed against Specific Foreign Countries: 1979 to the Present.* Congressional Research Service Report for Congress 88-612 F, rev. Washington, D.C., 9 September 1988.

———. *An Assessment of the Afghanistan Sanctions: Implications for Trade and Diplomacy in the 1980s.* Washington, D.C.: Congressional Research Service, 1982.

U.S. General Accounting Office. *Libyan Trade Sanctions.* Washington, D.C.: GAO,. 1987.

U.S. House of Representatives. Committee on Foreign Affairs; Subcommittee on Europe and the Middle East. Hearings on East-West Economic Issues, Sanctions Policy, and the Formulation of International Economic Policy: Statement by Under Secretary of State for Economic Affairs Allen W. Wallis. 98th Cong., 2d sess., Washington, D.C., 29 March 1984.

———. Committee on Foreign Affairs; Subcommittee on International Economic Policy and Trade and Subcommittee on Western Hemisphere Affairs. GAO Review of Economic Sanctions Imposed against Panama: Statement by Frank C. Conahan. 101st Cong., 1st sess., Washington, D.C., 26 July 1989.

van Bergeijk, Peter A. G. "Success and Failure of Economic Sanctions." *Kyklos* 42, no. 3 (Fall 1989): 385–404.

Venter, D. J. *South Africa, Sanctions, and the Multinationals.* Chichester: Carden Publications, 1989.

von Amerongen, Otto Wolff. "Economic Sanctions as a Foreign Policy Tool?" *International Security* 5, no. 2 (1980): 159–67.

Voorhes, Meg. *Black South Africans' Attitudes on Sanctions and Disinvestment.* Washington, D.C.: Investor Responsibility Research Center, 1988.

Wallensteen, Peter. "Economic Sanctions: Ten Modern Cases and Three Important Lessons." In *Dilemmas of Economic Coercion: Sanctions in World Politics,* ed. M. Nincic and P. Wallensteen. New York: Praeger, 1983.

Wasowski, Stanislaw S. "U.S. Sanctions against Poland." *Washington Quarterly* 9 (Spring 1986): 167–84.

Weintraub, Sidney, ed. *Economic Coercion and U.S. Foreign Policy: Implications of Case Studies from the Johnson Administration.* Boulder, Colo.: Westview, 1982.

Weisberg, Henry. "Unilateral Economic Sanctions and the Risks of Extraterritorial Application: The Libyan Example." *New York University Journal of International Law and Politics* 19 (1987): 993–1011.

White, Brian. "Britain and the Implementation of Oil Sanctions against Rhodesia." In *Foreign Policy Implementation*, ed. S. Smith and M. Clarke. London: George Allen & Unwin, 1985.

Wolf, Charles. *International Economic Sanctions*. Santa Monica, Calif.: Rand Corp., 1980.

Since 1990

Abbott, Kenneth W. Review of *International Economic Sanctions: Improving the Haphazard U.S. Legal Regime*, by Barry E. Carter. *American Journal of International Law* 85 (1991): 236–40.

Acevedo, Domingo E. "The Haitian Crisis and the OAS Response: A Test of Effectiveness in Protecting Democracy." In *Enforcing Restraint: Collective Intervention in Internal Conflicts*, ed. Lori Fisler Damrosch. New York: Council on Foreign Relations, 1993.

Alerassool, Mahvash. *Freezing Assets: The USA and the Most Effective Economic Sanction*. New York: St. Martin's Press, 1993.

Al-Samarrai, Bashir. "Economic Sanctions against Iraq: Do They Contribute to a Just Settlement?" In *Economic Sanctions: Panacea or Peacebuilding in a Post–Cold War World?* ed. David Cortright and George A. Lopez. Boulder, Colo.: Westview, 1995.

Alnasrawi, Abbas. "Iraq: Economic Consequences of 1991 Gulf War and Future Outlook." *Third World Quarterly* 13, no. 2 (1992): 335–52.

American Friends Service Committee, Working Group on International Economic Sanctions. *Dollars or Bombs: The Search for Justice through International Economic Sanctions*. Philadelphia: American Friends Service Committee, 1993.

Ascherio, Alberto, Robert Chase, Tim Cote, Godelieave Dehaes, Eric Hoskins, Jiliali Laaouej, Megan Passey, Saleh Qaderi, Saher Shuqaidef, Mary C. Smith, and Sarah Zaidi. "Effect of the Gulf War on Infant and Child Mortality in Iraq." *New England Journal of Medicine* 327, no. 13 (24 September 1992): 13.

———. *Infant and Child Mortality and Nutritional Status of Iraqi Children after the Gulf Conflict*. April 1992. Results of a community-based survey by an international study team.

Auerbach, Stuart. "Are Sanctions More Harmful than Helpful?" *Washington Post*, 28 March 1993, H1.

Bahgat, Gawdat. "Regional Peace and Stability in the Gulf." *Security Dialogue* 26, no. 3 (1995): 317–30.

Ball, Nicole. "Pressing for Peace: Can Aid Induce Reform?" Washington, D.C.: Overseas Development Council, 1992.

Barkan, Joanne. "War in the Gulf." *Dissent* 38 (Winter 1991): 5–6.

Bastos, Maria Ines. 1994. "How International Sanctions Worked: Domestic and Foreign Political Constraints on the Brazilian Informatics Policy." *Journal of Development Studies* 30 (January 1994): 380–404.

Becker, Charles M., and Jan H. Hofmeyr. *The Impact of Sanctions on South Africa.* Washington, D.C.: Investor Responsibility Research Center, 1990.

Bethlehem, Daniel L., ed. *The Kuwait Crisis: Sanctions and Their Economic Consequences.* 2 vols. Cambridge: Grotius Publications Ltd. Research Centre for International Law, Cambridge University, 1991.

Binder, David. "U.S. Suspends Trade Benefits for Yugoslavia." *New York Times,* 7 December 1991, 5, 7.

Blumenfeld, Jesmond. *Economic Interdependence in Southern Africa: From Conflict to Cooperation?* London: Pinter Publishers; New York: St. Martin's Press for the Royal Institute of International Affairs, London, 1991.

Bohr, Sebastian. "Sanctions by the United Nations Security Council and the European Community." *European Journal of International Law* 4 (1993).

Boutros-Ghali, Boutros. *An Agenda for Peace 1995.* New York: United Nations, 1995. (Includes *Supplement to An Agenda for Peace.*)

Bradsher, Keith."Two Democrats Offer Bill Requiring Trade Sanctions." *New York Times,* 5 November 1991, C2, D10.

"Bush's Sanctions Veto Snubs Foreign Relations Leaders." *Congressional Quarterly Weekly Report* 48 (24 November 1990): 3932.

Campbell, Barry R., and Danforth Newcomb, eds. *The Impact of the Freeze of Kuwaiti and Iraqi Assets on Financial Institutions and Financial Transactions.* London: International Bar Association Series, 1990.

Casimir, Jean. "Haiti after the Coup." *World Policy Journal* 9 (Spring 1992): 572.

Cason, Jim. "U.S. Policy toward Post-Apartheid South Africa." *Peace and Democracy News* 7, no. 2 (1994): 1.

The Children Are Dying: The Impact of Sanctions on Iraq. 1996. Reports by the UN Food and Agriculture Organization, Ramsey Clark, and world leaders. New York: World View Forum, 1996.

Christiansen, Drew, and Gerard F. Powers. "Economic Sanctions and the Just-War Doctrine." In *Economic Sanctions: Panacea or Peacebuilding in a Post–Cold War World?* ed. David Cortright and George A. Lopez. Boulder, Colo.: Westview, 1995.

———. "Unintended Consequences." *Bulletin of the Atomic Scientists* 49, no.9 (1993): 41–45.

Claude, Inis L., Jr. "The Gulf War and Prospects for World Order by Collective Security." In *The Persian Gulf Crisis: Power in the Post–Cold War World,* ed. Robert. F. Helms. II and R. H. Dorff. Westport, Conn.: Praeger, 1993.

Clawson, Patrick. *How Has Saddam Hussein Survived? Economic Sanctions, 1990–1993.* Institute for National Strategic Studies, McNair Paper no. 22. Washington, D.C.: National Defense University, 1993.

———. "Sanctions as Punishment, Enforcement, and Prelude to Further Action." *Ethics and International Affairs* 7 (1993): 17–38.

Cockburn, Alexander. "Servants to Murder: The Press, Bush, and Iraq Today." *Nation* (25 November 1991): 658–59.

Conlon, Paul. "The UN's Questionable Sanctions Practices." *Aussen Politik* 4 (1995): 327–38.

Constable, Pamela. "Haiti: A Nation in Despair. A Policy Adrift." *Current History* 93, no. 581 (March 1994): 108–14.

———. "Dateline Haiti: Caribbean Stalemate." *Foreign Policy* 89 (Winter 1992): 175–90.

Contreras, Joseph. "Is It Time to Lift Sanctions? An Interim Report Card on South Africa's Reforms." *Newsweek*, 1 July 1991, 37.

Cortright, David, ed. *The Price of Peace: Inducement Strategies for International Conflict Prevention.* Lanham, Md.: Rowman & Littlefield, forthcoming.

Cortright, David, and George A. Lopez. "Research Concerns and Policy Needs in an Era of Sanctions." In *Economic Sanctions: Panacea or Peacebuilding in a Post–Cold War World?* ed. David Cortright and George A. Lopez. Boulder, Colo.: Westview, 1995.

Cortright, David, and George A. Lopez, eds. *Economic Sanctions: Panacea or Peacebuilding in a Post–Cold War World?* Boulder, Colo.: Westview, 1995.

Crosette, Barbara. "U.S. Plans to Sharpen Focus of Its Sanctions against Haiti." *New York Times*, 5 February 1992, A8, A10.

Damrosch, Lori Fisler. "The Civilian Impact of Economic Sanctions." In *Enforcing Restraint: Collective Intervention in Internal Conflicts*, ed. Lori Fisler Damrosch. New York: Council on Foreign Relations, 1993.

Davis, Jennifer. "Sanctions and Apartheid: The Economic Challenge to Discrimination." In *Economic Sanctions: Panacea or Peacebuilding in a Post–Cold War World?* ed. David Cortright and George A. Lopez. Boulder, Colo.: Westview, 1995.

———. "Squeezing Apartheid." *Bulletin of the Atomic Scientists* 49, no. 9 (1993): 16–19.

Delbrück, Jost. 1992. "International Economic Sanctions and Third States." *Archiv des Völkerrechts* 30, no. 1 (1992).

"Dispute Stalls an Import Ban Aimed at Weapons-Makers." *Congressional Quarterly Weekly Report* 49 (12 October 1991): 2964–65.

Dorff, Robert H. "Conflict in the Post–Cold War International System: Sources and Responses." In *The Persian Gulf Crisis: Power in the Post–Cold War World*, ed. Robert. F. Helms. II and R. H. Dorff. Westport, Conn.: Praeger, 1993.

Dowty, Alan. "Sanctioning Iraq: The Limits of the New World Order." *Washington Quarterly* 17, no. 3 (1994): 179–98.

Doxey, Margaret P. *International Sanctions in Contemporary Perspective*, 2d ed. New York: St. Martin's Press, 1996.

Dreze, Jean, and Haris Gazdar. "Hunger and Poverty in Iraq, 1991." *World Development* 20, no. 7 (1992): 921–45.

Dumas, Lloyd (Jeff). "A Proposal for a New United Nations Council on Economic Sanctions." In *Economic Sanctions: Panacea or Peacebuilding in a Post–Cold War World?* ed. David Cortright and George A. Lopez. Boulder, Colo.: Westview, 1995.

———. "Organizing the Chaos." *Bulletin of the Atomic Scientists* 49, no. 9 (1993): 46–49.

Eaton, Jonathan, and Maxim Engers. "Sanctions." *Journal of Political Economy* 100, no. 5 (1992): 899–928.

Economist. "In the Eye of the Storm." 8 December 1990, 46.

Eland, Ivan. "Economic Sanctions as Tools of Foreign Policy." In *Economic Sanctions: Panacea or Peacebuilding in a Post–Cold War World?* ed. David Cortright and George A. Lopez. Boulder, Colo.: Westview, 1995.

———. "Sanctions: Think Small." *Bulletin of the Atomic Scientists* 49, no. 9 (1993): 36–40.

Ellings, Richard J. *Private Property and National Security: Foreign Economic Sanctions and the Constitution.* Washington, D.C.: National Legal Center for the Public Interest, 1991.

Elliott, Kimberly Ann. "Factors Affecting the Success of Sanctions." In *Economic Sanctions: Panacea or Peacebuilding in a Post–Cold War World?* ed. David Cortright and George A. Lopez. Boulder, Colo.: Westview, 1995.

———. "A Look at the Record." *Bulletin of the Atomic Scientists* 49, no. 9 (1993): 32–35.

———. "Nonmilitary Responses to the Iraqi Invasion of Kuwait: Use of Economic Sanctions." In *The Persian Gulf Crisis: Power in the Post–Cold War World*, ed. Robert F. Helms II and Robert H. Dorff. Westport, Conn.: Praeger, 1993.

Elliott, Kimberly Ann, and Gary Clyde Hufbauer. "Sanctions in the Post–Cold War Era." *International Economic Insights* 1 (September/October 1990): 8–9.

Fine, James. "The Iraq Sanctions Catastrophe." *Middle East Report* 22, no. 174 (1992): 36, 39.

Food and Agricultural Organization. *Evaluation of Food and Nutrition Situation in Iraq. Terminal Statement Prepared for the Government of Iraq by FAO.* Technical Cooperation Programme. Muhammad Manzoor Khan, Peter Pellet, Q-A. Ahmad, Sarah Zaidi, M.S. Fawzi. Mission from 25 July–1 September 1995. Rome, 1995.

Forland, Tor Egil. "The History of Economic Warfare: International Law, Effectiveness, Strategies." *Journal of Peace Research* 30 (1993): 151–62.

Galdi, Theodore, and Robert Shuey. *U.S. Economic Sanctions Imposed against Specific Countries: 1979 to the Present*. Washington, D.C.: Congressional Research Service, 1992.

Gann, Lewis H. *Hope for South Africa?* Stanford, Calif.: Hoover Institution Press, Stanford University, 1991.

Gavin, Joseph G., III. "Should Economic Sanctions Be Part of Foreign Policy?" *USA Today,* September 1990, 24.

George, Alexander L. *Bridging the Gap: Theory and Practice in Foreign Policy*. Washington, D.C.: United States Institute of Peace Press, 1993.

George, Alexander L., and William E. Simons, eds. *The Limits of Coercive Diplomacy*. 2d ed. Boulder, Colo.: Westview, 1994.

Glenny, Misha. *The Fall of Yugoslavia: The Third Balkan War*. London: Penguin, 1992.

Gordon, Michael. "Navy Begins Blockade Enforcing Iraq Embargo." *New York Times,* 17 August 1990, A10.

Hale, Terrel D., ed. *United States Sanctions and South Africa: A Selected Legal Bibliography*. Westport, Conn.: Greenwood Press, 1993.

Hanlon, Joseph, ed. *South Africa: The Sanctions Report*. Portsmouth, N.H.: Heinemann Educational Books, 1990.

Harvard Center for Population and Development Studies. *Sanctions in Haiti: Crisis in Humanitarian Action*. Cambridge: Program on Human Security, November 1993.

Harvard Study Team. "Harvard Study Team Report: Public Health in Iraq After the Gulf War." 1991.

———. "Special Report: The Effect of the Gulf Crisis on the Children of Iraq." *New England Journal of Medicine* (26 September 1991): 977–80.

Hatch, John. "Sanctions Must Stay." Interview with African National Congress President Nelson Mandela. *New Statesman & Society,* 27 September 1991, 12.

Hecht, Jeff. "Sanctions Hit Iraq's Ancient Sites." *New Scientist* 133, no. 1810 (29 February 1992): 13.

Hedges, Chris. "Outlook in Libya: Adapt, Improvise; Malta Becomes Transit Point as Travel by Sea Replaces the Banned Flights." *New York Times,* 17 April 1992, A5.

Helms, Robert F., II, and Robert H. Dorff, eds. *The Persian Gulf Crisis: Power in the Post–Cold War World*. Westport, Conn.: Praeger, 1993.

Hendrickson, David C. "The Democratist Crusade: Intervention, Economic Sanctions, and Engagement." *World Policy Journal* 11 (Winter 1994): 18–30.

Hengeveld, Richard, and Jaap Rodenburg, eds. *Embargo: Apartheid's Oil Secrets Revealed*. Amsterdam: Amsterdam University Press, 1995.

Herrmann, Richard. "Coercive Diplomacy and the Crisis over Kuwait, 1990–1991." In *The Limits of Coercive Diplomacy,* ed. A. L. George and W. E. Simons. Boulder, Colo.: Westview, 1994.

Hill, Kevin A. "The Domestic Sources of Foreign Policymaking: Congressional Voting and American Mass Attitudes toward South Africa." *International Studies Quarterly* 37 (June 1993): 195–214.

Hoskins, Eric. "Killing Is Killing—Not Kindness." *New Statesman & Society,* 17 January 1992, 12.

———. "The Truth behind Economic Sanctions: A Report on the Embargo of Food and Medicines to Iraq." In *War Crimes,* ed. Ramsey Clark et al. Washington, D.C.: Maisonneuve Press, 1992.

———. "Starved to Death." *New Statesman & Society,* 31 May 1991, 15.

Hufbauer, Gary Clyde. "The Impact of U.S. Economic Sanctions and Controls on U.S. Firms." Report to the National Foreign Trade Council . Washington, D.C., 1990.

Hufbauer, Gary Clyde, Jeffrey J. Schott, and Kimberly Ann Elliott. *Economic Sanctions Reconsidered: History and Current Policy.* 2d ed. Washington, D.C.: Institute for International Economics, 1990.

Human Rights Watch. "Iraq: Background on Human Rights Conditions, 1984–1992." New York: Human Rights Watch, Middle East Watch Committee, August 1993.

Hunter, David W. *Western Trade Pressure on the Soviet Union: An Interdependence Perspective on Sanctions.* New York: St. Martin's Press, 1991.

Hybel, Alex Roberto. *Power over Rationality: The Bush Administration and the Gulf Crisis.* Albany: State University of New York Press, 1993.

"The Impact of the International Community's Sanctions on the Health of the Population of FR Yugoslavia." *Yugoslav Survey* 35, no. 1 (1994): 97–110.

"In the Works: Sanctions." *Congressional Quarterly Weekly Report* 47 (30 September 1989): 2580.

International Federation of Red Cross and Red Crescent Societies. "UN Sanctions and the Humanitarian Crisis." In *World Disasters Report 1995.* Geneva: IFRC, 1995.

International Institute of Humanitarian Law. Meeting on humanitarian consequences of embargo measures, 1995.

"The Iraq Sanctions Dilemma." *Middle East Report.* Special edition. March/April 1994.

Jenkins, C. "Sanctions and Their Effects on Employment in South Africa." *International Labour Review* 130, nos. 5–6 (1991): 657–77.

Jentleson, Bruce W. *Economic Sanctions: Post–Cold War Policy Challenges.* Working paper prepared for the National Research Council's Committee on International Conflict Resolution, June 1996.

Johnstone, Ian. *Aftermath of the Gulf War: An Assessment of UN Action.* Boulder, Colo.: Lynne Rienner, 1994.

Joyner, Christopher C. "Sanctions and International Law." In *Economic Sanctions: Panacea or Peacebuilding in a Post–Cold War World?* ed. David Cortright and George A. Lopez. Boulder, Colo.: Westview, 1995.

———. "Sanctions, Compliance, and International Law: Reflections on the United States Experience against Iraq." *Virginia Journal of International Law* 32, no. 1 (Fall 1991): 1–46.

Kaempfer, William H., and Anton D. Lowenberg. "The Problems and Promise of Sanctions." In *Economic Sanctions: Panacea or Peacebuilding in a Post–Cold War World?* ed. David Cortright and George A. Lopez. Boulder, Colo.: Westview, 1995.

———. *International Economic Sanctions: A Public Choice Perspective.* Boulder, Colo.: Westview, 1992.

Karns, Margaret P., and Karen A. Mingst. *The United States and Multilateral Institutions: Patterns of Changing Instrumentality and Influence.* Boston: Unwin Hyman, 1990.

Kibbe, Jennifer. *Reconsidering South Africa: The Prospects for U.S. Investment.* Washington, D.C.: Investor Responsibility Research Center, 1993.

Kinzer, Stephen. "Sanctions Driving Yugoslav Economy into Deep Decline." *New York Times* (31 August 1992): A1–5.

Kirschner, Jonathan. "The Microfoundations of Economic Sanctions." *Security Studies* 6 (Spring 1997): 32–64.

Klotz, Audie. "Norms Reconstituting Interests: Global Racial Equality and U.S. Sanctions against South Africa." *International Organization* 49 (Summer 1995): 451–78.

———. "Transforming a Pariah State: International Dimensions of the South African Transitions." *Africa Today* 42, nos. 1–2 (1995): 75–87.

Knight, Richard. *State and the Municipal Governments Take Aim at Apartheid.* New York: American Committee on Africa, 1991.

———. *Unified List of United States Companies Doing Business in South Africa.* 3d ed. New York: Africa Fund, 1990.

Konovalov, Alexander, Sergey Oznobistchev, and Dmitry G. Evstafiev. "A Review of Economic Sanctions: A Russian Perspective." In *Economic Sanctions: Panacea or Peacebuilding in a Post–Cold War World?* ed. David Cortright and George A. Lopez. Boulder, Colo.: Westview, 1995.

———. "Saying Da, Saying Nyet." *Bulletin of the Atomic Scientists* 49, no. 9 (1993): 28–31.

Krinsky, Michael, and David Golove, eds. *United States Economic Measures against Cuba: Proceedings in the United Nations and International Law Issues.* Northampton, Mass.: Aletheia Press, 1993.

Lake, Anthony. *Confronting Backlash States.* Washington, D.C.: Executive Office of the President, 1994.

Lancet. "Starvation in Iraq." Editorial. 9 November 1991, 1179.

Lapidoth, Ruth. "Some Reflections on the Law and Practice Concerning the Imposition of Sanctions by the Security Council." *Archiv des Völkerrechts* 30, no. 1 (1992).

Laurence, Patrick. "Loosening Sanctions." *Africa Report* 36 (September/October 1991): 46–47.

Lavin, Franklin L. "Asphyxiation or Oxygen? The Sanctions Dilemma." *Foreign Policy* 104 (Fall 1996): 139–53.

Leich, Marian Nash. "Foreign Assets Control and Economic Sanctions." *American Journal of International Law* 84, no. 4 (October 1990): 903–7.

Leigh, Monroe. "The Political Consequences of Economic Embargoes." *American Journal of International Law* 89 (January 1995): 74–77.

Leyva de Varona, Adolfo. *Propaganda and Reality: A Look at the U.S. Embargo against Castro's Cuba*. Miami: Cuban American National Foundation, 1994.

Li, Chien-Pin. "The Effectiveness of Sanction Linkages: Issues and Actors." *International Studies Quarterly* 37 (1993): 349–70.

Licht, Sonja. "The Use of Sanctions in Former Yugoslavia: Can They Assist in Conflict Resolution?" In *Economic Sanctions: Panacea or Peacebuilding in a Post–Cold War World?* ed. David Cortright and George A. Lopez. Boulder, Colo.: Westview, 1995.

Lief, Louise. "Even in Hussein's Hometown, the Sanctions are Biting." *U.S. News & World Report*, 30 September 1991, 51.

Lopez, George A. and David Cortright. "'Smart' Sanctions on Nigeria." Working paper of the Joan B. Kroc Institute for International Peace Studies, Notre Dame, Ind., April 1996.

———. "Economic Sanctions in Contemporary Global Relations." In *Economic Sanctions: Panacea or Peacebuilding in a Post–Cold War World?* ed. David Cortright and George A. Lopez. Boulder, Colo.: Westview, 1995.

———. "The Sanctions Era: An Alternative to Military Intervention." *Fletcher Forum of World Affairs* 19, no. 2 (1995): 65–85.

———. "Sanctions: Do They Work?" *Bulletin of the Atomic Scientists* 49, no. 9 (1993): 14–15.

Lowenberg, Anton D. "Measuring the Effectiveness of Economic Sanctions on South Africa." *Africa Today* 4 (1990): 63–64.

Maas, Peter. "Serbian People, Politicians Scoff at West's Threats to Sanctions." *Washington Post*, 31 March 1993, A25.

———. "As Sanctions Bite, Serbs Look Warily toward Winter." *Washington Post*, 18 August 1992, A1.

Maguire, Robert, Edwige Balutansky, Jacques Fomerand, Larry Minear, William O'Neill, Thomas G. Weiss, and Sarah Zaidi. *Haiti Held Hostage: International Responses to the Quest for Nationhood, 1986–1996*, Occasional Paper no. 21. Providence, R.I.: Watson Institute, 1996.

Malloy, Michael P. *Economic Sanctions and U.S. Trade*. Boston: Little, Brown, 1990.

Manby, Bronwen. "South Africa: The Impact of Sanctions." *Journal of International Affairs* 46 (Summer 1992): 193–217.

Mansfield, Edward D. "International Institutions and Economic Sanctions." *World Politics* 47 (July 1995): 575–605.

———. "Alliances, Preferential Trading Arrangements, and Sanctions." *Journal of International Affairs* 48 (Summer 1994): 119–39.

Martin, Lisa L. "Credibility, Costs, and Institutions: Cooperation on Economic Sanctions." *World Politics* 45, no. 3 (1993): 406–32.

———. *Coercive Cooperation: Explaining Multilateral Economic Sanctions*. Princeton, N.J.: Princeton University Press, 1992.

Matthews, Ken. *The Gulf Conflict and International Relations*. London: Routledge, 1993.

Minear, Larry, and Thomas G. Weiss. *Humanitarian Politics*. New York: Foreign Policy Association, 1995.

———. *Mercy under Fire: War and the Global Humanitarian Community*. Boulder, Colo.: Westview, 1995.

Minear, Larry, Jeffrey Clark, Roberta Cohen, Dennis Gallagher, Iain Guest, and Thomas G. Weiss. *Humanitarian Action in the Former Yugoslavia: The UN's Role, 1991–1993*, Occasional Paper no. 18. Providence, R.I.: Watson Institute, 1994.

Minear, Larry, U. B. P. Chelliah, Jeff Crisp, John Mackinlay, and Thomas G. Weiss. *United Nations Coordination of the International Humanitarian Response to the Gulf Crisis, 1990–1992*, Occasional Paper no. 13. Providence, R.I.: Watson Institute, 1992.

Miyagawa, Makio. *Do Economic Sanctions Work?* New York: St. Martin's Press, 1992.

Montgomery, Ann. "The Impact of Sanctions on Baghdad's Children's Hospital." *War Crimes*, ed. Ramsey Clark et al. Washington, D.C.: Maisonneuve Press, 1992.

Nanda, Ved P., ed. "The Iraqi Invasion of Kuwait: The UN Response." *Southern Illinois University Law Journal* 15 (1991): 431.

Nelan, Bruce W. "Measuring the Embargo's Bite: Even If Some Countries Relent and Send Emergency Food and Medicine to Baghdad, Saddam Still Faces a Cash Crunch." *Time*, 17 September 1990, 32.

Ngobi, James C. "The United Nations Experience with Sanctions." In *Economic Sanctions: Panacea or Peacebuilding in a Post–Cold War World?* ed. David Cortright and George A. Lopez. Boulder, Colo.: Westview, 1995.

Nossal, Kim Richard. "The Symbolic Purposes of Sanctions: Australian and Canadian Reactions to Afghanistan." *Australian Journal of Political Science* 26, no. 1 (March 1991): 29–50.

Orkin, Mark, ed. *Sanctions against Apartheid*. New York: St. Martin's Press, 1990.

Patterson, Jack T. "The Political and Moral Appropriateness of Sanctions." In *Economic Sanctions: Panacea or Peacebuilding in a Post–Cold War World?* ed. David Cortright and George A. Lopez. Boulder, Colo.: Westview, 1995.

Pax Christi International. *Economic Sanctions and International Relations.* Brussels: Pax Christi International, 1993.

Payne, Richard J. *The Third World and South Africa: Post-Apartheid Challenges.* Westport, Conn.: Greenwood Press, 1992.

Pennar, Karen. "Will the Embargo Work? A Look at the Record." *Business Week,* 17 September 1990, 22.

Reed, Stanley. "Iraq May Not Starve, But Its Industry Will." *Business Week,* 17 September 1990, 28.

Reuther, David E. "UN Sanctions against Iraq." In *Economic Sanctions: Panacea or Peacebuilding in a Post–Cold War World?* ed. David Cortright and George A. Lopez. Boulder, Colo.: Westview, 1995.

Rich, Paul B. "Sanctions and Negotiations for Political Change in South Africa." *African Affairs* 89, no. 356 (July 1990): 451–55.

Rodman, Kenneth A. "Sanctions at Bay? Hegemonic Decline, Multinational Corporations, and U.S. Economic Sanctions since the Pipeline Case." *International Organization* 49 (Winter 1995): 105–37.

———. "Public and Private Sanctions against South Africa." *Political Science Quarterly* 109 (Summer 1994): 313–34.

Rosenthal, Robert W. "On the Incentives Associated with Sovereign Debt." *Journal of International Economics* 30 (February 1991): 167–76.

Rosenzweig, Laurie. "United Nations Sanctions: Creating a More Effective Tool for the Enforcement of International Law." *Austrian Journal of Public and International Law* 48 (1995).

Rouleau, Eric. "America's Unyielding Policy toward Iraq." *Foreign Affairs* 74 (January/February 1995): 59–72.

Rowe, David M. *Surviving Economic Coercion: Rhodesia's Responses to International Economic Sanctions.* Ph.D. diss., Duke University, 1993.

———. *The Domestic Political Economy of International Economic Sanctions.* Cambridge, Mass.: Center for International Affairs, 1992.

Rubenstein, Ed. "Can Sanctions Work?" *National Review,* 31 December 1990, 12.

"Sanctioned Trade: Breaking Embargoes Legally." *Geographical Magazine* 65 (June 1993): 19.

"Sanctions Compromise Reached on Chemical Weapons Makers." *Congressional Quarterly Weekly Report* 49 (28 September 1991): 2805–6.

Schachter, Oscar. "United Nations Law in the Gulf Conflict." *American Journal of International Law* 85 (1991): 452–73.

Scharfen, John C. *The Dismal Battlefield: Mobilizing for Economic Conflict.* Annapolis, Md.: Naval Institute Press, 1995.

Schmitt, Eric. "A Move to Block U.S. Aid to Amman; Jordan Suspected of Violating the Embargo against Iraq, Administration Says." *New York Times*, 8 December 1991, 10, 12.

"Senate Approves Export Bill Linking Sanctions, Weapons." *Congressional Quarterly Weekly Report* 49 (23 February 1991): 455.

"Senate Approves Sanctions Bill." *Congressional Quarterly Weekly Report* 48 (19 May 1990): 1572.

Shepherd, Anne. "Waiting for Investment." *Africa Report* 38 (November/December 1993): 17–19.

Shepherd, George W., Jr., ed. *Effective Sanctions on South Africa: The Cutting Edge of Economic Intervention*. New York: Praeger, 1991.

Simons, Geoffrey Leslie. *The Scourging of Iraq: Sanctions, Law, and Natural Justice*. New York: St. Martin's Press, 1996.

Smeets, Maarten. "Economic Sanctions against Iraq: The Ideal Case?" *Journal of World Trade* (Switzerland) 24 (December 1990): 105–20.

Smith, Jeffrey R. "Iraq Shipped Oil to Iran, U.S. Alleges." *Washington Post*, 31 March 1993, A1.

South Africa: U.S. Policy. Washington, D.C.: U.S. Dept. of State, Bureau of Public Affairs, Office of Public Communication, 1990.

"South African Chemical Workers in New York: CWIU Calls for Responsible Disinvestment." *Social Policy* 20 (Winter 1990): 11.

Spencer, Gary. "U.N. Official Discusses Sanctions' Viability." *New York Law Journal*, 24 January 1991, 1.

Stanley Foundation. *Political Symbol or Policy Tool: Making Sanctions Work*. Muscatine, Iowa: Stanley Foundation, 1993.

Stremlau, John. *Sharpening International Sanctions: Toward a Stronger Role for the United Nations*. A Report to the Carnegie Commission on Preventing Deadly Conflict. New York: Carnegie Corp., 1996.

Thomson, Alex. "Incomplete Engagement: Reagan's South Africa Policy Revisited." *Journal of Modern African Studies* 33 (March 1995): 83–101.

Tsebelis, George. "Are Sanctions Effective? A Game-Theoretic Analysis." *Journal of Conflict Resolution* 34, no. 1 (March 1990): 3–28.

Uchitelle, Louis. "Who's Punishing Whom? Trade Bans Are Boomerangs, U.S. Companies Say." *New York Times*, 11 September 1996, D1.

Ullman, Richard H. *The World and Yugoslavia's Wars*. New York: Council on Foreign Relations, 1996.

United Nations. *Report of the Special Committee on the Charter of the United Nations and on the Strengthening of the Role of the Organization: Draft resolution proposed by the Chairman of the Working Group, Implementation of the provisions of the Charter of the United Nations related to assistance to third states affected by the application of sanctions*. A/C.6/51/L.18, 25 November 1996.

————. *Letter dated 24 September 1996 from the Chairman of the Security Council Committee established pursuant to Resolution 724 (1991) concerning Yugoslavia addressed to the President of the Security Council, Report of the Copenhagen Roundtable on United Nations Sanctions in the Case of the Former Yugoslavia, held at Copenhagen on 24 and 25 June 1996.* S/1996/776, 24 September 1996.

————. *Report of the Special Committee on the Charter. Implementation of the provisions of the Charter of the United Nations related to assistance to third states affected by the application of sanctions under Chapter VII of the Charter, Report of the Secretary-General.* A/50/361, 22 August 1995.

————. *Yugoslav Sanctions Committee streamlines its procedures and facilitates legitimate shipping via Danube.* S/6063, 3 July 1995.

————. *Note verbale dated 13 July 1995 from the Permanent Representative of the Netherlands Addressed to the Secretary-General of the UN. "UN Sanctions as a Tool of Peaceful Settlement of Disputes." Submitted by Australia and the Netherlands at the first session of the subgroup on sanctions of the working group of the General Assembly on Agenda for Peace.* A/50/322. 3 August 1995.

————. *Strengthening of the Coordination of Humanitarian and Disaster Relief Assistance of the United Nations, including Special Economic Assistance: Special Economic Assistance to Individual Countries or Regions: Economic assistance to states affected by the implementation of the Security Council resolutions imposing sanctions against the Federal Republic of Yugoslavia (Serbia and Montenegro), Report of the Secretary-General.* A/49/356, 9 September 1994.

————. *Letter dated 15 July 1991 from the Secretary-General addressed to the President of the Security Council, Report to the Secretary-General on Humanitarian Needs in Iraq by a Mission led by Sadruddin Aga Khan, Executive Delegate of the Secretary-General,* 15 July 1991. Geneva: Office of the Executive Delegate of the Secretary-General for a United Nations Inter-agency Humanitarian Programme for Iraq, Kuwait and the Iraq/Turkey and Iraq/Iran Border Areas, S/22799, 17 July 1991.

————. *Letter dated 20 March 1991 from the Secretary-General addressed to the President of the Security Council, Report to the Secretary-General on Humanitarian Needs in Kuwait and Iraq in the Immediate Post-crisis Environment by a Mission to the Area led by Mr. Martti Ahtisaari, Under-Secretary-General for Administration and Management,* S/22366, 20 March 1991.

————. *Transnational Corporations in South Africa: Second United Nations Public Hearings.* New York, 1990.

United Nations High Commission for Refugees. *Effects of Sanctions on Refugees and Refugee Assistance Programmes in Iraq.* Baghdad, 1995.

U.S. General Accounting Office. *Serbia-Montenegro: Implementation of U.N. economic sanctions: Report to the Honorable Edward M. Kennedy, U.S. Senate.* Washington, D.C.: GAO, 1993. Microform.

————. National Security and International Affairs Division. *Economic Sanctions: Effectiveness as Tools of Foreign Policy.* Washington, D.C.: GAO, 1992.

U.S. House of Representatives. Committee on Foreign Affairs. *Roundtable on Haiti—October 1993: Briefing before the Committee on Foreign Affairs,* 103d Congress, 1st session. Washington: Government Printing Office, 20 October 1993.

————. Joint Economic Committee. Subcommittee on Education and Health. *Economic Sanctions against Iraq: Hearing before the Subcommittee on Education and Health of the Joint Economic Committee,* 101st Congress, 2d session. Washington, D.C.: Government Printing Office, 19 December 1992.

————. Select Committee on Hunger. *Humanitarian Conditions in Haiti: Hearing before the Select Committee on Hunger,* 102d Congress, 2d session. Washington, D.C.: Government Printing Office, 22 June 1992.

————. Select Committee on Hunger. International Task Force. *The Future of Humanitarian Assistance in Iraq: Hearing before the International Task Force of the Select Committee on Hunger,* 102d Congress, 2d session. Washington, D.C.: Government Printing Office, 18 March 1992.

————. Select Committee on Hunger. International Task Force. *Humanitarian Dilemma in Iraq: Hearing before the International Task Force of the Select Committee on Hunger,* 102d Congress, 1st session. Washington, D.C.: Government Printing Office, 1 August 1991.

————. Committee on Foreign Affairs. Subcommittee on International Economic Policy and Trade. *The Termination of Economic Sanctions against South Africa. Joint Hearing before the Subcommittees on International Economic Policy and Trade and Africa,* 102d Congress, 1st session. Washington, D.C.: Government Printing Office, 31 July 1991.

————. Committee on Foreign Affairs. Subcommittee on International Economic Policy and Trade. *The Status of United States Sanctions against South Africa: Hearing before the Subcommittees on International Economic Policy and Trade and on Africa of the Committee on Foreign Affairs,* 102d Congress, 1st session. Washington, D.C.: Government Printing Office, 30 April 1991.

U.S. President Clinton. *Status of Iraq: Communication from the President of the United States transmitting a report on the status of efforts to obtain Iraq's compliance with the resolutions adopted by the UN Security Council, pursuant to Pub. L. 102-1, sec. 3 (105 Stat. 4).* Washington, D.C.: Government Printing Office, 1996.

————. *Developments concerning the National Emergency with respect to Haiti: Message from the President of the United States transmitting a report on developments since his last report of October 13, 1994, concerning the national emergency with respect to Haiti, pursuant to 50 U.S.C. 1641(c) and 50 U.S.C. 1703(c).* Washington, D.C.: Government Printing Office, 1995.

————. *Status of Iraq: Communication from the President of the United States transmitting a report on the efforts to obtain Iraq's compliance with the resolutions adopted by the UN Security Council, pursuant to Pub. L. 102-1, sec. 3 (105 Stat. 4).* Washington, D.C.: Government Printing Office, 1995.

————. *Suspension of Sanctions Imposed on the Federal Republic of Yugoslavia (Serbia and Montenegro): Message from the President of the United States transmitting a copy of Presidential Determination no. 96-7: suspending sanctions imposed on the Federal*

Republic of Yugoslavia (Serbia and Montenegro), pursuant to Public Law 103-160, sec. 1511(e)(2)(107 Stat. 1840). Washington, D.C.: Government Printing Office, 1995.

————. *Actions and Expenses related to the National Emergency with Respect to the Federal Republic of Yugoslavia (Serbia and Montenegro): Message from the President of the United States transmitting a report on actions and expenses directly related to the exercise of powers and authorities conferred by the declaration of a national emergency in Executive Order no. 12808 and no. 12934 and to expanded sanctions against the FRY (S/M) and the Bosnian Serbs, pursuant to 50 U.S.C. 1641(c) and 1703(c).* Washington, D.C.: Government Printing Office, 1995.

————. *Developments concerning the National Emergency with respect to the Governments of Serbia and Montenegro: Communication from the President of the United States transmitting a report on developments since his last report concerning the national emergency with respect to the governments of Serbia and Montenegro, pursuant to 50 U.S.C. 1703(c).* Washington, D.C.: Government Printing Office, 1994.

————. *Status of Iraq: Communication from the President of the United States transmitting a report on the status of efforts to obtain Iraq's compliance with the resolutions adopted by the UN Security Council, pursuant to Public Law 102-1, section 3 (105 Stat. 4).* Washington, D.C.: Government Printing Office, 1994.

————. *Continuation of National Emergency with respect to the Federal Republic of Yugoslavia (Serbia and Montenegro): message from the President of the United States transmitting notification that the Federal Republic of Yugoslavia (Serbia and Montenegro) emergency is to continue in effect beyond May 30, 1993, pursuant to 50 U.S.C. 1622(d).* Washington, D.C.: Government Printing Office, 1993.

————. *Status of Iraq: Communication from the President of the United States transmitting a report on the status of efforts to obtain compliance by Iraq with the resolutions adopted by the U.N. Security Council, pursuant to Public Law 102-1, section 3 (105 Stat. 4).* Washington, D.C.: Government Printing Office, 1993.

van Bergeijk, Peter A. G. *Economic Diplomacy, Trade, and Commercial Policy: Positive and Negative Sanctions in a New World Order.* Aldershot, England, and Brookfield, Vt.: E. Elgar, 1994.

van Ham, Peter. Review of *Do Economic Sanctions Work?* by Makio Miyagawa. *International Affairs* 69 (July 1993): 576–77.

von Braunmühl, Claudia, and Manfred Kulessa. *The Impact of UN Sanctions on Humanitarian Assistance Activities: Report on a Study Commissioned by the United Nations Department of Humanitarian Affairs.* Berlin: Gesellschaft für Communication Management Interkultur Training mbH—COMIT, December 1995.

Walker, Peter. "Sanctions: A Blunt Weapon." *Red Cross, Red Crescent* 3 (1995): 18–19.

Weiss, Thomas G., and Cindy Collins. *Humanitarian Challenges and Intervention: World Politics and the Dilemmas of Help.* Boulder, Colo.: Westview, 1996.

Weiss, Thomas G., David P. Forsythe, and Roger A. Coate. *The United Nations and Changing World Politics.* Boulder, Colo.: Westview, 1994.

Weller, Marc. "Iraq's Sanctions Manoeuvres." *World Today* 50 (December 1994): 224–25.

Werleigh, Claudette Antoine. "The Use of Sanctions in Haiti: Assessing the Economic Realities." In *Economic Sanctions: Panacea or Peacebuilding in a Post–Cold War World?* ed. David Cortright and George A. Lopez. Boulder, Colo.: Westview, 1995.

———. "Haiti and the Halfhearted." *Bulletin of the Atomic Scientists* 49, no. 9 (1993): 20–23.

White, Nigel D. "Collective Sanctions: An Alternative to Military Coercion?" *International Relations* 12, no. 3 (December 1994): 75–91.

Woodward, Bob. *The Commanders.* New York: Simon & Schuster, 1991.

Woodward, Susan L. "The Use of Sanctions in Former Yugoslavia: Misunderstanding Political Realities." In *Economic Sanctions: Panacea or Peacebuilding in a Post–Cold War World?* ed. David Cortright and George A. Lopez. Boulder, Colo.: Westview, 1991.

———. "Yugoslavia: Divide and Fall." *Bulletin of the Atomic Scientists* 49, no. 9 (1993): 24–27.

World Council of Churches. "Memorandum and Recommendations on the Application of Sanctions." Central Committee, Document 3.2, September 1995.

Worth, Roland H. *No Choice but War: The United States Embargo against Japan and the Eruption of War in the Pacific.* Jefferson, N.C.: McFarland, 1995.

Wren, Christopher S. "African-Americans, Visiting Mandela, Back Sanctions Plan." *New York Times,* 3 November 1991, 4, 14.

Zimmermann, Tim. "Coercive Diplomacy and Libya." In *The Limits of Coercive Diplomacy,* ed. A. L. George and W. E. Simons. Boulder, Colo.: Westview, 1994.

Zupan, Dusan. "America, Serbia, and New World Order." *TANJUG,* 19 April 1992, and *Foreign Broadcast Information Service,* 20 April 1992, EEU-92-076.

Index

About the Contributors

LAKHDAR BRAHIMI is UN under-secretary-general for the Secretary-General's Preventive and Peacemaking Efforts and former foreign minister and ambassador of Algeria. He has conducted numerous missions for the United Nations. As Special Representative of the UN Secretary-General, he led two UN missions: in spring 1994, the UN Observer Mission in South Africa for elections that saw the birth of a nonracial South Africa; and from September 1994 until March 1996, the UN Mission in Haiti that contributed to the return of the democratically elected government and the organization of peaceful legislative and presidential elections.

DAVID CORTRIGHT is president of the Fourth Freedom Forum in Goshen, Indiana, and fellow at the Joan B. Kroc Institute for International Peace Studies at the University of Notre Dame. He has authored several books, including *Peace Works: The Citizen's Role in Ending the Cold War* (1993), and has coedited two books, including, with George A. Lopez, *Economic Sanctions: Panacea or Peacebuilding in a Post–Cold War World?* (1995). His most recent scholarly articles appear in *Fletcher Forum, Bulletin of the Atomic Scientists, Peace Review,* and *Peace and Change.*

NETA C. CRAWFORD is assistant professor of political science at the University of Massachusetts, Amherst. She is the author of *Soviet Military Aircraft* (1987) and coeditor, with Audie Klotz, of the forthcoming book *How Sanctions Work: South Africa.* She is currently doing research on normative change and world politics.

JALEH DASHTI-GIBSON is a doctoral candidate in the Department of Government at the University of Notre Dame. Her dissertation is titled "Sharpening the Bite: Monitoring Multilateral Sanctions in the Post–Cold War World." She has coauthored an article on sanctions in the *American Journal of Political Science.*

JULIA DEVIN is an attorney specializing in international human rights and humanitarian law. She was the CIET international program coordinator (1994–1995) and executive director and founding board member of the International Commission on Medical Neutrality (1990–1994). She has worked with physicians in the former Yugoslavia, coordinated the first international investigations of the health and humanitarian impacts of war and sanctions in Iraq, and drafted a code of medical neutrality in El Salvador. While a grant recipient with Physicians for Human Rights, she reported on human rights abuses in China, Israel, Somalia, and Guatemala. She has worked as a consultant for the U.S. Congress and the United Nations and has published numerous monographs and articles in the *New England Journal of Medicine*.

ERIC HOSKINS, trained as a physician and a social scientist, is an associate member of the Center for International Health at McMaster University in Canada. As an epidemiologist and public health specialist, he has worked extensively in conflict areas including Sudan, Eritrea, and Iraq. In 1992, he was awarded Canada's most prestigious humanitarian award, the Lester B. Pearson Peace Medal.

GEORGE A. LOPEZ is a faculty fellow at the Joan B. Kroc Institute for International Peace Studies and professor of government and international studies at the University of Notre Dame. His research concerns humanitarianism, violence and the use of force, economic sanctions, and human rights issues. Most recently, he coedited, with David Cortright, *Economic Sanctions: Panacea or Peacebuilding in a Post–Cold War World?* (1995) and, with Nancy Myers, *Peace and Security: The Next Generation* (1997). He serves on the editorial boards of *Bulletin of the Atomic Scientists, Human Rights Quarterly,* and *Mershon International Studies Review.*

LARRY MINEAR is senior fellow at Brown University's Watson Institute for International Studies, where he is principal researcher and, along with Thomas G. Weiss, codirector of the Humanitarianism and War Project. He has worked on humanitarian and development issues since 1972. His latest books are *The Media, Civil Wars, and Humanitarian Action* (1996, with Colin Scott and Thomas G. Weiss), *Soldiers to the Rescue: Humanitarian Lessons from Rwanda* (1996, with Philippe Guillot), and *Humanitarian Action and Politics: The Case of Nagorno-Karabakh* (1997, with S. Neil McFarlane).

THOMAS G. WEISS is research professor and director of the Research Program on Global Security at Brown University's Watson Institute for International Studies and also executive director of the Academic Council on the United Nations System. Previously, he held several UN posts (at the UN Conference on Trade and Development, the UN Commission for Namibia, the UN Institute for Training and Research, and the International Labor Organization) and also served as executive director of the International Peace Academy. He has authored or edited twenty-five books on aspects of development, peacekeeping, humanitarian action, and international organization. He is on the editorial boards of *Global Governance* and the *Third World Quarterly.*

SARAH ZAIDI is one of the founders and science director of the Center for Economic and Social Rights in New York City and a former research fellow at the Harvard Center for Population and Development Studies. She grew up in Pakistan, studied at Brown University, and received her Ph.D. from the Harvard School of Public Health. She has focused her research in the areas of public health, population dynamics, maternal and child health, and international human rights law; she has worked extensively on the humanitarian impact of sanctions on Iraq, and more recently on Haiti.